TEACHING SELF-HYPNOSIS

An Introductory Guide for Clinicians

TEACHING SELF-HYPNOSIS

An Introductory Guide for Clinicians

David A. Soskis, M.D.

The Institute of Pennsylvania Hospital
and
University of Pennsylvania

W · W · NORTON & COMPANY · *NEW YORK* · *LONDON*

Published simultaneously in Canada by Penguin Books Canada Ltd, 2801 John Street, Markham, Ontario L3R 1B4

Printed in the United States of America.

Library of Congress Cataloging-in-Publication Data

Soskis, David A.
  Teaching self-hypnosis.

  Bibliography: p.
  1. Autogenic training—Study and teaching.
I. Title. [DNLM: 1. Hypnosis—methods. WM 415 S715t]
RC499.A8S66 1986   615.8′512   85-29856

ISBN 0-393-70010-0

W. W. Norton & Company, Inc., 500 Fifth Avenue, New York, N.Y. 10110
W. W. Norton & Company Ltd., 37 Great Russell Street, London WC1B 3NU

  4 5 6 7 8 9 0

Foreword

Hypnosis has traditionally been seen as induced by the hypnotist. Research conducted over the last three decades, however, has established that the ability to enter hypnosis is largely a function of the patient's capacity to focus attention, fantasize vividly, suspend disbelief, and to "think with" suggestions. The person's motivation to be hypnotized is important insofar as hypnosis probably never occurs when an individual chooses to resist. The skills of the hypnotist consist largely in creating a context where the patient can feel comfortable, trusting, and willing to allow himself or herself to respond. Already before the turn of the century, Coué argued that there is no suggestion other than self-suggestion and that there is no hypnosis other than self-hypnosis. While such a view is reasonable and fits much of what we now know, it may be equally true that all self-hypnosis, at least at the training stage, is hetero-hypnosis in that its success and continued usage seem to depend upon an actual or implied relationship with someone who is seen as the hypnotist.

The relationship between self-hypnosis and hetero-hypnosis has never been fully resolved but it is not merely a semantic game, nor is it like the question, "Which came first, the chicken or the egg?" Though there are a large number of books on self-hypnosis with a very wide distribution among the lay public, there are few patients who learn self-hypnosis solely from a book, and virtually none who learn it from a book continue to practice regularly and derive benefit from it over time. This is not only true of self-hypnosis but also characteristic of other meditative disciplines. Despite the ready availability of literature, few if any individuals learn meditation from a book. It is the rule rather than the exception that one learns to meditate under the guidance of an experienced and often wise teacher. It takes many years of training before the neophyte is able to continue to meditate successfully, that is, truly on his own.

The paradox of self-hypnosis is that it depends on the patient's skill and is thought of as belonging exclusively to the patient, and yet the interpersonal context is important for the skill to be acquired and probably also to be maintained. This is, however, not as surprising as it may seem because just about any highly developed skill requires a coach or teacher to perfect it. Rare is the individual who becomes an outstanding athlete, or a chess master, or a great musician, without a teacher and extensive opportunities to practice the skill in a context where performance is reinforced. Nevertheless, no one would question that the athlete's performance depends primarily on his native ability and training. By the same token, however, some coaches and teachers turn out to be more successful than others in facilitating the development of a particular unique skill.

In this book the author provides a manual for the psychiatrist or psychologist interested in using self-hypnosis with patients. It is to be recognized that neither hypnosis nor self-hypnosis involves an independent science or discipline; rather these are techniques — tools — to be used in the area of the therapist's expertise. In other words, it is inappropriate for the health professional to treat any problem or condition that he or she could not comfortably treat using techniques unrelated to hypnosis. There can be no substitute for extensive knowledge about the diagnosis, natural history, and prognosis with different approaches, in order to appropriately use hypnosis in therapy.

The present manual evolved from the author's work in collaboration with a research project where a detailed manual was essential. The author is well aware of the need for concrete instructions and the importance of attending to the many details which all too often make the difference between success and failure.

Among therapists there is a tendency to look askance at "cookbooks." Indeed, they have little use unless one tries to cook. Then they become invaluable. A cookbook, however, does not make a great chef. It is only after the recipes are thoroughly mastered that the chef's true ability can become apparent. This book provides directions which, if followed, will enable the reader to teach the skill of self-hypnosis to others. Once this is learned, the therapist will undoubtedly further adapt these procedures to his or her own particular style and talents.

The therapeutic use of self-hypnosis does not occur in a vacuum and should only be employed as a component of an overall treatment program. As such, it can be a uniquely effective, relatively easily taught procedure, particularly if the patient has the natural ability to respond. It would be unfortunate, however, to be misled by a dramatic initial positive response and to assume that the patient will, in the future, continue to use the skill he has acquired. On the contrary, follow-up is an essential part of using self-hypnosis as an effective therapeutic modality. Beyond providing feedback to the therapist and reassurance to the patient, continued contact may be critical for the patient's motivation and his or her ability to utilize self-hypnosis effectively. A few patients require little or no continued contact, while many require a continuing therapeutic relationship that must be terminated quite gradually if self-hypnosis is to remain effective over time. Only the therapist who insists on following his or her patients will ultimately learn how self-hypnosis can be most meaningfully integrated into psychotherapy and/or other aspects of medical treatment.

This book will provide the reader with an opportunity to acquire a useful therapeutic technique, but unless the therapist as much as the patient is highly motivated to understand and continue learning, he or she may all too readily become disillusioned because the patient's initial gains may not be maintained.

Patients vary greatly in the amount and type of support they require. We must learn what kind of support is needed by a particular patient and how to provide it in ways that are acceptable to both the patient and ourselves. We need to strike that delicate balance between making patients unduly dependent versus having them feel forced to be prematurely on their own. This book will provide the basics, but it will ultimately be our patients who must teach us how to become truly effective teachers!

Martin T. Orne, M.D., Ph.D.
The Institute of Pennsylvania Hospital
and
University of Pennsylvania Medical School

Contents

Acknowledgments

I am grateful to all those who have helped me develop the system of teaching self-hypnosis that is described in this book. Above all, Martin Orne has guided and inspired my work in the field of hypnosis with his unique combination of rigorous scientific thought, clinical ethics and experience, and the ability to integrate them with creativity, humor, and common sense. Since 1981, when I first came to work at the Unit for Experimental Psychiatry of the Institute of Pennsylvania Hospital and the Department of Psychiatry of the University of Pennsylvania, I have had the chance to benefit firsthand from his leadership and example.

Emily Carota Orne and David Dinges, Co-Directors of the Unit, have also given unselfishly of their time and advice in guiding my efforts and broadening my perspectives. The staff of the Unit have provided invaluable assistance, especially John Powell and Stephen Fairbrother, in the intricacies of computer programming and word processing. In addition, a steady stream of consultants, colleagues and visitors to the Unit have influenced this book through their ideas and suggestions. In particular, I would like to thank Matthew Erdelyi, Peter Bloom, Fred Frankel, and Ernest Hilgard. Dr. Hilgard's research workshop at the 1982 International Society of Hypnosis 9th Congress in Glasgow provided a unique opportunity to share ideas and experiences concerning self-hypnosis with colleagues from all over the world.

This book would not have been possible without the many patients, medical students, residents and workshop participants from all clinical disciplines who shared their experiences, both good and bad, with me and offered ideas and suggestions for the refinement of the Brief Hypnotic Experience exercise and its clinical applications. In their clinical examples and case histories throughout this book, I have tried to communicate some of the human richness of working with clinical hypnosis. All the case histories and examples describe real people and

xi

events, but the details have been intentionally changed to protect the privacy of those who have helped and taught me. Often I have combined several related case histories into one to provide a particularly clear example of a process or problem.

My own development as a clinician, teacher, researcher and writer has been fostered by many people. In particular, I want to thank my own teachers: Abraham Hurwitz, William Coles, Theodore Greene, Malcolm Bowers, John Romano, Charles Shagass, Joseph Wolpe, Anthony Panzetta, and Abraham Kaplan. My parents, Ann and Philip Soskis, wisely and lovingly controlled and channeled my early interest in hypnosis as a teenager, and as social workers helped me to integrate it into a professional identity of disciplined caring. My wife Carole has provided both intellectual and emotional support, and my sons Benjamin and Michael have helped me by being, and enjoying, themselves.

Susan E. Barrows, my editor at W. W. Norton, has seen this book through from the beginning with a wise and helpful professional approach.

Finally, I want to acknowledge the support of the National Institute of Mental Health for the major research project in which a modified form of this book will be used as a treatment manual (Studies of Hypnosis and Its Clinical Application, MH 19156, Martin T. Orne and David F. Dinges, Co-Principal Investigators), and the support of a grant from the Institute for Experimental Psychiatry Research Foundation for computer facilities, Unit for Experimental Psychiatry library, and other resources.

David A. Soskis
Philadelphia
February 1986

Introduction

This is a book for beginners at hypnosis. When you have read this book through and tried the exercises that it suggests, you will have taken an important and enjoyable step in your professional development — you will be able to use hypnosis to help some of your patients with some of their problems.

I have written this book to ensure that this step actually takes place. It is based on years of experience as a medical school faculty member and in specialized workshops teaching medical students, physicians, psychologists, and social workers how to use hypnosis. The mechanics of hypnosis are easy to learn, as you will soon discover. But like a handshake, or a hug, or a right hook, the trick with hypnosis is knowing when and with whom to use it.

All we have learned about learning points to the fact that behaviors that are rewarded are more likely to be repeated. I want your initial experiences with hypnosis to be rewarding, because I know that this is the only way that hypnosis will be integrated into your day-to-day practice. Hypnosis often shares a common fate with other specialized treatment techniques that are taught in workshops — what I call the weekend romance phenomenon. A clinician is introduced to a glamorous-sounding and supposedly potent technique (hypnosis, paradoxical psychotherapy, sex therapy, etc.) by an expert who makes it look easy and demonstrates with selected volunteers or videotapes of his own patients. Often the workshop is held in an attractive location far from the duties of home. The clinician returns after the workshop with fond memories and full of enthusiasm for the newly acquired technique, only to have his balloon punctured when the second patient he uses it with gets worse, or when the first patient asks, "Have you ever done this before?" The workshop materials then go on file, and the clinician returns to the techniques he or she knows best. Good weekend romances often make bad marriages.

To make sure this does not happen to you, I have stacked the deck in your favor. Based on my own experience teaching and doing research on hypnosis, I have chosen *one hypnotic technique* to teach you: a simple self-hypnosis exercise that you will learn to do yourself and that you will be able to teach to your patients. The exercise is called the Brief Hypnotic Experience (abbreviated B.H.E.), and is described in Chapter 5. I have also intentionally chosen *a narrow range of clinical problems* for your first uses of the self-hypnosis exercise. All this is for one purpose: to make your first experiences enjoyable for you and effective in helping your patients. If I as teacher and you as student achieve these goals, the rest will follow on its own. You will want to learn more about hypnosis through reading, workshops, lectures, videotapes, individual supervision, or other educational means. The appendices at the end of this book will give you some suggestions along these lines. You will also be able to deal with therapeutic failures when they occur, as they always do in the real world, without unrealistic anger at yourself or your patients, or premature abandonment of the use of hypnosis. You will be ready to master more hypnotic techniques and to extend their application to other clinical problems.

If you examine the table of contents, you will notice that half of this book is devoted to issues and procedures that come before the formal induction of hypnosis and instruction in the self-hypnosis exercise. This distribution is deliberate. It reflects the fact that the preliminaries of patient and target symptom selection, introductory discussions, negotiation of a therapeutic contract, and trying and discussing the hand-separation test play a role equal to formal hypnotic induction in determining the overall results of your treatment intervention. If you follow this method carefully, you will have much of the actual induction of hypnosis done before you even begin your formal induction.

I have chosen self-hypnosis rather than hetero-hypnosis for two reasons. First, understanding and explaining hypnosis as self-hypnosis correspond with a large body of clinically relevant research that has identified and measured the hypnotic responsivity of the subject as a major contributor to what happens in hypnotic interactions. In practical terms, even a beginning hypnotist can help a talented subject experience dramatic and effective hypnotic phenomena. On the negative side, even an able and experienced hypnotist may get limited results from a subject whose hypnotic responsivity is low. Using self-hypnosis helps the beginning hypnotist, as well as his patients, keep this perspective and avoid fruitless efforts and unproductive blame.

My second reason for choosing self-hypnosis as your initial hypnotic technique is that it minimizes some of the risks associated with the clinical use of hypnosis. These risks, as we shall see, reside not in the nature or consequences of hypnosis *per se*, but in what hypnosis *means* to patients and to therapists and in how this interacts with the intricate intimacies of their relationship. Teaching a patient a self-hypnosis exercise that you have learned yourself can help with these transference/countertransference issues. You interact with the patient in the role of a more experienced teacher, not in the role of an all-powerful Svengali doing something to the helpless and passive patient. Even using this approach, there is plenty of magic and mystery to hypnosis — but you should be in control of these features, so that they work for you rather than against you.

My selection of the initial applications for the self-hypnosis exercise has been made for similar reasons — maximum potential benefits with a minimum of risks. Anxiety, tension and stress are part of all of our lives, and their control has obvious benefits for the individual patient and for those around him. Self-hypnosis is an ideal technique for dealing with this problem, and can hold its own quite well with standard psychotherapeutic and pharmacological approaches. Dysfunctional pain, the second initial application, is somewhat more challenging for the clinician, especially in terms of patient selection. The dramatic positive results in responsive and appropriate patients justify these efforts, however. Pain relief through a self-hypnosis exercise gets to the heart of hypnosis's power to heal — the attainment of clinically significant modifications in the patient's subjective experience.

Anxiety, tension, stress, and pain complicate many other clinical conditions and life situations. This fact can be useful in other applications of self-hypnosis, such as its use in psychosomatic disorders, depression, and habit disorders. I have included brief discussions of these applications following the primary chapters on clinical applications to give you some ideas as to how the basic principles that you will learn can be applied to other situations where hypnosis has a much more limited, but still potentially useful, role in the total treatment approach.

It is time to be specific on some of the things that this book is *not* meant to do. This is an introductory guide for clinicians concerned with a specific, limited, clinical tool: self-hypnosis. I am assuming that you have had basic training in the areas of evaluation, diagnosis, and treatment that are fundamental to your own professional discipline. This is not a "do it yourself" book for those who need help with health or personal problems and think that hypnosis might be the answer; if that is your situation, you should find a competent and caring physician, psychologist, or social worker who can review your problem with you and help you to decide what treatment is appropriate. The best treatment might, or might not, include hypnosis.

This book is also not a substitute for the personal interaction with a live teacher/supervisor in learning hypnosis — or any other clinical skill for that matter. Hypnosis, including the teaching of self-hypnosis, is a complex and emotionally charged interpersonal event. It is impossible to simultaneously manage this transaction, observe yourself and your patient, and provide appropriate feedback so that you may correct your errors and refine your skills. Videotaping your sessions or, if that is impossible, audiotaping them is an invaluable part of the learning experience. This book will help you most, however, if it is combined with a live workshop experience, or personal supervision, or, preferably, both. Appendix A will give you some concrete suggestions about how to acquire these crucial learning experiences in a way that is practical for you.

If you are a workshop leader or training director and have read this far, you know my position on the role of this book in a training program in clinical self-hypnosis. This book has emerged from my own experiences in teaching beginners' workshops, and provides in one package the materials and information that I usually hand out or dictate to students. There is enough to do in preparing for a workshop ("I know the air conditioner drowns out the microphone, sir; which one would you rather have?"), so that anything that you can be sure of in advance helps. There is some controversy over the use of a script for initial training; I myself have found that its benefits in reducing initial student anxiety and ensuring that "all the bases are covered" far outweigh its disadvantages in reducing spontaneity and free interaction. For some beginning students, it is clearly the *only* approach that will get them to actually try hypnosis with a patient of their own.

The exercise and applications presented in this book are both geared towards the low end of hypnotic responsivity. In practical terms, this means that the student is likely to be able to use the material that I have presented with a wide range of patients without a large number of failures based on a lack of hypnotic talent in the patient. On the negative side, these techniques do not explore or exploit the many fascinating and clinically useful phenomena that occur only in the high range of hypnotic responsivity and that are sampled in several of the standard hypnosis scales.

Even the best-prepared book is inadequate for several of the key issues in clinical hypnosis. Adapting even the simplest self-hypnosis training to the student's personal and professional style and circumstances, individual questions or concerns, and case presentations for the possible use of the techniques you are teaching are all outside the range of what a written manual can deliver. The heart of learning, and of teaching, is still personal and is still in your hands.

Despite the considerable amount of careful scientific research that has been done on hypnosis during the last 30 years and its general acceptance by the clinical community, it remains an extremely controversial field; and there is much about it that we understand imperfectly, if at all. Devoted and well-meaning researchers and clinicians who are recognized experts still attack each other in a tone that has changed little since the days of Mesmer. I have presented the teaching approach that I have found works best for me and for my students. Some readers may be surprised, or even annoyed, by the detail with which I have presented a number of procedures. I have done this at the specific request of many students and trainees, who found these details helpful in getting started. As their experience with self-hypnosis grew, they were able to modify the procedures that I suggested to suit their own needs. If you are using this book for a workshop or course, you may want to utilize some of the material and omit or disagree with other sections. This is a training manual, not a book about the nature of hypnosis, and I have not done justice to the many valid alternative approaches that may be equally useful heuristically and clinically. Some of these can be found in the reading materials listed in Appendix B.

Whether you are a student or a teacher, this book will be most useful to you if you approach it with critical curiosity, a sense of humor, and common sense. After years in the field, I still share the wonder, excitement, and fun of hypnotic experiences and of their use in healing. I hope that this book can help you to do the same.

TEACHING SELF-HYPNOSIS

An Introductory Guide for Clinicians

ONE

Understanding and Explaining Self-Hypnosis

There was once a young clinician who became fascinated with hypnosis. He read all the books he could find on the subject and finally wrote to one of the authors to ask the question that still intrigued him: What *was* hypnosis, really? The expert wrote in reply that, although reading could help in gaining an understanding of the nature of hypnosis, actual experience and practice were far more important. So the young man attended all the workshops and training courses he could, but still failed to find a really satisfying explanation of the true nature of hypnosis. At several of the workshops he had attended, however, mention was made of one wise, old man (wiser, even, than the legendary Milton Erickson) who had supposedly penetrated as far as possible to the core of this mystery. The clinician used most of his surplus resources to gain an interview with this wise old man in his office in a remote community.

Finally, face to face with the master, he asked: "Do you know the true nature of hypnosis?" The old man nodded. "What is it, then?" "Hypnosis is pure experience," the old man replied. The young clinician was dumbfounded. "Do you mean to tell me that I've studied for years and come all these miles to hear you tell me that hypnosis is pure experience?" The old man thought for a few moments, looked at the young clinician, and replied: "You mean hypnosis *isn't* pure experience?"

Although this story ends up as a joke, like many jokes it is not far from the truth of the situation it pokes fun at. Experienced researchers and clinicians are far from having a coherent, comprehensive, and generally accepted theory of the true nature of hypnosis. Gurus and catchy phrases abound. Hypnosis has always been, and remains, an

3

area that fascinates and draws people on. Above all, a gentle skepticism and a healthy sense of humor are called for and will serve you well.

With these caveats in mind, we can proceed to a consideration of the substantive issues involved at a level that will be useful and practical for you as a beginner. We do know many things about what hypnosis is and about how and where it works. You need to know enough to get started safely and to answer appropriate questions from your patients. The concepts that you use should be helpful tools that get the job done and that talk about hypnosis in ways consistent with current research. But remember what the old man said: "Hypnosis is pure experience." Like the rest of the story, there is some truth in that statement, which brings us to your own experience of hypnosis and how it interacts with the experiences you will be providing for your patients.

Your Personal Experience of Hypnosis

I believe that your use of hypnosis with patients will be more effective if you are able to experience hypnosis yourself. To answer a question that would surely come to my mind if I were reading this chapter for the first time: I myself use the exercise that I will be teaching you regularly. I use it (mostly for relaxation and for an occasional headache) because I find it effective, fun, and simple to do. I communicate this fact verbally and nonverbally to my patients, and this communication plays a major role in determining what hypnosis means within the therapeutic relationship.

This approach is certainly not unique or unusual, but it does differ sharply from several of the more common stereotypes of what hypnosis is and how it is used. If it seems totally foreign to your personal or therapeutic style, this book may not be for you. But read on for a while before you decide.

I do not claim that everyone who prescribes lithium must take it himself so that he speaks with the empathy born of personal experience. But when, as with self-hypnosis, the therapeutic technique per se is enjoyable, risk-free, and relevant to the stresses of normal life, the argument for at least giving it a try is stronger. Having experienced hypnosis, you will be able to offer reassurance that is genuine, and you will find ways to rephrase some of the explanations and strategies offered in this book so that they sound like (and are) your own.

How to experience hypnosis yourself will depend on who and where you are. If you have had past experiences with hypnosis in an academic, clinical or entertainment setting, review them in the light of what you read here. Does what I say about hypnosis make sense to you now? If not, can you reconcile the differences yourself or with the help of peers or teachers? The differences that are of most clinical concern are covered in the questions and answers that appear later in this chapter. Try the procedure I suggest for those with no previous experience; incongruent concepts or feelings may reflect earlier settings or developmental issues that are ready to be integrated and perhaps outgrown. Hypnosis, like psychotherapy, brings out the child in us. The trick is to retain the sense of adventure and play and at the same time avoid childish ways of perceiving and behaving.

If you think you have had no previous experience with hypnosis, you are wrong. Almost everyone in our culture has had *some* contact with hypnosis as a spectator or participant. Have you ever watched children's cartoons on television? Since they are repeated endlessly, you are sure to have seen the one in which Elmer Fudd, as a hunter, tries to hypnotize Bugs Bunny but is himself mesmerized into thinking he is a rabbit. Although the interaction is genuinely funny, it does present hypnosis as an unfriendly struggle between hunter and prey in which one side wins while the other side loses. Experiences like this leave a residue that influences subsequent experiences — including your reaction to what you are reading now. This issue is addressed in much greater detail in Chapter 3. Although that chapter prepares you as a clinician to deal with and use your patients' previous experiences with hypnosis, it might be a good idea to review it for yourself before you try the exercise. If some of the issues it raises resonate with your own past experiences, you may be able to eliminate some preventable interference.

After reviewing your own past experiences with hypnosis and the conceptual material and explanations presented in this chapter, you are ready to experience hypnosis for yourself. If you are using this book as part of an instructional workshop, or plan to take one, this personal experience will usually be built into the workshop structure in parallel with more didactic presentations. One popular way to do this is to have the workshop participants pair up in the roles of hypnotist and subject and go through the various hypnotic procedures: preliminary "waking" suggestions, induction, selected hypnotic suggestions, instruction in a self-hypnosis exercise, etc. After each step the subject can give the hypnotist feedback on his or her style (e.g., were descriptions vivid enough; was his speech audible?) before reversing roles. Some workshop leaders prefer to administer the procedures themselves or through a tape to the group as a whole, with subsequent opportunities for sharing and questions. In general, I believe that a well-conducted workshop is the best way for a beginner to learn hypnosis. Such workshops are available worldwide, and are discussed in detail in Appendix A.

If for some reason you are unable to attend a workshop, you can derive some of the benefits of the workshop format (consensual validation, feedback, support, economy) by learning together with a group of your colleagues. You might want to consider having a senior clinician whom you all respect, preferably with some knowledge and experience in hypnosis, serve as leader of your group. You can use this book as your text.

Other alternatives, though less desirable, are possible. Two beginners can learn together, or you can learn hypnosis, like other clinical skills, as part of an ongoing relationship with a clinical supervisor. If none of these is feasible, it is possible, though far from optimal, to learn hypnosis on your own using this book. To do this, simply record the various procedures in Chapter 5 on an audiotape and play them back to yourself. You will be able to experience all the phenomena described in this book and have the chance to hear yourself as others do — a highly instructive, though sometimes unsettling, experience.

Ideally, you should have a chance to experience and practice for yourself the procedures described in Chapters 4, 5, and 6 before you use them with others. This includes the hand separation test, the Chevreul pendulum, the Brief Hypnotic Experience (B.H.E.) Induction, Evaluation and Exercise. If you are learning in a group, this personal experience will have included both sides of the hypnotist-subject relationship. If you are learning alone, or if you are still a little unsure of yourself after the formal learning period, you should practice the role of hypnotist and teacher of the exercise a few times with non-patients before you use it with patients in your role as clinician.

It is possible, and reasonable, to provide a subject with the experience of hypnosis and teach him the B.H.E. exercise without applying it to any specific problem or defining your role in the situation as a therapist. In choosing these practice subjects it is best to avoid people with whom you have a real love relationship (e.g., spouses, children) or where the relationship is otherwise emotionally charged. You are, after all, a beginner at hypnosis and don't need to complicate your training more than necessary. You might know someone very well and still not know what hypnosis means to him or her or how. it will be interpreted within the dynamics of your relationship. The ideal practice subject would be someone you know but do not work with or socialize with regularly.

Don't let all these cautions and logistic issues scare you off. Hypnosis as presented in this book is fascinating and *fun*. Go ahead and give it a try!

The Nature of Hypnosis

The information you need about hypnosis falls into two broad categories. The basic functional understanding of what hypnosis is and how it works will emerge from your own personal experiences with this phenomenon. I have chosen a question and answer format to provide some conceptual tools to help you shape and express that understanding. I chose this format because it helps with one of the most common sources of distress for beginning clinicians using hypnosis for the first few times with patients: questions that you cannot answer or answer so hesitantly that you reveal more of your newness in this area than you want to.

The second broad category of information that you may need relates to an in-depth understanding of hypnosis and its applications to a wide range of clinical problems. Consideration of these issues goes far beyond the scope of this book, which is a manual for beginners aimed at getting you started in the right direction. But what if your first pain-relief patient is a child with cancer? Doesn't it make sense to learn something about the special factors involved in using hypnosis with this group before you begin actual work with your patient? The answer to this question is clearly yes, and I have provided Appendix B to both help you with these kind of specialized clinical issues and provide you with several resources for exploring the extensive research and clinical literature on the nature of hypnosis. When working with patients you should feel comfortable answering the questions I have given with the answers I have provided or with your own versions of them. You should also feel comfortable saying that you don't know the answer to a sensible but more advanced question, and, if appropriate, trying to find that answer if it is available.

The answers to common questions have been phrased carefully, as you will soon see. They reflect both my view of the balance of evidence on these issues and the way of presenting this information that will be most likely to contribute to the clinical success of the self-hypnosis procedures presented in this book. *All* definitions and explanations have an instrumental as well as an abstract explanatory function, and this instrumental function of explanation is amplified when controversial or emotionally charged subjects, such as hypnosis, are involved. If you decide to give very different answers to these questions or to make up your own definitions of key terms, be sure that they fit with the hypnotic experiences that you will be providing for your patients. The answer to each question is followed by a discussion of the choice of phrasing and/or of related clinical issues.

1) *What is hypnosis?* Hypnosis is a process that allows us to experience thoughts and images as real.

You should understand the details of how this fundamental definition has been phrased, since it expresses the theoretical and clinical positions on which this book is based. By defining hypnosis as a "process," we are steering clear of the extreme forms of both the state and trait views of hypnosis. The term process implies some activity and leads easily into the use of a self-hypnosis exercise. The major clinical issues that arise from the state and trait views will be covered in other questions.

The verb "allows" introduces the elements of facilitation and permission, and the subject/object "us" prepares the way for the interaction around your patient's learning the self-hypnosis exercise being structured as a voluntary and collaborative one. Try to get into a frame of mind geared towards voluntary collaborative effort and sensitive to factors that might interfere with it. If you have used this definition or a similar one early in your interaction with your patient, you may be able to return to it later to "explain" problems that you encounter in a way that comes across as professional and does not mobilize excessive defensiveness.

What is it that hypnosis allows us to do? Hypnosis allows us to *experience* thoughts and images as real—not to behave as if they were real. The work of Martin Orne and his colleagues has conclusively demonstrated that untrained, unhypnotizable subjects simulating hypnosis can fool experts in the field by their behavior. Although the hypnotic techniques presented here fit well with a behavioral approach, they are not primarily aimed at modifying behavior. Hypnosis modifies experience. The patient's behavior is likely to change if it is related, as it well may be, to the experiences that have been modified.

The definition I am using gives a central role to what has been called phenomenology, an approach that has been developed more in Europe than in the United States, but which has been incorporated into several of the recent research efforts to understand the nature of hypnosis. It is possible to measure and even to quantify subjective experiences — the Brief Hypnotic Experience Evaluation Form that you will be using later is a simple version of this methodology.

In fact, the position that identifies reality as something "out there" and associates experience with subjective perceptions alone may be putting the cart before the horse. Reality is our name, given in faith, for what we know. What we know is our experiences and perceptions. Objectivity, in the last analysis, is a consensus of intersubjectivity. The philosophical ramifications of this issue are not of concern here; the important point for the clinician is to be able to see the patient's experiences as tools for change as well as sources of diagnostic information.

The traditional term "suggestion" has not been retained in my definition, which might have been phrased "hypnosis is a process that allows us to experience suggestions as real." It is possible to define a suggestion as bringing to mind a thought or image that you actively concentrate on, but this definition is far from the semantic loading of the term for most patients. Specifically, the term suggestion carries implications of influence (power, domination, manipulation), prompting or cueing, and supplicating or entreating that are counterproductive in my view. The meaning that involves introducing an idea to a person indirectly or deviously is contained in the Latin root, *suggestus*, which means, among other things, "placed under." Eliminating this term from your own definition of hypnosis will not, unfortunately, eliminate all these implications from your patients' minds. They pervade the associations surrounding the term hypnosis in the minds of most laypersons and many hypnotists.

What does it mean to experience a thought or image as real? We are not referring here to acceptance of a logical or experimental truth or the basic process of sensory perception. Stop reading for a few moments and try to answer this question based on your own experiences: Have you, yourself, ever experienced a thought or image as real? See if you can come up with one or two examples before you continue.

The examples that you came up with will be useful to you in teaching patients self-hypnosis. If they correspond with the ones that I will be discussing here, they indicate that your own interpretation of the definition is congruent with the one to be presented in this book. Variations of your own that keep the same basic idea are *better* than the ones I will present — they come from your own experience and you will be able to communicate them to your patients with more genuineness and enthusiasm than if they came from someone else. If your examples are very different in concept or direction from the ones I will give, try to understand the differences before you proceed. You may want to reread this chapter or even refer to some of the literature on the nature of hypnosis mentioned in Appendix B.

The example that I use most frequently is an experience while watching a good movie. *Chariots of Fire*, for instance, is a film about two competitors in the 1924 Olympics. Near the end of the movie, Ben Cross playing Harold Abrahams prepares for and wins the 100 meter dash. Much of what has gone on in the movie has led up to this moment. As I watch him dig in for the start, my heart begins to beat faster. With the sound of the gun, my fists are clenched and I find myself leaning forward in my seat, just as his coach has told Harold to lean forward. As Harold breaks the tape at the finish line, I feel a tremendous sense of exultation and relief of tension. I feel swept up in the excitement of the crowd as they pour onto the track. While I am watching the movie, I am experiencing parts of it as real. The quality of reality is reflected in the intensity of my emotional reaction, my pounding heart, and the way I move my body in sympathy with what is happening on the screen. To use a popular slang term, I am really "into" the movie.

That is what I mean by saying that hypnosis allows us to experience thoughts and images as real. Let's say that for some reason I did not get "into" this movie, did not experience it as real. What would that be like? I can easily describe that, because that is what happens when I go to what I consider a bad movie. Under those circumstances, the movie does not absorb my entire attention. I am very aware that I am in a theater watching a movie, and a very poorly made one at that. I look at my watch occasionally and wish that the time would go by faster. I am angry at myself, or at whoever convinced me to come, for wasting my time and money. I notice that I have to go to the bathroom, and welcome the interruption. I may even look around at the other people watching the movie to see if they find it as boring as I do. If I lean forward and clench my fists in relation to the movie, it is only as I realize it is about to end and prepare to make a dash to get out of the theater first.

There is nothing special about *Chariots of Fire* as an example; any movie that you have enjoyed would do just as well. I sometimes use Walt Disney's *Bambi*—when the Great Prince of the Forest says to Bambi, "Your mother can't be with you any more; you must learn to walk alone"—or the escape scene from *Stalag 17*, or any number of moving scenes from *Goodbye Mr. Chips*. I try to think ahead a little and match the movie to the patient I am talking to; it helps if he or she has also seen the film and had a similar reaction. It does not help if the subject matter of the movie would upset the patient just through your mentioning it or otherwise strain your relationship. If you know the patient well, any performance medium can make the point—opera, ballet, the "soaps" on daytime TV, Broadway theater, etc.

The example of a moving and absorbing performance is useful in understanding self-hypnosis because it presents the potentially frightening reality issue in the context of what Coleridge called "the willing suspension of disbelief for the moment." Involvement with a performance is clearly voluntary and temporary; when it is all over, we get up, leave the theater, and go home to go on with our lives, hopefully better for the experience. That is just what the patient is going to do after he has learned the self-hypnosis exercise you will be teaching him. There is also a subtle message in using what is usually a shared social experience as the basic example—indirectly, the analogy may allay worries that trouble some patients about being singular or strange for trying self-hypnosis at all.

The second example that I commonly use is the absorption and personal involvement that I can experience while reading a good book ("Where have you been, David? I called you to supper ten minutes ago!"). Although I sometimes use a work of fiction, I more often use this example to illustrate the possible relationship of the experiences that can occur through hypnosis to subsequent performance—a common goal of many applications of hypnosis within behavioral treatments for phobias or maladaptive inhibitions. A favorite example of mine is a book I read when I was learning about fly fishing. I sat down with it after tangling myself up with my new equipment several times, finally ready to acknowledge that I had to read the instructions *first*. The book's author, an expert fisherman and a good teacher, described how to cast a fly line in the context of fishing a small woodland stream. Through his description I could hear the water splashing on the rocks and smell the pine trees near the bank. I felt the coolness of the stream on my legs, and joined in his excitement as he spotted the tell-tale swirls of a feeding fish in a pool. As he described his cast, my hands moved with him. I was completely absorbed in the world he had created as he hooked and landed a sleek trout.

After finishing the chapter I ran outside to try my casting technique. To my delight, I was able to get the line out without snagging my hat or the grass. I still was not, nor am I now, an expert fly fisherman. But I had taken the first step, and was able to go on to improve my skill and enjoy myself in the process. Participating in the reality that the book's author had created helped me overcome a troublesome obstacle and begin to master a new skill.

As you can see, the quality that unites these two examples is a kind of "imaginative involvement" in the experiences. Josephine Hilgard and her colleagues have explored and developed this concept as central to hypnosis, including work with both reading and theater. Again, the specific type of experience is not important—the goal is an example that you can describe with conviction and that is comprehensible to your patient. Unfortunately, many people today seldom get involved in reading a good book; don't use a reading example with a patient who is essentially a non-reader.

One final note about the definition. Hypnosis is described here as *a* process that allows us to experience thoughts and images as real, not *the* process. This reflects my own theoretical position on the relationship of hypnosis to meditation, prayer, "psyching up" in sports, and other similar experiences. The definition gives you latitude in answering questions of the "isn't that the same as . . . " variety without attacking beliefs or practices that may be important and useful for your patient. These related practices, in fact, may provide important alternative pathways to hypnosis for reaching your clinical goals.

2) *Can anyone be hypnotized? Can I?* Almost everyone can have some hypnotic experiences if he wants to and puts some effort into it. It's a lot like sports or music—some people have a special talent and turn out to be naturals, but everyone who wants to can usually participate in some way.

I have provided only a general answer to these two questions, and left the second one essentially unanswered. The second question was included because it is always there whether it is asked or not whenever a patient asks you about hypnotizability. Both you and your patient will discover the answer to the second question in the course of your work together; how you handle it at this stage depends more on your own style and your patient than upon any fixed rules.

People vary widely in their ability to experience hypnosis, and this ability, like intelligence, tends to be a stable characteristic of the individual. This is the "trait" aspect of hypnosis. Of all the names for this trait, "hypnotic responsivity" seems to have the best implications for a self-hypnosis setting, in comparison with alternate names such as "hypnotic susceptibility" or "hypnotizability." Using the analogy to athletic or musical talent both puts the issue in positive terms and relates hypnosis to other skills that may be familiar and acceptable to your patient.

Ernest Hilgard and his colleagues have devoted many years to delineating and refining our understanding of this trait and our ability to measure it reliably. Among the results of this work are a number of standardized scales (the Stanford Scales) for use with adults and children in both research and clinical settings. The basic concept of the Stanford individual scales was extended to a group using a tape recorded induction in the Harvard group scale of Ronald Shor and Emily Orne. These scales have played a crucial role in the major advances in hypnosis research over the last 20 years. They allow us to examine any measureable phenomenon claimed to be hypnotic and evaluate its correlation with a generally accepted measurement of this dimension. The scripted induction and standardized evaluation form used in this book will give you a taste of this approach to hypnosis. If you want to explore this approach further or get into formal research in the field, you will be ready for the Stanford, Harvard, and other standardized scales which are described in Appendix B.

Disciplined research into self-hypnosis is in a much earlier stage than hetero-hypnosis. One of the issues for inquiry is whether and how these two phenomena differ from each other. Despite the questions that remain open on this, I believe that at present it makes sense to take what is known about hetero-hypnosis as a reasonable starting point. From this considerable research literature, we can draw some useful generalizations. The ability to experience hypnosis does not correlate to a clinically useful degree with any of the standard personality measures.

Whether a person is shy or outgoing, affiliative or a loner, etc., does not make a crucial difference in his ability to respond to hypnosis. Patients who are disoriented because of an organic brain syndrome, grossly psychotic, or severely mentally retarded will have trouble learning and practicing a self-hypnosis exercise, but this reflects much broader problems with tasks and learning. Certain diagnostic groups, such as paranoid schizophrenics, may be poor candidates for hypnosis, but this is likely to relate more to nonhypnotic issues than to an inherent inability to experience hypnosis.

Standard demographic variables (e.g., age, sex, race, religion, and social class) are also not crucial. There are some changes relating to age, with children around age 10 responding better than those younger or older, and some problems experiencing hypnosis for the very young (below age four) and very old (over 80). These age differences are usually less than differences *within* an age group, however, and problems with children or the aged seem less significant to clinicians who are accustomed to working with patients in these age groups.

Two specific features of the approach presented in this book justify a relatively positive answer to patients' questions about their ability to experience hypnosis. First, because it is a clinical approach, the ability of anyone other than the patient you are working with to experience hypnosis is of distinctly secondary importance. The question is whether what *that particular patient* can experience is enough to accomplish or move toward the agreed-on clinical goals. Many patients who have low levels of hypnotic responsivity as measured by standard scales can nevertheless gain substantial clinical benefit from learning and practicing a self-hypnosis exercise. Thus, the suggestion that things will go well is an appropriate one, as it usually is in low-risk therapeutic procedures.

Second, because this is a book for beginners, the Brief Hypnotic Experience induction and exercise are biased towards the low end of hypnotic responsivity. The basic item is an ideomotor response (this will be explained in Chapter 4) that has a very high pass percentage and can even be experienced without a hypnotic induction. I have structured the procedure this way to assure as much as possible that both you and your patients will have successes in your initial experiences with hypnosis. There are no items involving challenges, eyes-open hallucinations, amnesia or post-hypnotic suggestion. These items are fascinating in themselves, allow us to chart the upper ends of the responsivity dimension, and are included in the standardized scales I have mentioned. You can learn about them and use them once your basic skills have been consolidated.

3) *Will I be asleep?* or, *Is hypnosis like sleep?* Hypnosis is different from sleep. We have learned a great deal about sleep through the study of brain wave patterns, and these patterns have also been studied in hypnosis. The brain wave (EEG or electroencephalogram for more sophisticated patients) pattern in hypnosis resembles that of a person who is awake and doing whatever the person in hypnosis is doing (e.g., imagining a scene with his eyes closed, talking to another person). The pattern does not resemble any of the stages of sleep, including the stage in which most dreams occur (REM or rapid eye movement sleep).

A lot of the confusion about this subject has arisen because older styles of hypnosis used the word sleep and began with suggestions of eye heaviness. Although this may be useful for some people, it is not necessary for hypnosis, and the exercise that we will be using does not mention sleep at all. You will be awake and alert during the exercise, and able to respond if necessary to things that are going on around you. We usually teach the exercise with eyes closed to help people concentrate and imagine more easily, but the exercise can be done with eyes open.

It is, of course, possible and even easy to fall asleep while doing the exercise. Some people who have trouble falling asleep use the exercise for just this purpose. When this happens, you awaken normally just as you would from a nap or from a night's sleep.

The above answer covers the most important points that you and your patients should know concerning the relationship of hypnosis to sleep. Along with the next question on trance, these are the major practical aspects of the "state" aspect of hypnosis. Many of the traditional sleep-oriented inductions are quite useful clinically and the technical misnomer does not seem to produce any harm. Since you will be learning one induction method to start with, I have chosen one that does not involve sleep. Elements of relaxation and dream-like experiences are included in this induction, but I have never been impressed that the addition of sleep terminology promotes either of these processes in a uniquely potent way. For a number of patients, the idea of being "put to sleep" by anyone has negative emotional associations (often from childhood surgery) that are best left alone.

The relationship of the clinical benefits derived from doing a self-hypnosis exercise to the benefits of napping is another matter entirely. Planned, controlled napping has much in common with the approach presented in this book (a brief procedure that the patient does on his own to restore or improve his function, to combat a problem, or to promote health). I have encountered several patients who regularly fell asleep almost as soon as they began the exercise, but clearly benefited from a regularly scheduled refreshing nap although they were not doing self-hypnosis in the usual sense. All were hardworking, dutiful people who would never have introduced a nap into their daily routines on their own. The combination of "doctor's orders" and the structure of the exercise made the procedure acceptable. For such patients it is clearly not helpful to emphasize the differences between hypnosis and sleep.

This issue underscores the importance of a regular sleep history in any clinical investigation. Sleep and its disorders are beyond the range of this book, but a number of recent investigators have explored both sleep and hypnosis. The paper by David Dinges cited in Appendix B will provide a brief introduction for clinicians without any prior background in the physiology or psychology of sleep.

4) *Will I be in a trance?* Many people describe the feeling of hypnosis as different in a pleasant way from their usual experience. Just like the notion that hypnosis is sleep, however, the idea of a hypnotic trance or state in many people's minds is more related to something they saw in an old movie than to the reality of hypnosis itself. You will not be walking around like a zombie with your arms out in front of you or speaking in a mechanical voice like a robot. You will be able to move around if you want to and will not be frozen in some kind of weird pose.

All of the above are common notions of how people behave in hypnosis. None of them is necessary or helpful to your use of the self-hypnosis exercise with patients. In actual practice, the opposite experience is more likely to be problematic, i.e., patients who are able to experience and benefit from the B.H.E. exercise but who have doubts that they were "really hypnotized" because they didn't do or experience anything overtly weird. This possibility is heightened by the use of high-pass items in the exercise you will be using. Some patients find the B.H.E. items unusual enough to be convincing; the remainder need to be reassured that you don't have to be weird, feel weird, or act weird to be hypnotized.

You should be aware that many questions around the nature and measurement of the "state" aspect of hypnosis remain unanswered. In fact, considering the remarkable changes that hypnosis can produce in experience, it is impressive how *little* documented evidence of a unique physiological (as opposed to an experiential) state has emerged after extensive research efforts, including studies of brain waves, corticosteroids, galvanic skin responses, and endorphins. This is one of the reasons why the state aspect of hypnosis is not emphasized in this clinical presentation and the word trance is not used.

5) *Will I remember what happens to me in hypnosis?* Yes. We will not be changing your memory at all.

Alterations in memory may be produced in hypnosis, but this is not an area for beginners. This answer will help prevent amnesias related to previous ideas or experiences with hypnosis.

6) *Can someone in hypnosis be made to say or do something that he doesn't want to?* No, he cannot. Some people worry about this issue because of movies they have seen about hypnosis, stories they have read, or impressions they have gotten from watching a stage hypnotist perform. In these settings hypnosis is sometimes presented as something that a powerful person does to innocent victims or trusting audience members so that he can later take advantage of them. People can certainly be taken advantage of, but this has nothing to do with the use of hypnosis in a legitimate clinical or research setting. To be specific for your own case, you will remain aware and in control while you are learning the self-hypnosis exercise and when you practice it at home on your own. I will not be asking you to do anything that will harm or embarrass you. When you do the exercise at home, no one will be able to take control of you in any way against your will. In fact, if someone in hypnosis is asked or told to do something that he believes is dangerous or wrong, he will refuse and usually come out of hypnosis as well.

This question and its many variations are never asked by patients in a vacuum. Behind the general question there are concerns about one or several possible revelations or behaviors. Patients vary in how conscious they are of these specific concerns, which can range from subjects of waking worry and rumination to thoroughly repressed sexual or aggressive fantasies: Will I blurt out something about the affair I am having and starting to feel guilty about? About what we did with the taxes last year? Will he make me dependent on him so I can never end the treatment? Will he try to have sex with me?

These concerns are not unique to hypnosis, but arise regularly in psychotherapy and in any intimate relationship. How to explore and to manage issues of confidentiality, dependency/control and sexuality within clinical relationships is or should be part of basic training in medicine, psychology and social work. Although these broad issues are beyond the scope of this book, some specific suggestions for beginners at hypnosis concerning the issues of sexuality and dependency/control will be discussed in Chapters 2 and 3. Obviously, if you want to explore the specifics of the patient's concerns, it makes sense to ask a question like "What kinds of things might someone do or say?" in response to the initial query. Whether or not you make this inquiry at that point or save it for later depends on the specifics of the particular patient and even of the particular session. Some patients not socialized to insight-oriented psychotherapies resent having questions answered with questions and expect a reply. The answer I have given here addresses that part of the question that is related to conscious concerns and previous misinformation. This kind of overt cognitive restructuring is necessary but not sufficient for gaining the patient's optimal participation and consent.

The experimental studies of this issue, as well as the investigation of alleged cases where crimes or other forbidden activities occurred in hypnosis, present a picture more complicated than any answer appropriate for a concerned patient. Several examples from this area will help to round out your own view. Some subjects participating in experiments on hypnosis have reached into a cage and grabbed an agitated rattlesnake at the suggestion of the hypnotist. This would seem to be an example of someone doing something dangerous under the control of the hypnotist. This experiment does not demonstrate this—the snake is, in fact, harmless, although the subject had no obvious way of knowing this. But the lack of an obvious way does not mean that there is no way. The subject knows he is in an experiment and that the researcher is subject to scrutiny, and correctly trusts the researcher not to endanger him. Thus, the interaction or relationship that determines the subject's behavior is really outside of hypnosis.

This is, in fact, usually the place to look in evaluating any question of this type: Is there anything in the overall relationship of the two people involved or in the life of either that would give a sensible explanation of what has happened? If there has been a sexual encounter in a dormitory room during an informal "experiment" with hypnosis, is the unusual occurrence in that room sex, or is it hypnosis? Does the encounter seem characteristic or uncharacteristic of the participants? When was the encounter reported in relationship to when it occurred, and why is it being reported right now?

The answers to questions like these can usually clarify what is going on, and they generally reinforce the reassuring reply concerning hypnosis presented earlier. Let's conclude with the most extreme example: the role of hypnosis in producing criminal behavior. Hypnosis has been used as an excuse for just about everything, and ingenious defense attorneys have tried it regularly as an absolving explanation of why their clients did something wrong. But the bottom line of these cases is the same as the one for the examples we have already considered: The explanations for the behavior can usually be found much more sensibly in factors beyond and outside hypnosis per se. In fact, there has *never* been an adequately documented situation in which a person committed a crime under hypnosis that benefited only the hypnotist.

The primary purpose of these additional examples is to allow you to provide reassurance with confidence. The whole issue is of minor relevance anyway to the hypnotic procedure that you will be using, since this procedure does not involve alterations in memory, post-hypnotic suggestions or unusual behavior, and is based on a self-hypnosis exercise that intentionally emphasizes the patient's executive role.

7) *How is it possible for a person to hypnotize himself?* Remember the original definition of hypnosis as a process that allows us to experience thoughts and images as real. The end result of this process, the heart of hypnosis, is *your own experience* of thoughts and images. It takes place within you. The fact is that there can be no hypnosis *unless* a person hypnotizes himself by participating actively and voluntarily in the process. In that sense, all hypnosis is self-hypnosis.

Older ideas about hypnosis, including some held by people today, did not recognize the crucial role of the subject in producing hypnosis. Instead, they concentrated on the personality or role of the hypnotist.

In some of the earliest forms of this thinking, it was believed that the hypnotist posessed a kind of "animal magnetism" through which he influenced his subject. We now know that these ideas do not accurately portray what happens in hypnosis, even in demonstrations of stage hypnosis where they may seem to apply. In our own use of hypnosis to help you, I will be acting as a teacher or coach in helping you learn the self-hypnosis exercise. I will be introducing you to the exercise through a number of preliminary procedures and then guiding you through your first experience with it. After you have learned the exercise you will be initiating and controlling the hypnotic process yourself.

This reply combines an expansion on the original definition with an introduction to what the patient can expect in his work with you. The procedure that you will be using does not cover the full range of phenomena that are usually considered hypnotic, but you should know that *all* phenomena within this range, including amnesias and post-hypnotic suggestions, have been produced through self-hypnosis. Thus, even though we know much less about self-hypnosis than about hetero-hypnosis, there is no reason for feeling that self-hypnosis is not the "real thing."

The reply steers clear of one of the major debates concerning self-hypnosis, but it is one that you should know about because the Brief Hypnotic Experience induction itself illustrates one aspect of the problem. The debate concerns the role of a formal hypnotic induction in hypnosis, and whether any procedure that uses such an induction can truly be called self-hypnosis. In the Brief Hypnotic Experience induction, for example, the initial hypnotic experience is clearly best described as hetero-hypnosis: You are giving a series of suggestions of arm lightness, physical relaxation and experience of a pleasant scene at the beach to which the patient responds. Later in the induction, the patient is taught how to go through the exercise himself without you (the hypnotist) being physically present.

One could say, and some researchers have, that this procedure and all like it are generating elaborate post-hypnotic suggestions (performing and experiencing the exercise) rather than teaching the patient self-hypnosis. Thus, whether or not you are physically present, the patient will be following a post-hypnotic suggestion that you have administered in hetero-hypnosis every time he does the exercise. In this sense all hypnosis of this type is hetero-hypnosis. If you wanted to really do self-hypnosis, you would have to create conditions that enabled the patient to learn and to practice the exercise *completely* on his own.

The problem with this point of view becomes clear as soon as you begin to try to design just such a "pure" self-hypnosis procedure. Is the hypnotist's role removed by putting the induction on tape? That seems like a step in the right direction, but the hypnotist is clearly still present in some senses during the induction. What about having the subject read the induction to himself from written instructions (it *can* be done), or tape record an induction himself using his own phrasing and voice? What about introjected parental figures? You begin to get the idea: It is much harder to distill the hypnotist out of hypnosis than it might seem at first glance.

For this reason, and because the answers from this stream of research are just beginning to come in, I have chosen to structure the Brief Hypnotic Experience induction along relatively traditional hetero-hypnotic lines. It is still aimed at teaching the patient a self-hypnosis exercise that he will be able to practice on his own. The aim is to make your presence during the induction, and afterwards, a helpful and healing one. But you *will* be there.

8) *Can hypnosis cure cancer?* I don't know of any reliable scientific evidence that hypnosis can cure cancer. But many cancer patients, particularly those who suffer from pain, have been helped by hypnosis.

No discussion of the nature and uses of hypnosis would be complete without a consideration of this and similar distressing questions. They often arise after you have been working with a patient for a while, and frequently refer to a loved one with a malignancy or some other serious medical condition. In the case of questions concerning cancer, patients may notice several genuine similarities between the self-hypnosis exercise you have taught them and several visualization and relaxation procedures that are sometimes used with cancer patients. Unlike the questions that express distrust and hesitation concerning hypnosis, these questions express hope concerning the procedure and confidence in you as an expert. There is also usually a residue of the magical aura that has surrounded hypnosis down through the ages and which your educational efforts can modify but not erase. It is from people like these, and questions like these, that quacks make a living.

The details of how to handle such questions are outside the domain of hypnosis, but a response similar to the one I have provided is usually called for. Given kindly, it can protect the patient against exploitation without destroying vital hope.

TWO

Optimal Uses
and Risks

Your First Self-Hypnosis Patients

Once you have acquired a basic conceptual understanding of hypnosis and have had a chance to experience it yourself and teach it in a workshop or supervision format, you will be ready to begin your work with patients. The secret of success at this stage is simple: play only a game you know well, and with the deck stacked in your favor. Obviously, most clinicians do not usually have the luxury of being able to practice (or even play) this way. But what I am suggesting here is not a permanent state of affairs. I am talking about how you choose the first three patients with whom you use hypnosis. If you are at all successful with two out of these three, or very successful with one, your learning experiences up to this point will have been rewarded sufficiently for you to go on.

Let's start with the first element: playing a game that you know well. When applied to hypnosis this is clearly a relative statement, since you are a beginner at this technique. More to the point is the necessity to avoid the complete opposite of the approach I am advising. Let me describe this mistake in advance for you, so that you can recognize if you are at risk and change your course in time. Don't be offended or discouraged if this description fits you exactly; it applies to many eager or curious beginners who have gone on to do things right and succeed in their clinical uses of hypnosis.

The pitfall here is easy to describe: it is making your *first* use of the Brief Hypnotic Experience exercise a session with one of your patients. If you do this, you are literally asking for failure both in terms of the experience of hypnosis and your relationship with your patient. If you are reading this book in sequence, you may wonder why I am making this point again. In the previous chapter, I suggested various options for experiencing and learning to apply the exercise in the section on

22

"Your Personal Experience of Hypnosis." These options range from the ideal of a well-conducted workshop with ample opportunities for paired practice to learning the procedures from your own audiotapes and some practice teaching with a few non-patients.

How could anyone make this mistake after what I have just said? Easily, and unfortunately, all too commonly. For some it is simply the coincidence of newly kindled excitement over a new technique with a patient who seems ideal. For others it is resentment at feeling locked in to what seems like a restrictive protocol. The exercise itself, they reason, provides all the structure they need.

All I can do is to share my own experiences as a teacher in this area with you: the failure/abandonment rate is unacceptably high when the exercise is used with patients without any prior practice. This does not seem to depend on the age or general clinical experience of the learner. When I have had the opportunity to review what has gone wrong with students, it has usually boiled down to the direct or indirect communication to the patient that the clinician had literally never done this before. Hypnosis is still too controversial a technique to introduce in this way. Please, do not assume that what I have just said could never apply to you, so that you can go ahead and use the exercise right "out of the box" with patients. If these last paragraphs are truly unnecessary for you, i.e., if you have practiced, or plan to practice, please accept my apologies.

Let's assume, then, that you know your game well enough to start playing. Now you're ready for the second element: stacking the deck in your favor. For your first three patients you want the odds to be heavily on your side. Remember that you and your patient *both* win when things go well. After this, the spectrum of optimal to less than optimal to risky uses will serve as a context in which you can make sense of your experiences with hypnosis. You will use it to get perspective on when you probably could have done better than you did and when a minimal improvement is about all you can expect. Let's begin by considering the end of the spectrum where you want to be for your first three cases: the optimal uses for self-hypnosis.

*Problems That Self-Hypnosis
Is Likely to Help*

Self-hypnosis is most likely to prove helpful when applied to problems that:

1) are perceived, accepted, and presented to you as problems by the patient;
2) are relatively recent, or, if longstanding, the patient is ready and able to have them diminished;
3) have a central element that can be seen as a subjective experience of the patient;
4) can be influenced by helpful thoughts or images.

Each of these factors deserves some elaboration. To help you put these principles in a realistic clinical perspective, here is a case where self-hypnosis was successful that illustrates all of them:

Walter P. sees himself as a man stuck on the ladder to success. He is 29 years old, happily married, and with pride shows off a picture of his two-year-old daughter; another child is on the way. Walter was into computers before it became the "in" thing to do, and has accumulated both an academic and practical head start in the field of computer applications to business and medical forms. He has a good job with a major computer manufacturing and sales company, and his supervisors have admitted to him that people like him who know what they are doing technically and can apply their knowledge creatively to specific client problems are very hard to find. Walter describes his problem as the only thing that is blocking a series of promotions that would bring him a significantly higher salary. Both he and his wife feel ready to buy a house and have even begun exploring neighborhoods. They know exactly what they want to do with the money that promotion would bring.

For the last two months, Walter has noticed himself getting increasingly nervous when he has to present his proposed system to the client company's executives. He has never before had any problems with these kinds of presentations, but in the past they were infrequent and he had plenty of time to prepare and to practice. Now he has to make one about once every two weeks. Walter's nervousness is expressed as a pounding heart, a feeling of fear, and an embarrassing tremor that shows when he picks up a paper or points to something on one of his overheads. He has been to see his internist, who has given him a thorough physical exam and laboratory studies, including a thyroid evaluation. His internist asked me to see Walter to evaluate him for possible use of hypnosis or some other anti-anxiety treatment.

Walter has had no recent changes in his relationships or in his patterns of eating, sleeping, or recreation. He denies any past or family history of anxiety or depression, and his mental status is normal as he speaks to me in my office. After reviewing a number of options for handling his performance anxiety, Walter expresses a desire to try self-hypnosis. He prefers to avoid any medications, is skeptical about exploratory psychotherapy, and has a good friend who got considerable relief from post-operative pain from a self-hypnosis exercise taught to him by the anesthesiologist.

Walter had no trouble with the hand-separation test (described in Chapter 4), which I taught him at the end of our first session. At our second session, I taught Walter the Brief Hypnotic Experience exercise (described in Chapter 5). He responded very well to the exercise, describing it as "incredible." He was particularly impressed with how vivid the beach scene was for him, right down to a salty taste in his mouth and the sound of the gulls. Walter was assigned to practice the exercise twice daily during the two weeks before our next session. If he wished and felt comfortable with it, he could try out the exercise right before a presentation he was going to make in the middle of the second week to see if the peace he felt at the beach would neutralize the tension he felt during his presentations. Walter understood that we might be using the exercise directly in this way, or as part of a desensitization program.

Walter came in to his third session smiling broadly. He had practiced the exercise regularly and noted that he actually looked forward to the practice sessions as a break from sitting in front of his video display terminal. He was curious and a little apprehensive when he tried out the exercise before his presentation, but he knew as soon as he was finished with the exercise that this presentation would give him no problems. The relaxed, warm feeling from the beach was exactly the opposite of the worried and uptight feelings that had bothered him during his presentations.

Sure enough, the presentation went well and Walter was able to concentrate on the nods and exchanged smiles of his audience rather than on wondering if they were noticing how nervous he was. He pronounced himself cured, and required some convincing to return for a fourth session a month from the second. At this session he reported that he now only did the exercise when he was tired or before a presentation, and that the last two presentations had gone well. At a telephone follow-up six months after he had learned the exercise, Walter reported that his cure had endured. He had received a promotion and jokingly spoke of sending his two subordinates to see me so that they could learn to be more relaxed when they made presentations.

Let's go back to the four factors now and review them one by one using Walter's case as an illustration:

1) *Problem for the patient.* The treatment method taught in this book is embodied in an exercise that the patient learns from you and then applies to his problem on his own. You will have a significant role in tailoring this application, but when compared to other forms of psychotherapy, much more of the action here is going on outside of your office and thus outside of your direct control. This is helpful in generalizing the results to the patient's real life situation, but it makes the treatment highly vulnerable to mixed motivation on the patient's part.

For Walter, his anxiety in situations where he had to present his program orally was clearly a problem. Whatever the unconscious factors underlying this reaction, on the conscious level Walter wanted to be rid of it. He had a clear idea of what he stood to gain and lose, and was ready to work hard at learning the exercise and applying it to the troubling situation. That made my work rather easy, and yours will be made easy or easier when this kind of strong, unambivalent conscious motivation is present.

Not everyone you see will be like this. For example, if Walter had been badgered into treatment by a supervisor who himself was responding to pressure from above, the situation would have been quite different. Then the problem would have been identified as Walter's mostly by others. Or Walter's nervousness in the presentations might be a signal to him that he was trying to do too much too soon. Perhaps he was better off in direct service rather than as a supervisor. Under these circumstances the results of self-hypnosis are likely to be poor; there are too many opportunities with this treatment technique for mixed motivation to take its toll. In my own practice, I usually will not even try self-hypnosis under these conditions — if I am lucky enough to have spotted them in advance.

2) *Recent/ready to release.* Walter's problem was clearly of recent origin, so it was easy to decide that this factor was present in his case. But I still would have considered self-hypnosis a reasonable treatment strategy if the anxiety in public speaking situations had been longstand-

ing and the impetus to treatment had come from a change in the importance of these situations in Walter's life. Walter might still have been ready and able to work collaboratively with me on diminishing his anxiety to a level where it no longer blocked him from achieving his own goals.

Evaluating a patient's readiness to live without a chronic symptom is not an easy or foolproof process, and you should expect to make some mistakes. What you want to avoid is blaming *everything* that goes wrong in treatment on the patient's inability and/or unwillingness to abandon his symptoms. This can become a self-serving approach that is impervious to contradictory data, cuts off the opportunity to learn from mistakes and succeed with an alternative strategy, and destroys the mutual trust and respect that makes collaboration possible. This issue is covered in detail in Chapter 7, since it is a central one in developing a workable therapeutic contract for patients with pain.

3) *Subjective experience.* In my description of Walter's problem I identified it with the broad term "nervousness." I was able to get Walter to describe the elements of this nervousness: a pounding heart, a feeling of fear, and a tremor. In fact, they all occurred together, so that little was gained in being overly specific. Each of these can be seen as a subjective experience. Certainly the pounding heart could be described as a pulse rate or electrocardiogram, the tremor measured electromyographically or observed by someone else. But for purposes of self-hypnosis, you want to concentrate on the subjective and use the patient's self-reports as your major measuring device. Some suggestions for identifying and recording appropriate target symptoms for self-hypnosis are presented in Chapter 3.

If Walter had asked me to improve his public speaking, I would have wanted to redefine the problem, if possible, in experiential terms. If *performance* is to be a criterion, the patient must have the talent and training that are necessary conditions for success. A course in public speaking, some rehearsal, or learning more about the subject itself might be much more efficient than self-hypnosis in improving performance. (If these elements sound familiar, they are the exact procedures I have encouraged you to follow so that your performance as a beginning hypnotist is a success for both of us!) Let's consider two cases where this factor of behavior or performance vs. experience was an issue: one where self-hypnosis was eventually helpful, and another where it was not.

David E. was a generally well adjusted college student and an outstanding middle distance runner. His father, whom I knew, suggested that he see me to get some help with "the wall," a term familiar to athletes like himself but which I never heard of before. David described the wall for him as a feeling of overwhelming fatigue and almost physical resistance that came over him about three-quarters of the way through a race. Lately, he had been getting so tense in anticipation of this feeling that his performance at the start of the race was off what he considered his best.

David had no trouble learning the self-hypnosis exercise and was diligent in following my instructions for our first application. There was no difficulty in identifying the problematic subjective experience here — the wall. My first suggestion was that David do the exercise right before a race in an attempt to reduce his anticipatory anxiety and, by extension, help him break through the wall. By doing this I shifted the focus of the exercise to an area that I was familiar with — anticipatory anxiety — in an approach similar to the one that had worked with Walter.

David tried to be polite in describing the results, but his disappointment showed. Although he felt calm while doing the exercise and a little better about his starts, there was no real change in the wall. He wondered out loud whether he might have wasted his carefully budgeted time in learning and practicing the exercise. I acknowledged my failure and decided to try a more direct approach to the wall itself First, we abandoned any effort to do the exercise right before a race. David was relieved at this, since it had taken some effort to conceal what he was doing from his teammates. He was not anxious to tell them about his self-hypnosis, especially if it was unsuccessful, and I did not challenge this position.

Next, we worked together on the exercise itself to find a "key phrase" associated with the relaxing beach scene that would help with the wall. With some coaching from me, David finally came up with "strong and steady," two words that both described the waves as he watched them from the beach and the opposite of how he felt when he ran up against the wall (weak and faltering). Our strategy was to use regular practice of the exercise to imprint this phrase and its implications in David's mind; he would then repeat the phrase to himself during the race as he neared the place where he usually encountered the wall.

This second strategy was much more successful. David reported that his pace in the last third of his races was much steadier, and that he had picked up a second or two in his overall times. Soon the use of the phrase "strong and steady" became almost automatic, and David began to be able to devote his attention to positioning himself for the finish. He lost interest in the self-hypnosis exercise and stopped practicing it after a few months, but his father reported that he continued to use the phrase through his college running career. Although he talked freely with his father, none of his college classmates or friends ever knew about his use of self-hypnosis.

In Chuck M.'s case, the ending was not so happy. I first met Chuck in the prison ward of a city hospital, where he was brought after being shot by a police officer during an unsuccessful armed robbery. He was able to learn and effectively use a self-hypnosis exercise to deal with post-operative pain following removal of the bullet and part of his small intestine. Although he described himself as mean and dangerous, he was always friendly to me and seemed to get a kick from showing off his exercise to the other prisoners and to the guards.

I did not see or hear from him for another three years. Then I was called by the intake worker at the outpatient clinic, who told me that Chuck had asked specifically to be assigned to my team because he wanted hypnosis. He was now out on parole, unemployed, and living with his girlfriend and her infant daughter. His problem, as he saw it, was his temper. His angry oubursts and readiness to fight were assets on the street, but made him impossible to live with according to his girlfriend. Although he had not struck her or her child, she was threatening to kick him out if the outbursts did not stop. According to Chuck, his girlfriend had a good influence on him; he was much less likely to hang around with his bad friends while he was living with her. He wanted to save the relationship if possible. Chuck reasoned that hypnosis, which had been so helpful with his pain, was the answer. Could he hypnotize himself to get rid of his temper?

In exploring the problem, it was clear that both members of the couple contributed to the outbursts. Chuck's girlfriend came in for one session with him, but he called a few days later to say that she had been very uncomfortable and did not want to come back. He emphasized that it was hypnosis, not "just talking" that he wanted to try. The outbursts were not associated with intoxication, and had no features suggesting a seizure disorder. Chuck could clearly identify a number of physical sensations and emotions regularly associated with the outbursts: a tightness in his chest, tension, rapid breathing, and a feeling of rage. Although the beach scene was not particularly meaningful to him, Chuck was able to construct a similar peaceful scene based on a pond in a local park where he had played as a boy. As he had in prison, he enjoyed demonstrating the self-hypnosis exercise in front of medical students and residents.

Unfortunately, Chuck's hypnotic talent and mastery of the exercise could not be brought to bear on his anger "attacks." The problem was that he became aware of the physical sensations and emotions only *after* the actual outbursts, which usually lasted only a few seconds to half a minute. There were no warning signs that he could spot beforehand. We even tried having him do the exercise every few hours during the times when the outbursts occurred, but this too failed. The problem, then, remained basically an unacceptable (to his girlfriend) behavior and we never could translate it functionally to an intervening subjective experience that we could work with.

Chuck remained friendly and cheerful through these unsuccessful trials, but finally called up to cancel his appointment and say, "Thanks, doc, but I guess it's not going to work on this like it did with the pain." Several months later, a medical student who had run into Chuck's girlfriend at another clinic gave me a follow-up: she had indeed kicked Chuck out about a week after his last appointment. About a month later he had been arrested for selling stolen goods. No one was hurt during the arrest, but Chuck was back in jail. His own assessment of the success of hypnosis in one situation, where the problem was an experience, and its failure in another, where the problem was a behavior, was right.

4) *Helpful thoughts/images.* For Walter, the beach scene he was able to experience while doing his self-hypnosis exercise brought with it a relaxed, warm feeling that effectively neutralized his performance anxiety. Whether you call David E.'s "strong and steady" phrase a thought or an image (it probably, as with many hypnotic phenomena, has elements of both), it was enough to give him the feeling that he had broken through the wall. For Chuck, the peaceful thoughts and images associated with his self-hypnosis exercise did not influence his problem.

Many problems can be influenced by helpful thoughts or images, ranging from the normative stresses that life brings to the symptoms of critical or terminal illness. Notice that I use the term influenced, not removed or cured. Self-hypnosis is far from the only established systematic method that makes use of helpful thoughts or images: prayer and meditation are two others. If you are at all familiar with religious or meditative practice, these perspectives may help you to understand this factor and how it can be applied to a wide range of human problems. Wise members of the clergy of all faiths and experienced teachers of meditation are well-versed in the creative potential, and the limitations, of helpful thoughts and images.

The relationship of self-hypnosis to meditation and prayer is a fascinating topic beyond the scope of this introductory book. An article by Herbert Benson and his colleagues on "The Relaxation Response and Hypnosis" compares hypnosis to a widely practiced meditative technique; it can be found in the special issue on self-hypnosis (July 1981) of the *International Journal of Clinical and Experimental Hypnosis* referenced in Appendix B. In Chapter 9 I have tried to deal with some of the more common religious issues raised by patients who are using self-hypnosis.

Clearly, the four positive factors that I have outlined and discussed interact with each other and in fact may overlap. They are meant to give you a set of criteria that you can apply yourself to the patients you see. Where all are present, self-hypnosis will probably be helpful; where none is present, it is probably not worth a try. Most patients will fall somewhere between these extremes.

There are two items that are conspicuous for their absence from my list: hypnotic responsivity and diagnosis. The Brief Hypnotic Experience exercise is geared towards the low end of hypnotic responsivity. To be more specific, it is based on an ideomotor response with a very high pass percentage, and features a pleasant, relaxing scene that is imagined with eyes closed. These features both make your work as a beginning hypnotist easier (you will have few complete failures) and take the pressure off you to find highly talented subjects for your first efforts.

If you are beginning to suspect that a large part of the benefit of learning and practicing the self-hypnosis exercise has nothing to do with hypnosis per se, then you are absolutely right. The same is true of the relationship of clinical improvement to taking antidepressant medications, as well as a host of other physical and psychological treatment methods. Calling these aspects of treatment "nonspecific" or placebo effects gives them an undesirable taint and grossly misrepresents their importance in healing. You want to be able to use these nonhypnotic elements intelligently and ethically to help your patients; it is only in the research context that it becomes crucial to tease them out of the fabric of treatment with devices such as placebo controls and double-blind conditions.

The most prominent nonhypnotic elements that are involved in the exercise you will be teaching are the meaning of hypnosis to the patient, learning a self-help procedure, physical relaxation, and use of the exercise as a time-out from usual problems or activities. I will be going over each of these in detail in subsequent chapters, but you should be aware of them now as additional screening criteria for patients and problems likely to be helped by self-hypnosis. Do any of these elements click with your perception of the patient's resources and needs?

I have also not included any specific diagnostic categories in my list. This is not because I disapprove of the whole idea of medical model diagnoses in favor of some alternative scheme of psychodynamic, behavioral, or cognitive analysis. I make diagnoses, and find them useful. But except for a few obvious exceptions (such as profound mental retardation or acutely manic bipolar disorder), skilled clinicians have used the Brief Hypnotic Experience exercise or a number of similar procedures with patients falling in almost every diagnostic category, including schizophrenic, somatoform and personality (DSM-III Axis II) disorders.

As explained in the Introduction, I have selected two common diagnostic categories as ideal initial applications for the self-hypnosis exercise: 1) anxiety, tension or stress, and 2) dysfunctional pain. The reasons for this selection have already been outlined. You should realize, however, that this does not mean that anxiety or pain must be the *only* diagnoses of your first patients. This may be particularly impractical if you work in a specialized treatment setting. A patient with cancer may have anxiety, or dysfunctional pain, or both. A recovering alcoholic may benefit from nonpharmacological anxiety reduction during his first week back on the job after a month in a detoxification center. A bipolar patient on lithium may also have a bad back. Just keep the four positive factors in mind, and make sure that other diagnoses or problem areas don't entirely negate them.

*Problems That Self-Hypnosis
Is Unlikely to Help*

Self-hypnosis is unlikely to prove helpful when applied to problems:

1) that are founded in disturbed current interpersonal relationships;
2) of patients who cannot or will not practice the exercise on their
own between sessions;
3) that have not responded at all to three or more different treatment approaches applied by competent professionals.

Case examples may help here as well. I am going to give examples
for this section from the cases of clinicians who came to me for consultation or supervision concerning hypnosis. I have had my own share
of failures and mistakes and have already shared the case of Chuck
M. with you; I will mention another in Chapter 6. The potential
mistakes and failures that I am most concerned about at this point are
the ones you should see coming *before* you try hypnosis. Let's start
with Ellen G.

Ellen is 43 years old and describes herself as a potter. Her two
children (both girls) are in their sophomore and senior years of college and are described by Ellen as a delight and a source of pride to
her and to her husband, a successful cardiologist. Ellen's oldest daughter has just been accepted to a prestigious medical school. She has been
referred imformally by her husband to a psychologist who has had
some success with hypnosis in alleviating anxiety in a number of the
husband's post-heart-attack patients.

Ellen had presented as an intelligent, articulate woman who was
highly motivated to learn self-hypnosis. The target symptom was anxiety attacks that occurred at first in airplanes but soon spread to all
travel situations beyond her local community. An evaluation by her
internist and a brief trial of diazepam (Valium) had not been particularly helpful. The psychologist established quickly that the first attack
occurred on a flight with her daughter to look over a medical school
and that some features of panic disorder and agoraphobia were present.

Ellen easily learned a self-hypnosis exercise but got absolutely no
relief from it. Several reasonable approaches had been tried, including
twice daily use, concentrated use during travel situations, and a cog-

nitive message focusing on relaxation and calm control. I could find nothing wrong with the hypnosis aspects of the treatment and suggested some further exploration of the relationship side.

Two weeks later, the psychologist called to tell me what had happened. After only the most superficial inquiries, Ellen had broken down in the psychologist's office and weepingly described her dilemma. In brief, she was caught between the role of successful suburban home-maker/artist that her parents had raised her for and her husband admired and the possibilities of a new relationship that she herself knew was risky and dangerous. She had met and been attracted to a potter in his thirties who shared her interest in some of the same glazing techniques and actually earned his living from his craft. He was divorced and had no real contact with his former wife and child who now lived in a distant city. He was a gentle, considerate person who was much more relaxed than Ellen in talking about their mutual attraction but put no pressure on her sexually.

About a week before the airplane trip with which her symptoms began, Ellen and her friend had shared a bottle of wine at lunch and done some "touching under the table" as she put it. She had declined an invitation to return to his apartment, but thoughts and fantasies of this man began to occupy her increasingly. She described the only real benefit of the self-hypnosis exercise as its ability to produce extremely vivid and arousing masturbatory fantasies for her—all of which involved this one man.

Ellen did not consciously blame her daughter, but did recognize the daughter's unwitting contribution to upsetting her equilibrium. Here was an attractive young woman breaking down the role boundaries that had provided the structure for Ellen's marital and personal self-image. It didn't help matters any that her daughter discussed her own relationship problems freely with her mother, whom she saw as arty and tolerant. Ellen had never seriously considered talking about any of this with her husband. She knew that he had had two brief affairs during their marriage, both with nurses. One he had told her about after it was over; another she had found out about on her own. Although they had never discussed it explicitly, Ellen felt (and the psychologist, who had worked with her husband, agreed) that he would be enraged and seriously upset by any extramarital relationships on Ellen's part.

At this point, the psychologist abandoned efforts to work on the self-hypnosis exercise and devoted the rest of the session to a pre-liminary exploration of Ellen's options. For the time being, Ellen decid-ed that she did not want to consummate the sexual aspects of her new relationship; she realized that the excitement she now felt might be the best that this particular relationship had to offer. She also realized that she was embarked, for better or worse, on an examination of her roles and values. Although she called herself a potter, wasn't she really from an economic point of view a doctor's wife? Was she willing to be poor? On her own? Was adultery permissible, regardless of what her hus-band or anyone else said or did? The psychologist was able to help her work out an appropriate matrix for examining these issues: sessions with another clinician who was wise and mature, could work with couples if that became appropriate, and had no professional or per-sonal connections to her husband. She decided to keep the sessions to herself, and pay for them from her own savings. By the time the referral was completed, Ellen's anxiety attacks were significantly reduced, but not gone. There was still much work to be done.

Relationship-based problems are the most common source of failures in cases that, like Ellen's, seem ideal for self-hypnosis. I am not im-plying that all candidates for self-hypnosis must be happily married or single — only that the target problem for self-hypnosis not be a direct expression of the disturbed relationship. Marital and parent-child issues also influence practice significantly after patients have learned a self-hypnosis exercise; these aspects will be covered in Chapter 9.

Patients who cannot or will not practice the exercise on their own between sessions are easy to spot after you have already taught the ex-ercise; the trick is to spot them in advance. By the time the psychiatrist treating Mark R. had run out of small talk, it was obvious to both of us that Mark was not going to show up for our session. The psychiatrist already had a sense that self-hypnosis might not help much with Mark's drug abuse problems, but he was willing to give it a try and had been pressured by Mark's parents, who had read an optimistic article in the newspaper. The psychiatrist had asked me to sit in with him to evaluate both Mark and his own technique.

The no-show was no surprise. Mark had failed to show up for slight-ly over half of his appointments. His parents paid for the sessions whether he came or not; this was the only way they had been able to get competent clinicians to see him. Mark was the spoiled and unstable scion of a wealthy old moneyed family. He had completed prep school and two years of college, but the two years had taken him four to finish because he quit classes frequently after losing interest or being criticized by the teacher. He sarcastically claimed that he was the best living argument against academic freedom: no one at school was free to expel him as long as his father was providing the money for the new dorm. His peer relationships were generally superficial and based on fascination with or efforts to get a piece of his great wealth. He felt most comfortable, and had the best relationships, with some of his old prepschool classmates who came from similar families.

After waiting half an hour we both left, having decided that there was very little likelihood that Mark would practice a self-hypnosis exercise even if he was able to learn one. Any patient whose life and/or personality is significantly unsteady or unmotivated may not practice a self-hypnosis exercise enough to make it a preferred treatment option. In cases like these you are much better off setting very modest goals and sticking with a treatment method that takes place more directly under your control.

Mark, it turned out, also illustrated the last of my fundamental negative factors: the psychiatrist now treating him was the last in a series of at least half a dozen physicians, psychologists and social workers, all well-qualified and all with excellent records of previous successes. It is slightly more negative if the three previous treatment efforts have been made by three different therapists, each doing what he or she felt was needed, but I would still call this factor present if the different approaches had been tried by the same competent therapist.

This last factor would seem to be so self-evident as to not even merit mention — a long past history of treatment failures predicting another failure; yet the combination of hypnosis as the method and a beginner as the teacher seems to be especially vulnerable to these cases. Often, as with Mark, the impetus for treatment comes from a distressed and caring parent, spouse or child. People have always turned to magic when their usual methods of explanation and control did not work, and hypnosis carries a considerable magical heritage. A beginning hypnotist, anxious to try out a new technique, may mistake desperation for realistic enthusiasm. Easily understandable burnout in clinicians caring for difficult patients may lead to referrals that function more as respite for the therapist than realistic treatment. Sometimes the "dumping" can be more blatant, especially with naive younger clinicians. One psychiatric resident realized only in retrospect that a senior supervisor had referred a chronically chaotic borderline personality disorder patient to her for training in self-hypnosis only to buy some time while he was on vacation out of the country.

This last factor is a relative, not an absolute, one. Some seemingly hopeless cases with long histories of treatment failures have benefited significantly from self-hypnosis, especially if it was taught using a low-key "let's try this and see if it helps you feel any better" approach. Still, it is probably best not to include such patients among your first.

Risks of Self-Hypnosis

Considering all the controversy that has surrounded it and its prominent role in drama and literature, hypnosis is a remarkably risk-free procedure when used by a well-trained therapist. The common Svengali misconceptions (complete control of subject, sexual domination, criminal manipulation) have been discussed in Chapter 1. The inherent safety of hypnosis is amplified by the particular structure of the Brief Hypnotic Experience exercise: it is a self-hypnosis procedure that the patient learns from the hypnotist and then applies *himself* under supervision to his own problems. Thus, the hypnotist's treatment strategy can at least potentially be examined by the patient or by others outside of the therapist's office.

If I had to give you only one expression of the risks of self-hypnosis to take away from your reading of this book, I would choose a warning phrase used in his many workshops for clinicians by a clinician-researcher who has served as one of my own principal teachers and role models in the use of hypnosis: Dr. Martin Orne. Martin has put it so concisely and well that the only thing to do is to quote him directly. The concept is so important that it cannot be emphasized too much: *"Never treat any patient using hypnosis whom you would not treat without it."*

This principle, intelligently applied, will protect you and your patients even more than the few specific warnings that follow. Let's make sure that you understand this phrase completely. Notice that no specific diagnosis, patient group, or target symptom is mentioned. Whatever the category, someone, somewhere, will consider it a routine practice problem.

This is always brought home to me most graphically when I conduct workshops that include a variety of clinicians. One of the best features of these workshops is the chance to meet and learn from people whom you wouldn't ordinarily encounter. Under these circumstances, each person presents the kinds of problems and patients that are of personal concern and to whom the newly acquired hypnotic skills are to be applied: discomfort from dental prostheses after all reasonable adjustments have been made; addicts in a methadone maintenance program; graduate students unable to defend their theses because of public speaking anxiety ; terminally ill patients in a hospice program; people struggling with the stresses of a hostile and legally entangled divorce. It takes only a few presentations to get the message: what one clinician feels perfectly comfortable with would give the person next to him that "Uh oh!" feeling that precedes fantasies of humiliating headlines or lawsuits.

I do not mean to imply that you have to be an oncologist to treat a cancer patient or a divorce attorney to help someone going through one. What you want to steer clear of are situations where your still-to-be-established expertise in hypnosis is the *only* thing qualifying you to work in any way with a particular patient, or where you enter a new consultation area for the first time as a hypnotist. In borderline situations I would advise you to do the same thing that I do: work conjointly with a clincian who *is* an expert in the given field. This may be an awkward or expensive arrangement, but it will prevent the kind of avoidable mistakes that might later prove more awkward or expensive, mistakes that usually have nothing to do with hypnosis per se. If you have questions about a particular application and are seeking a consultation or a second opinion, the expertise you want to be sure of relates to the patient group or clinical problem; if you can find hypnotic expertise in the same person, you are lucky.

Now that you understand the most important caution, we can go over a few specific problem areas. There are a few situations and types of patients where I feel hypnosis should probably not be used even if the patient and/or someone else wants it and the requisite hypnotic talent, motivation and willingness to practice are present. These are:

1) paranoid patients with persecutory tendencies;
2) patients who have current problems with basic reality contact, especially interpersonal reality;

3) unusually sexually charged situations between therapist and patient;
4) attempts to retrieve factually accurate memories.

As before, let's go over each of these briefly.

1) *Paranoid patients*. The cultural implications of hypnosis interact in a very unhelpful way with persecutory paranoid systems. Including in those at risk are patients with true paranoid disorders; schizophrenia, paranoid type; and paranoid personality disorder. These patients latch on to real, suspected or delusional hypnotic experiences and continue to pursue them long past the point of any benefit to themselves or others. Hypnosis shares this place with a number of other phenomena and institutions: radio transmissions, lasers, the F.B.I., the Mafia, and other structured variants on the paranoid "they."

I have seen a number of patients who requested hypnosis in order to "undo" an alleged prior hypnosis that was making them hear voices or think evil thoughts, or was blamed for snatching thoughts out of their minds. Just as often, patients have been sent to me for a second opinion by clinicians who have given up on trying to convince them on their own that hypnosis is neither the cause nor the treatment of their problems.

George L. had been laid off from his factory job along with a number of other employees due to production cutbacks. Before this, his supervisors had valued his steady, reliable work in a relatively routine job far below his formal educational level. They knew of his several past psychiatric hospitalizations, and that he took medications "for his nerves." About a month after he was fired, George stopped his medication and became preoccupied with the idea that he had been influenced through a video display terminal at work in order to "screw up my mind so that I couldn't find another job."

George found a lay hypnotist through the Yellow Pages who he claimed had hypnotized him in an effort to "clear my mind of whatever had been done to me." Following this experience, he decided that the mainframe computer at work had hypnotized him through the video display terminal, and that the hypnotist might be involved in the plot as well. When he called one of the other employees who had been fired to confirm his suspicions, that employee immediately called George's brother (the closest person to him), who immediately called George's psychiatrist.

George reluctantly agreed to restart his antipsychotic medication, but the relief of his agitation did not get rid of his newly acquired paranoid delusion. I interviewed him at his psychiatrist's request, and tried to reassure him that he had not been hypnotized by the computer. I refused, as had his psychiatrist, to hypnotize him again to "straighten the whole thing out." George was rehired a few months later, but his delusion persisted; he required a good deal of reassurance to work near the computer. He called me again a year and a half later to request hypnosis; I again refused and referred him back to the psychiatrist who had been caring for him. Like others in this group, he was a sad, tormented person whom hypnosis had harmed much more than it had helped.

2) *Reality problems*. The patients in this group are different from the paranoid patients I have just discussed, although a paranoid delusion is certainly a problem with reality and there may be some overlap. The quality I want you to be watching for is one described as "spacey," "wifty," or "in a world of his own." Diagnoses are usually along Axis II of DSM-III, especially schizotypal personality disorder, or mixed personality disorders that feature schizoid, borderline or avoidant traits in adults. For adolescents (and these patients are often adolescents or young adults), the diagnosis is usually schizoid or avoidant disorder of adolescence, or identity disorder. When frankly psychotic features such as hallucinations or delusions are present, hypnosis is not usually sought as a treatment by these patients themselves or by family members trying to help them.

The picture is often complicated by past, suspected or current substance abuse or dependence. Patients may have tried membership in cults or more conventional religious groups as a way of mastering their turmoil. The clinician thinks of self-hypnosis under these circumstances, or has it suggested to him or her by family members, as a relatively harmless substitute for drugs, exotic religious rituals or meditation, or as an antidote to suspected brainwashing.

With such patients self-hypnosis, or any other practice that focuses attention on inner experiences (remember our definition: a process that allows us to experience thoughts and images as real), may do more harm than good and should be undertaken cautiously, if at all. It is certainly not an application for beginners. What these patients often need is a return to more normal patterns of socialization that will permit consensual validation and social feedback. Where some kind of unusual socialization experience, such as a cult, is the issue, a gradual reintroduction to family and community may take a good deal of time and patience. Many communities have support groups that can be very helpful both to former members and their families. Where social isolation and peculiar thinking are indications of more serious individual psychopathology, a careful psychiatric evaluation and treatment program are indicated. Such a program might very well include structured supportive psychotherapy and psychotropic medications where appropriate.

Linda S. had left her sophomore year of college to join a religious community that many people considered a cult. Her conventionally religious parents were angered and upset by her move, but maintained contact with her on the advice of the family minister, who had counseled several families in similar circumstances. After five months away, Linda returned home around Christmas time, saying she "needed some space to figure things out." She entered psychotherapy voluntarily with a clinician who taught her a self-hypnosis exercise to replace the meditative ritual that had filled so much of her time recently. Linda spent several hours a day "in self-hypnosis" alone in her room, and seemed to be avoiding any realistic planning for work or for a resumption of her education.

After about two weeks of this routine, a crisis occurred during which Linda became panicked by "terrible, evil, thoughts" that would come to her as she did the self-hypnosis exercise. The clinician wisely advised Linda to stop the exercise and increased the frequency and structure of the psychotherapy sessions. Linda went through a period of considerable turmoil, but was able to work through the crisis with her therapist without any need for hospitalization or medications; the family minister was helpful in reassuring her about her spiritual quest, and she got considerable comfort from attending weekly church services. The self-hypnosis exercise was not an ongoing therapeutic issue, and Linda returned to college uneventfully at the beginning of the next school year.

Linda's relatively favorable outcome might have been quite different (and less happy) had the clinician responded to her crisis by deciding that more hypnosis was needed rather than less. In addition, family and religious factors worked for her and against isolation. If these factors had not been working in the right direction, the mistaken use of hypnosis might have caused more harm.

3) *Sex.* The meaning of hypnosis in our popular culture still carries a significant sexual load. Much of this has its origin in the Svengali/Trilby story (in a novel by George Du Maurier published in 1894) and its many variants. The themes that seem to occur most often are the use of hypnosis by a powerful male figure to seduce and/or control a younger woman, and the hypnotic state as a disinhibiting condition where denied or repressed sexual impulses are blurted out or acted out (often with subsequent amnesia). Alcohol has a similar reputation in both these areas.

The sexual risks of the self-hypnosis situation you will be teaching are generally small. The self-hypnosis paradigm itself gets away from the Svengali model, since you are empowering the patient by teaching him something rather than imposing your will on him through a procedure that always is done by you. Consequently, my warning centers on the therapist-patient relationship rather than on the procedure itself, and is restricted to situations that are unusually sexually charged *for that particular therapist.*

All well-trained clinicians are aware of the sexual feelings that go along with the therapist-patient relationship. An understanding of transference and countertransference, an appreciation and acceptance of the ethics of therapy, and a character able to resist the inevitable temptations are the factors that protect us and our patients. All I am saying is that the sexual implications of hypnosis should lead you to avoid its use where you can foresee sexual trouble *in advance.*

What are the kind of warning signs to look for? Here are a number provided retrospectively by clinicians who experienced problems in this area:

1) a patient whom you find unusually attractive, or who appears in your sexual fantasies or dreams; a good self-screening may be to ask whether this patient would arouse jealousy in a current or recent sexual partner;
2) a patient with a past history of sexual relationships with clinicians and/or teachers;
3) a patient who persists in emphasizing the sexually controlling

or disinhibiting aspects of hypnosis even after thorough discussions;

4) a patient who acts in an overtly sexually provocative way during the early phases of self-hypnosis training (e.g., inappropriate "loosening" of clothing).

All these factors may seem pretty obvious, but they have been present in situations that caused problems for other clinicians and you should have them somewhere in your mind as a cue for scrutiny.

There are also a number of factors within the hypnotic situation itself that can act as sexual stimuli. For some beginning clinicians the induction of hypnosis itself is experienced as highly arousing sexually; they usually are surprised and sometimes are frightened by the arousal, which most often occurs as the patient begins to respond behaviorally to the induction suggestions (e.g., as the arm begins to rise or as obvious muscular relaxation occurs). Sometimes specific factors can be identified, such as eye closure and relaxed posture in a patient who always sits and talks upright; in other situations the stimulus is clearly originating in the meaning of hypnosis for the clinician. These reactions often disappear with practice, but may require some structured supervision or psychotherapy for the clinician if they are severe or persistent. Sometimes patients will discover erotic possibilities in self-hypnosis on their own, as did Ellen G., described earlier in this chapter. The psychologist working with her was able to listen to her description of vivid masturbatory fantasies professionally, and to fit this into a broad understanding of Ellen's personal resources and current situation.

Sex is a part of life, and sexual issues can be legitimate foci for clinical self-hypnosis. Chapter 8 contains an introduction to the use of self-hypnosis in sex therapy. To fix the risk factors in your mind, here is the case of a beginner who was not aware of them:

Craig M. took a workshop in hypnosis, including self-hypnosis, during his first year of residency training in psychiatry. He correctly recognized that the psychotic inpatients with whom he worked were not ideal as his first hypnotic cases, so he decided to try hypnosis on one of his few outpatients, a graduate student in English at the university, whom he had seen about ten times on a weekly basis.

Looking back on it later, Craig realized that it was no accident that he had chosen Laura A. as his first hypnosis patient. She had come seeking "psychotherapy for self-understanding," and seemed in excellent psychological health compared to the patients he usually dealt with. He had identified a repetitive pattern of unsatisfactory relationships with men, including a brief romance with one of her professors. Laura was the first patient who had reported dreams to him (she believed that this was part of psychotherapy), but Craig was not sure what to do with them. He planned on using hypnosis to allow Laura to generate dreams in the office that might be more accessible to both of them.

Although Craig had dealt with a number of young women patients on the inpatient unit, he had perceived Laura immediately as different. She was like him in social background, single, and he was fascinated by her literary interest. Laura was strikingly good looking, and came to their sessions dressed revealingly. After the first two sessions, Craig found himself wondering before he went out into the waiting room what she would be wearing. Often he had to exert conscious effort to keep from looking at her nipples during the psychotherapy hour. He had himself had erotic dreams about her several times.

Craig discussed hypnosis with Laura and found her open and interested. He planned an exploratory session where he would do an induction, suggest that Laura have a dream, and then teach her a self-hypnosis exercise if the process seemed promising. Laura came dressed for this session in a thin T-shirt and jeans. About five minutes into the induction, she suddenly opened her eyes and smiled broadly at Craig. His eyes were clearly fixed on her breasts, and he had an obvious erection. Craig described that moment as one of the most painful in his life. He looked away from Laura's gaze, crossed his legs, and asked Laura what the problem was. Craig did not remember Laura's reply or what he said in his desperate efforts to get through the time remaining in their session. He was relieved when Laura did not show up for their next regular appointment and did not call her to follow up. Not surprisingly, many of her dreams had been about her father.

4) *Accurate memories.* Using self-hypnosis, or any other hypnotic technique, in an attempt to retrieve *factually* accurate memories is dangerous in a different sense than the other risk factors that I have mentioned. The risk here is not so much to the patient as to the memory itself, and to any third party who might suffer the consequences of decisions based on that memory. This may all sound rather technical, but a case example will make it quite clear:

Bob O. had been convicted of a bank robbery in his twenties, and had served seven years in prison for the crime. Now in his late thirties, he seemed to be doing well in his job as a truck driver and in his relationship with his wife and two children. Then he was suddenly arrested and charged with a bank robbery in a nearby town in which an assistant bank manager had been shot and killed. A teller at the bank identified him both in a line-up and later in court. Another criminal who couldn't stay straight.

Or so it seemed. As the trial progressed, it emerged that the teller had been unable to give a clear description of the robber when she was first interviewed by police. The manager who had been killed had been the person who hired her, and he had helped her through several tough situations. She was sick with grief and rage. The detectives working on the case were under intense pressure to solve it, and were becoming uncomfortable with the repeatedly unproductive interviews of the distraught teller and the endless reviews of mug shots. One of them had heard that hypnosis could help retrieve memories, and brought in a local psychologist who used hypnosis in his practice for relaxation and habit control.

In a dramatic session, the psychologist hypnotized the teller and the detectives interviewed her again under hypnosis. She was told that she would now be able to see the face of the robber clearly, and that this picture would remain with her so that she would be able to identify him later. The detectives began talking her through the robbery scenario. Suddenly she screamed out loud, "That's him! That's him!" and began weeping hysterically. She described a person who fit Bob's description perfectly and was later able to pick him out of the mug-shot book and in a line-up. When asked why she could not recall or identify him earlier, she replied, "I had a picture, but it wasn't clear yet; the hypnosis made it clear."

The prosecution had presented its initial arguments, and the defense was preparing to present expert testimony questioning the accuracy of hypnotically refreshed memories when the trial ended abruptly. Bob's alibi for the time of the robbery was quite weak: he said that he had been on the road, but admitted that he had been in the vicinity of the robbery at the time. Everyone, including Bob, was surprised when another trucker came forward to support his alibi. This man had been driving behind Bob at the exact time of the robbery; he could be sure of this because the robbery was reported and discussed by several people on the C.B. channel he was using at the time. He remembered Bob and his rig clearly because they had both been involved in a multi-truck accident several months earlier in which several rigs had been scraped by another. The other driver had pulled up beside Bob and seen him clearly in the cab of his truck before settling in behind him. He was shocked when he read of the trial in the newspapers, and immediately called the police.

Bob put his life back together, but it took some time for his young children to get over the trauma and they retained a suspiciousness of police that reminded him painfully of his own past. The detectives, the teller, and the psychologist were bewildered by what had happened. "I can still see the picture in my mind," the teller insisted, "It's *him!*" The defense experts who had never had to testify, and others who have conducted legitimate scientific research on memory, hypnosis, and their interactions knew what had happened. The details of this fascinating and complex subject are beyond the scope of this book, but let me summarize the essential points. If you are aware of these factors you will be able to steer clear of high-risk situations and avoid putting yourself in the position of the psychologist in this case — a well-meaning and generally competent clinician who had confused clinically useful memories with factually accurate ones.

Memory, as most clinicians realize, is a dynamic process in every sense of the word. The view of memories as a set of videotapes in the brain that can be retrieved and replayed under the right conditions is naively inaccurate. Where clear memories are not available and where pressure to remember is applied, people will confabulate memories to fill these gaps. This process is obvious in patients with amnestic syndromes based on organic brain disease, but it occurs regularly in less dramatic forms. The sources for confabulation are usually mixed: cues from the current environment (e.g., mug shots, biased questioning) mixed with related and unrelated past memory traces.

The same voluntary suspension of disbelief and critical thinking that allows a patient to experience his hand as light and floating or feel that he is on the beach makes confabulation more likely in hypnosis than in the nonhypnotic state. To make matters worse, both those who have undergone hypnosis and those who have observed them mistake the vividness of hypnotic experiences for accuracy, and are more confident in hypnotically refreshed memories than in ordinary ones. Using hypnosis may indeed overcome emotional blocks to remembering, but confabulations are mixed in with accurate memories. No one, no matter how expert he or she is in hypnosis or memory, can tell which memories reported in hypnosis are accurate and which are confabulations. Worst of all, the memory itself is changed by the use of hypnosis and the distortion cannot be undone ("I can still see the picture in my mind; it's *him!*").

There are a number of guidelines for the investigative use of hypnosis that can somewhat reduce, but not eliminate, the risk of serious distortions. The hypnotist and all those present should know nothing of the details of the case so that they do not inadvertently cue the subject and shape his response to fit their own preconceptions. (The detectives who did the interview had suggested Bob as a possibility early in the investigation, but the teller had not been able to make even a tentative identification—she had, however, spent a long time looking at Bob's picture.) No suggestions of enhanced memory should be given, and the less obtrusive the recall technique the better. Complete videotape recordings of all sessions (which were not available in this case) can be examined by impartial experts for instances of cueing.

Clinicians, including most clinicians who use hypnosis, would never think of applying such procedures to their work with patients. Any clinician who has worked with both members of a couple individually and then seen them together in marital therapy is aware of the range of individual difference in how a single event is perceived and remembered. Who said or did exactly what is less important than the improvement of the relationship. From the time of Freud, clinicians have been aware of the complex mixture of historical fact, confabulation, and unconsciously determined fantasy in the memories all of us have of the important people and moments of our lives. Again, relief of suffering, finishing unfinished psychological business, and the resolution of debilitating conflicts are the goals. Clinicians are not evaluated for the factual accuracy of their patients' memories as experienced in therapy.

By now you should have the picture: this is an area in which hypnosis should be used cautiously, if at all, and then only by specialists. A number of states have already disallowed the use of hypnotically refreshed memories as evidence in court, and more are likely to follow. Self-hypnosis, the hypnotic technique you will be starting with, is not usually used for memory retrieval.

If you are interested in pursuing this area further after you have acquired general experience with hypnosis, the relevant issues and techniques are covered in the chapter by Orne, Soskis, Dinges and Orne cited in Appendix B. The major hypnosis societies (see Appendix A) often have advanced workshops on forensic hypnosis at their annual meetings. In this area even more than in others it is important to acquire scientifically based training: I would advise you to stick to workshops sponsored by the International Society of Hypnosis or its constituent societies or by recognized universities or hospitals. These same societies usually also offer advanced workshops on hypnoanalysis (which may employ techniques such as age regression, automatic writing or dream induction) and other applications of hypnosis to clinical (as opposed to forensic) situations where memories are important.

THREE

Preparing
the Patient

The First Session

The goals and methods of your first session with a patient devoted to hypnosis are harder to specify than the other areas discussed in this book. In this part of the hypnotic task the characteristics of the individual patient, the presenting problem, and your own work setting will play a larger role than the specifics of the task. In Chapter 2 I discussed the factors, both positive and negative, that should influence your decision about using self-hypnosis as part of your treatment plan. Telephone contacts with the patient or with a referring clinician can give you an idea about these factors, and may help you screen out clearly inappropriate applications. But information gathered this way is inevitably limited, and in any case should lead to a personal evaluation by you. The issue of treatment with hypnosis has been raised, and you are sitting across from your patient. How do you begin?

Here is a working outline for what you want to accomplish in the first session:

1) confirmation of diagnosis and presenting problem;
2) exploration of previous experiences with hypnosis and expectations for treatment;
3) translation of the presenting problem into specific target symptoms appropriate for treatment with self-hypnosis;
4) establishing a workable therapeutic contract;
5) preliminary procedures (Chevreul pendulum and/or hand-separation test).

Only the preliminary procedures (which are discussed separately in the next chapter) are highly specific to hypnosis. In this chapter I will provide some general guidelines to help you with the first four stages. They represent my own perspectives on these issues and the approaches I have generally found most useful for beginners. Let me reiterate, however, that these are the areas where you will be most likely to diverge legitimately from the material offered in this book. If your ideas for handling any of these issues are *very* different from the ones I have presented, you may want to review them with a trusted supervisor or colleague who knows you and the setting where you work. With these limitations in mind, let's go through the preparatory stages one by one.

Diagnosis and Presenting Problems

After introducing yourself and making sure that your patient is comfortable, it makes sense to spend a few minutes of your first session reviewing the basic circumstances that bring the patient to you. Obviously, this will not be necessary if you are teaching self-hypnosis to an established patient, but even here you might want to ask yourself the same basic questions: Do I have an adequate diagnostic formulation for this patient, based on my own work with him or on that of another clinician whom I trust? Does the use of self-hypnosis make sense under these circumstances?

When you are serving as a consultant, it is particularly important to go through this step, even if briefly. I have been on both sides of consultations where a colleague, by simply being a different person with a different perspective, has provided a correct diagnosis that often suggested a different therapeutic direction. I feel embarrassed and even a little resentful at such corrective consultations, but I know that I (and every other professional) need them. Don't be afraid to say, and do, what you believe to be the right thing. Remember, however, that a revised diagnosis does not necessarily exclude a legitimate helping role for self-hypnosis.

Much more common than a completely revised diagnosis is the identification of a presenting problem that, even with a good deal of work, is not an appropriate target for self-hypnosis. The most common of these are the job and relationship consequences of serious and/or chronic health and behavioral problems. In these situations you can see in advance that although the patient may very well be satisfied with the modest results of self-hypnosis on his own experience, others in his life may not be. Sometimes you can reach an understanding under these circumstances, but sometimes it is best not to proceed with hypnosis because your real customer is not going to be satisfied no matter how good a job you do. The real customer is sometimes hard to identify, but a useful initial question is who is paying the bill. The farther removed the source of your fee is from the patient to whom you will be teaching self-hypnosis, the more important this issue becomes.

I usually try to get only a "ballpark" feeling about the presenting problem — enough so that I feel comfortable going on — before I begin discussing hypnosis with the patient. The translation of the presenting problem into target symptoms for self-hypnosis is more effective if it is done collaboratively with the patient. It is unfair to expect meaningful collaboration if the patient's ideas and feelings about hypnosis are significantly unrealistic, as they often are.

Exploration of Previous
Experiences and Expectations

Begin this exploration by asking in an open-ended way about your patient's previous experiences with hypnosis (e.g., "I'd like you to tell me about your previous experiences with hypnosis"). Then wait and let the patient talk, remembering that you will not get an accurate feeling for the nature and extent of misconceptions if you interrupt the description to offer interpretations or corrections. Significant misconceptions and fears about hypnosis are so common in the general population that you should not be surprised by them or waste time blaming others for misinforming or scaring your patient.

Remember that previous experiences with hypnosis may have been entirely outside of a professional context. Tom G. denied any previous experiences with hypnosis when I first asked him. When I extended my question specifically ("You mean you've never seen *anything* about hypnosis on TV or watched a stage hypnotist perform?"), Tom immediately described an experience about ten years previous to our session where he was in the audience for a performance of a stage hypnotist at a summer resort. He enjoyed the show, but did not participate directly. Now that he was about to have a hypnotic experience himself, however, he was glad that his eyes would be closed so that he would not have to observe or be embarrassed by his own "performance."

Tom was telling me in no uncertain terms that even though he felt that he might be able to respond hypnotically, to do so meant that he must abandon his usual standards of behavior. He expected to look silly to others in the hypnotic situation and preferred not to observe himself. The implied options are to keep his dignity intact by not responding or minimize the damage by having his eyes closed. A no-win orientation such as this one is much easier to correct at this stage than after the induction goes poorly.

Although statements like Tom's indicate that there is a problem, only further inquiry will make it clear how much work will be required to change the patient's orientation enough to proceed. For some, including Tom, a relatively superficial approach may be all that is needed. This would involve clarifying the difference between stage hypnosis and hypnosis used in a clinical or research context, assuring the patient that he will not be asked to do anything which he finds embarrassing and letting him know that he can stop the procedure at any time. For Tom, it was particularly helpful to know that the procedure could be modified if he wished so that it could be done with eyes open.

Sometimes the past experiences are not so benign. Evelyn O. looked obviously uncomfortable when I asked my rather low-keyed initial question about previous experience with hypnosis. It took some gentle reassurance to make her comfortable enough to tell her story. As a rather naive college freshman she had consented to serve as a "practice subject" for a junior who was taking an abnormal psychology course. The hypnotic induction conducted in his dormitory room was a thin excuse for an attempt at seduction. The induction and the seduction both failed, and Evelyn was left angry and ashamed of herself for being so gullible. She had put the fiasco out of her mind and gone on to a series of more sincere relationships and marriage, but the idea of hypnosis still conjured up this unpleasant old memory.

In Evelyn's case, a simple set of reassurances was not enough. It took our entire first session to work through the college experience and some resonating themes that had come up in other clearly analogous relationships. I then went on to clarify the nature of the self-hypnosis exercise and answer her reasonable questions about how it would be taught, learned, and practiced. At the end of the hour she herself said, "I think I'll be ready to give it a try next time." She was.

Evelyn had come to me as a specialized referral for instruction in self-hypnosis, not for psychotherapy. I judged, correctly in this case, that resolving the potential blocking issue would not extend our work by more than one session. That standard is a reasonable one for deciding whether to work through a persistent misconception or negative past experience.

Although you may consider yourself far from an expert about hypnosis, the material in Chapter 1 is enough to provide you with a sensible nontechnical explanation of hypnosis and self-hypnosis under these circumstances. In fact, having read that chapter you already know more about this subject than the vast majority of citizens and most health-care professionals. It is much more effective to impart this information to patients while discussing a previous experience with hypnosis or while answering a question than to deliver it as a sort of lecture to an audience of one. Patients resent these "canned" presentations, and they should. Avoiding even the appearance of this kind of approach is especially important for you, since you will be using a standardized script as the basis for your first induction.

Sometimes your problems with the patient's past experiences are not related to any negative aspects at all. Not infrequently patients will have been told about a positive experience with hypnosis by a friend or relative, or have had one themselves. Remember that hypnosis is done by all sorts of people, in all sorts of ways, and that all of these have probably been judged to have helped someone, somewhere. The patient's positive expectation is desirable, but beware that it does not include very specific expectations about how the procedure will be conducted, how long it will take, and how much it will cost. This happens to me frequently enough so that I take it in stride with a sense of humor. If the discrepancy in expectations is sufficiently large in a referred patient, you may want to end the session right there and let the patient think over your way of doing things and/or discuss it with the source of the referral before proceeding any farther.

Once you have had a chance to review the patient's past experiences with hypnosis and correct any glaring misconceptions or discrepant expectations, you are ready to move to a translation of his presenting problem into target symptoms appropriate for treatment with self-hypnosis. Don't be surprised if other significant past experiences emerge in this or later stages and require further discussion. By simply having opened the subject of past experiences early in your interaction with the patient, you will have avoided a crucial omission that has been responsible for many preventable failures among beginners at hypnosis.

Target Symptoms for Self-Hypnosis

The ability to translate presenting problems into appropriate target symptoms is central to any specialized treatment technique. We have already covered the basic concepts that you will use in this part of your first session in the section entitled "Problems That Self-Hypnosis Is Likely to Help" in Chapter 2. Presumably, you have chosen to use self-hypnosis with this particular patient because all or at least some of these factors are present. To refresh your memory, appropriate target symptoms for self-hypnosis are:

1) problems for the patient;
2) ready to be diminished;
3) subjective experiences;
4) able to be influenced by helpful thoughts or images.

Even a skilled clinician who is also an expert at hypnosis cannot give certain answers about these factors very early in his or her encounter with a patient. Your goal at this point should be to set up a conceptual structure for thinking about the treatment that will provide you and your patient with these answers in a way that you can both agree upon. The central elements in this structure are an accurate descriptive name for the target, an estimate of baseline occurrence, and a system of recording. Let's consider these one by one.

An *accurate descriptive name* should include the elements of the patient's problem that you feel might be helped directly by self-hypnosis. Ideally, that is all it should include. Remember that you are concerned with the meaning of a term for your patient, not with dictionary definitions. Walter P., whom you may remember from Chapter 2, used the term "nervousness" to describe attacks of performance anxiety that were interfering with his business presentations. When I asked him to elaborate on this, he mentioned a pounding heart, feelings of fear, and a tremor. He was aware of all three of these during his presentations, and worried that others could see his hands shake. Sometimes one element would be more prominent, but they were all present at every recent presentation, and none of them had troubled him in the past.

In our work together using self-hypnosis, I decided to retain Walter's own term: "nervousness." The goal of the treatment, then, was to decrease this nervousness as much as possible. Before I settled on this term, I made sure that Walter was not using it so broadly that it would include entirely normal autonomic arousal and apprehension before an important talk. No, replied Walter, he did not expect to be laid back and sleepy when he gave his talks; he was known, and valued, as a hard-driving worker and he expected to be psyched up for a big sales presentation. "Psyched up" for Walter meant tense, talking fast, and with a clear agenda that didn't waste time. When I asked him about the normal apprehension before an important presentation he replied, "Sure, you'd have to be crazy not to be worried about something like that!" This was what I needed to proceed. Although I might have used the term "nervousness" to describe normal apprehension and arousal (which self-hypnosis couldn't, and probably shouldn't eliminate), Walter used it as a consistent name for maladaptive performance anxiety and had another term ("psyched up") for the normal reactions.

When you can, it is preferable to use the patient's own term for his problem. Doing this helps the patient to "own" the treatment, as well as any changes in the target symptoms that may occur. David E.'s term, "the wall," was new to me but it exactly described what turned out to be an appropriate target symptom for self-hypnosis. What you want to avoid are overly broad terms (e.g., "my presentations" for Walter P. or "the 440" for David E.) that may conceal a helpful treatment effect in a complicated social or work situation. It's not the end of the world if you need to rename a target symptom later in your work with the patient to appropriately narrow the focus of treatment. But you should try to avoid this if you can, since patients sometimes interpret it as an effort to cover up a failure by changing the terms of the original agreement. As a beginner I'd advise you to err on the side of narrowness in naming initial target symptoms. You can move on later to other related narrow targets if your first efforts succeed.

How will you know if you succeed? This is where an estimate of baseline occurrence and a system of recording come in. These components do not have to be complicated, but they should be identifiably present to make your work as easy as possible and to avoid miscommunication between you and your patients. To get an idea of *baseline occurrence*, simply ask your patient, "how often does X occur?" where X is the target symptom you have named for treatment. For Walter P., the answer was every time he had to make a presentation, which was about once every two weeks. If the nervousness had occurred during only half of his presentations, the interval would have stretched out to once a month. Under these circumstances, you could either use a time framework (once a month) or a percentage (50%) as the baseline figure for how bad the problem was before treatment. Notice that here the target symptom would be relatively infrequent, though not necessarily unimportant to the patient; it might be some time before you knew whether the treatment had worked or not.

Don't be surprised if patients have some trouble giving you an even roughly quantitative idea of how often a target symptom occurs. Under these circumstances I simply try to get a "ballpark" figure and work on from there. For a target symptom that seems frequent, I might ask: "Does X occur once an hour, a few times a day, about daily, or less often than that?" For a less frequent symptom my question would be something like: "Does X occur once a week, a few times each month, monthly, or less often than that?" Be patient in this phase and stick with it until you have an estimate, however rough. If you can't get even this, it might be a good idea to review your treatment plan and choice of target symptom.

The arrival at an estimate of baseline occurrence leads naturally into a *system of recording*. This is a way of keeping track of the frequency and/or intensity of the target symptom so that the effects of treatment can be evaluated. For relatively well-organized patients who carry an appointment book or jot things down on a desk or wall calendar, this is usually not a problem. Several techniques can be helpful in keeping track of things, and will also suggest that you have done this before. It may be useful to use a code letter (e.g., P for pain) with a number for intensity (e.g., from 1 for mild to 4 for severe), and circle the entry and/or write it with a colored pen or pencil to make it easier to find when results are being tabulated before a session.

Some obsessive patients can turn this practical idea into overly elaborate quantitative recording systems, but the more usual problem is at the other extreme, with the patient who has trouble keeping track of things in general and needs considerable help and encouragement to keep even the simplest records. In these cases, I will construct a recordkeeping system in the office, often on a 3 by 5 card that I give to the patient to keep in his wallet or her pocketbook and bring back to the next session. Sometimes I write the patient's next appointment on the same card as a reminder that this "homework" will be gone over in "class." Here is how such a card might look for a middle-aged woman with anxiety symptoms she calls "attacks." She has told me that the attacks occur several times daily, and our next meeting is in one week:

```
┌─────────────────────────────────────────────────────────────┐
│   Arlene Jones              SYMPTOM RECORD                    │
│  Date            Brief Description of Attacks                 │
│  Wed 2/5         heart skipped beat in bus                    │
│  Thurs 2/6       short of breath in laundromat/couldn't sleep—heart │
│  Fri 2/7         heart pounding in bus/too nervous to go to meeting/ │
│                     faint at night                           │
│  Sat 2/8         scared in laundromat                        │
│  Sun 2/9                                                     │
│  Mon 2/10                                                    │
│  Tue 2/11                                                    │
│  Wed 2/12                                                    │
│     NEXT APPOINTMENT: WED. 2/12/86 AT 10 AM                 │
│                                                             │
└─────────────────────────────────────────────────────────────┘
```

At our next meeting I would go over the card with the patient to confirm the baseline rate of occurrence; at later sessions I would use it to measure the effect of doing the self-hypnosis exercise on the target symptom. I usually take the cards back and keep them so that they are not lost and do not influence subsequent ratings.

Occasionally you may encounter a patient or a treatment situation where even this simple form of recordkeeping is impossible. Under these circumstances it is still worthwhile to ask the patient, at each session, whether his target symptom is better, worse, or the same since the last time you met. If it is better or worse, ask him "a little better/worse or much better/worse"? The answers to these two questions give you a five-point scale for rating the target symptom from session to session:

1-much worse/2-little worse/3-same/4-little better/5-much better

This very simple rating scale may not seem like much, but it has helped me elucidate a number of otherwise difficult clinical problems. For some patients things are always worse—the only variation is between a little worse and much worse. Some of these patients suffer from hypochondriasis with or without a depressive component, and often they have the kinds of subjective physical symptoms that seem like they would respond well to treatment with self-hypnosis. This may indeed be true, and these patients are often responsible, hardworking people who will learn and practice the exercise diligently. The problem comes when you try to link practice of the exercise to change in the target symptom.

In this situation, even this simple recordkeeping system will allow you to work with the patient on the actual problem — whether he is ready or able to feel better — rather than tinkering unproductively with the self-hypnosis exercise. Most often, the levels of physical and psychological health in these patients are relatively stable at an unsatisfactory level, although they are often productive workers and generous community members.

When I review five or so consecutive ratings by such a patient of his target symptom as "a little worse" or "much worse," I often use a simple graph to illustrate the symptom "going off the paper." If this is done kindly and with an appreciation of the reality of the patient's suffering, it sometimes produces a shared smile of recognition and the beginning of a more productive collaboration with the patient. Because so much of self-hypnosis is subjective, the patient who wants to prove how bad things are or are getting can *always* win. But it is a Pyrrhic victory in a game that both of you don't really want to play. Even a simple system of recording is the best protection against getting caught up in such unproductive partnerships. This is true whether they are based on a psychological problem of the patient or simply on the fact that self-hypnosis is not working in that particular situation.

Establishing a Workable
Therapeutic Contract

Once you have identified an appropriate target symptom and set up a system of recordkeeping, you are in a position to say what you propose to do and how you and your patient will know if it is working or not. In the conventional uncomplicated treatment situation, you propose to teach the patient a self-hypnosis exercise which he will practice and apply to the target symptom that has been identified. If the treatment works, it will be reflected in a decrease in the intensity and/or frequency of this target symptom as recorded by whatever system the two of you have worked out together.

Those are the basic elements of your side of the therapeutic contract. If you communicate these elements clearly to your patient, you will avoid some of the worst misunderstandings that I have seen concerning the clinical use of hypnosis. In most of these, the lack of clear communication and explicit methods and goals did not appear unique to hypnosis, but rather were characteristic of the clinician, the patient, or both. In my own experience, these problems are *not* related to the school of therapy practiced by the clinician: psychoanalysts, cognitive therapists, and family therapists can do equally well, or poorly, at this task.

Implied in the summary that I presented of your side of the therapeutic contract is one element of the patient's side that is unique to self-hypnosis: he will be expected to practice the exercise on his own outside of your time together. For some patients this element of learning and mastering a self-help procedure on their own is just what they want. It represents a collaborative, relatively nonpaternalistic treatment relationship that empowers the patient and gives him real control over what happens and when.

You will have no trouble recognizing the positive response of such patients to the exercise as you present it. They themselves will often contrast the self-hypnosis exercise favorably with other treatments they have had, whether office-based psychotherapies, narcotic medications for pain, or surgical procedures. They will be willing to practice the exercise on their own.

Patients at the opposite extreme will usually eliminate themselves from self-hypnosis training as soon as they understand this part of the treatment contract. For them, the idea of having responsibility and control over much of the treatment is a contradiction in terms. They, or their insurance carrier, are paying a supposed expert good money to be treated, not sent home with a piece of paper and a pep talk. Treatment occurs in a hospital, or in the doctor's office — period.

Most patients in the real world fall between these two extremes, and the realities of your own practice will determine how you handle this issue. Perhaps you will have to be satisfied with a provisional agreement from the patient to practice the exercise for a week ("only because you say it may help with the pain"). Perhaps the patient may want to stop after this session and explore some other treatment alternatives, free to return in the future if he is interested in trying what you have to offer. The only absolute here is the need for some explicit communication around this issue during the first session, *before* you begin the preliminary procedures and training in the Brief Hypnotic Experience exercise.

Not infrequently, patients will comment that the whole idea of hypnosis, let alone self-hypnosis, is so strange and new to them that they don't feel able to predict much about what they will or won't be able to do with it. This is a perfectly reasonable position and should not be contradicted or punished. You can usually proceed in such cases with the preliminary procedures (hand-separation test with or without the Chevreul pendulum) and do some more talking when you have some concrete things to talk about. In fact, I usually try to have *something* actually hypnotic included in the first session, even if most of it is taken up with the issues described in this chapter. There is something to be said for breaking up blocks of psychological exploration and clarification with what under the circumstances may be refreshing episodes of "hands-on" practice.

Another helpful interlude that should be inserted in all discussions and practice sessions is an opportunity for the patient to ask questions. "Do you have any questions about what we've just discussed (or just done)?" should suffice. The more information about hypnosis in general and about your work with that patient in particular you can present in answer to a patient's questions, the better. Because the patient has chosen to ask that question, you can assume more than usual that he is listening to you when you reply.

Some mention should also be made of the other standard element of the patient's side of the therapeutic contract: payment for your professional services. As with a number of the subjects covered in this chapter, the nature of your own practice will be a greater determining factor here than any special features of self-hypnosis. In general, patients are no less willing to pay for clinical services involving hypnosis than they are for other treatment procedures. Two special features of payment for self-hypnosis training deserve mention, however, because misunderstandings relating to them are much easier to correct before than after the training has taken place.

If your patient has any kind of health-insurance coverage and expects that it will pay for all or part of your services to him, he should check in advance to determine whether therapeutic hypnosis is a covered procedure. The tremendous variation in the professional qualifications of people offering treatment with hypnosis has led to its exclusion in a number of otherwise liberal policies. If you are well qualified and well trained you can sometimes get such an exclusion reversed on an individual basis, but this usually involves the expenditure of a significant amount of effort and long delays. If hypnosis is not covered, the patient will have to decide whether he is willing to pay for the treatment himself.

If your use of hypnosis is part of a broader professional service that is covered (e.g., psychotherapy, office visits for cancer treatment), this exclusion will not be a serious problem for you. The problem arises when your contact with a particular patient is *only* for hypnosis. If you are a mental health professional, a particularly difficult variant of this problem concerns patients who for various reasons do not want to be identified in any way as having gotten psychological help. Even hypnosis may be too exotic for them to want it listed on the insurance claim forms that may be seen in their work setting, for instance. In these cases patients are often perfectly willing to pay for their own treatment and thereby avoid any needed documentation of their visits with you.

I would tend to charge for self-hypnosis training done by you personally on the same fee for time unit basis that you use for the other professional services you deliver. If you have never billed a particular patient before, be sure to let him know your fee structure. This is especially important with self-hypnosis training, since patients can come with preconceptions based on a friend's or relative's experience with a nonprofessional hypnotist whose fee may be a small fraction of what you usually charge.

One aspect of payment for self-hypnosis training is easier than usual: giving the patient an estimate of how many sessions are involved. I usually devote two sessions to the training, including the materials covered in this and the next two chapters. Two more sessions for supervision of practice and follow-up (often shorter than the first two) complete the basic initial treatment plan. Most often, you can reassure your patient that he will have a good idea whether treatment with self-hypnosis is going to help his problem at the end of these four sessions, which may be spaced out over a month or two. If further sessions are needed, the patient will be able to make a decision about them based on some real results.

There is another positive aspect of the payment situation, a particularly appropriate one with which to end this chapter and put you into the right frame of mind for the preliminary procedures that begin the task of hypnosis. I am referring to the broad risk/benefit/cost equation that usually underlies informed consent for any treatment procedure. One of the major reasons I have devoted so much time and effort to self-hypnosis is that the risks of the procedure itself are insignificant (see Chapter 2), the potential benefits are large (almost unbelievable in a procedure that is actually *fun*), and the cost is *far* below what is usual for other treatments delivered by the same clinician. This very favorable equation is another reason for insisting on a system of recording target symptom occurrence: even a modest (e.g., 25%) decrease in a troublesome target symptom may be a bona fide success *because it is achieved relatively quickly and with low risk and cost to the patient*. When it works even a little bit, self-hypnosis does quite well compared to the alternatives.

FOUR

Preliminary
Procedures

The Hypnotic Task and
The Hypnotic Voice

The procedures described in this chapter would not be considered "hypnosis" by most laypersons or clinicians. This is fine for you, because it means that you can accomplish a large part of the task of inducing hypnosis with your patient and teaching him the self-hypnosis exercise free from the inevitable performance anxiety associated with the "real thing." Researchers still debate the nature and boundaries of the hypnotic state, and the responses to outside-of-hypnosis test suggestions, such as the hand-separation test and the Chevreul pendulum, are popular foci for their arguments.

It may help you understand where we are headed to briefly summarize the current state of these investigations. Almost all the phenomena usually associated with hypnosis, including ideomotor responses, anesthesia, vivid sensory experiences, and challenge suggestions, have been produced in some subjects without a prior formal hypnotic induction. Where controlled studies have compared responses to the same suggestion with and without an induction, the induction seems to exert a surprisingly small but nevertheless definite enhancing effect. This summary statement is my own; strong proponents and opponents of the state theory of hypnosis might very well argue with it. If you are interested in pursuing this matter further, the books by Kenneth Bowers, by Ernest Hilgard and by Peter Sheehan and Campbell Perry mentioned in Appendix B contain balanced discussions by eminent researchers.

Now where does all this leave you as a clinician? Probably the most useful way to think of these procedures is that they comprise the first part of the actual hypnotic task as you will be undertaking it — the part that immediately precedes the formal induction of hypnosis. You have already arrived at your diagnostic formulation and treatment plan, and reached a workable therapeutic contract with your patient that includes instruction in self-hypnosis. You have explored his past experiences and tried to deal with his questions and concerns. It's time to get going.

I have presented the hand-separation test before the Chevreul pendulum in this chapter because it is the preliminary procedure I *always* use with patients. I also use the Chevreul pendulum regularly under two circumstances: when I am introducing self-hypnosis gradually to a patient in ongoing therapy, and where I have information either from my own interviews or from the referring clinician that the patient may be unusually worried or suspicious about the use of hypnosis.

In the first situation, the extra step provided by the pendulum lets the patient make a more gradual transition to the collaborative teacher/ student role that I use in teaching self-hypnosis. Time is not crucial here, since there is ongoing therapy work to be done at each session in addition to the hypnotic task. In the second situation the extra time consumed by work with the pendulum is well spent even if it entails a full additional consultation session. A highly nervous or suspicious patient is unlikely to respond to a hypnotic induction, and the Chevreul pendulum is the least threatening way I know to lead into the hypnotic task. When the pendulum is used, of course, it is taught *before* the hand-separation test.

You should try both procedures yourself, and may want to have the pendulum equipment ready in your desk or pocket even if you had not planned initially on using it. Sometimes the hand-separation test, which is much closer to traditional hypnotic procedures, scares patients or arouses memories or associations that make you want to back off a little bit. It's useful to have a fall-back position ready.

Why, you may ask, don't I *always* use the pendulum? The answer brings us back to an important perspective on any treatment procedure: practical limitations on time. If you follow the guidelines in this book you will, I believe, be using hypnosis in a clinically effective and scientifically appropriate way. Unfortunately, this is not always the way it is used. Many different clinicians ranging from exceptionally well-qualified experts to complete quacks use hypnosis: there are 27 listings under "hypnotists" in the current edition of the Philadelphia Yellow Pages, and other cities are even more prolific! You want to do the best job you can for each patient. You also have to be careful not to set up such a complex and lengthy protocol that you keep *no* patients at all, or quickly tire of and abandon the intricate ritual.

This is not a real problem in ongoing therapy because instruction in self-hypnosis becomes one of several treatment approaches going on concurrently. The situation may be quite different, however, when you are functioning primarily in the role of a clinician who teaches the patient self-hypnosis. Assuming that you have realistic confidence in the referring colleague, you cannot take forever to do your thing. In general, when I deal with uncomplicated and appropriate referrals, I try to devote two sessions to getting the patient to the point where he has learned the Brief Hypnotic Experience exercise and goes home to practice it. This includes the general and hypnotic history, correction of misconceptions, establishing a treatment contract, preliminary procedures, and the initial administration of the Brief Hypnotic Experience induction.

The mathematics of this situation should become clearer to you now: there is barely enough time in two standard 45-50-minute sessions to complete these tasks. You can get around this, as I sometimes do, by having longer sessions — 90 minutes, say, or by adding an additional one. I try to do something that the patient can identify as hypnotic in the first session: this is usually the hand-separation test, which he then practices and reports on at our second session. If you add the Chevreul pendulum to this sequence you may find yourself pushed for time. This is one of the areas where I can only raise the issues that others have reported and leave you to work out the procedure that works best for you. Some clinicians move through the pendulum and the hand test at a brisk pace and feel that doing both is worth it; others like to stick with one and explore it in greater depth. Not infrequently, you will have different protocols in different practice settings (e.g., when consulting on a surgical inpatient vs. seeing someone in your own private office).

Don't let all these worries about time pressure and scheduling make these preliminary procedures sound painful. Far from it, they are often perceived as fascinating and fun by patients, including some who are usually tense and/or depressed. They *are* fascinating and fun, as you will discover when you try them for yourself. Communicating this to the patient, both directly and by your behavior, is a positive factor in clinical success. Moreover, these will be the hypnotic "souvenirs" that your patients will be able to share with friends or relatives if they want to; we will cover this in Chapter 9.

Both procedures involve the principle of ideomotor action. I usually introduce this concept to patients explicitly with a statement something like this:

"We are now going to begin your introduction to self-hypnosis using a principle known as ideomotor action: the fact that thinking about a movement or about an image associated with that movement causes a tendency to make it. This will give us a chance to explore together the ways in which we work with thoughts and images in hypnosis."

At this point, you begin the actual hand-separation test or Chevreul pendulum procedures. In both procedures a primitive form of amplification is used to get a visual expression of the small movements involved. The hand-separation test uses a simple lever arm: small movements in the shoulder and upper arm muscles are visible in the separation of the hands, just as with the pointer on an electrical meter. The pendulum adds its own characteristic transformations of energy and momentum to make very small movements of the hand muscles clearly visible in regular patterns.

For more sophisticated patients I will explain these factors in some detail, adding that we could also record and display these small movements electronically in a manner similar to a biofeedback apparatus, using a tone or a visual display on a screen. Interestingly, this scientific approach seems to make the actual ideomotor response more rather than less remarkable — but that may just be an expression of the fact that for most people today technology and scientific jargon are the external forms of believable magic.

Both procedures will give you and your patient a concrete sample of the interactions of experience and behavior, thinking and doing, in a specifically hypnotic context involving the two of you. Almost all of the problems most likely to interfere with the success of clinical hypnosis will arise in this early phase where they can be examined and often corrected without interrupting a formal induction.

Both procedures also lead naturally to a discussion and review of the necessary conditions for responding to hypnosis. These conditions apply equally to these preliminary procedures and to any formal hypnotic induction:

　　1) active concentration (focusing attention on the thought or image is what you *do* in that period of time);

2) willingness to be receptive and to respond ("giving it a try," feeling comfortable with the response itself);
3) absence of external or internal interference (noise, distractions, worried about people watching, distrust of hypnotist, etc.).

Working out the particulars of these conditions as they apply to your patient is one of the major roles of these preliminary procedures.

As soon as you actually begin to talk your patient through the hand-separation test (and to a lesser extent with the Chevreul pendulum) you should begin using your hypnotic voice. The truth about the hypnotic voice probably lies somewhere between the "relax, my dear; now you are totally within my power" myth and the contention that there is no such thing. Certainly, the hypnotist's voice is the transmitting process, if not the content, of most hypnotic inductions, the Brief Hypnotic Experience included. At an extremely obvious but important level, the hypnotic subject's attention is focused disproportionately on the hypnotist's voice during any eyes-closed induction (such as the B.H.E.) or during the portion of any hypnotic experience during which the eyes are closed — there are no nonverbal visual cues to amplify or clarify the communication.

There is more to it even than this. Many people who have experienced hypnosis, including a fair number who are quite assertive and sophisticated in their everyday lives, describe their experience of the hypnotist's voice as qualitatively special. Each person's description of this quality is his own, and clearly depends both on the realities of the current hypnotic situation and the memories and associations it calls forth. I have heard effective hypnotists' voices of both sexes described as regular, soothing, monotonous, deep, soft, insistent, didactic and reassuring. Some extremely talented hypnotists speak with strong foreign or regional accents, and many use a tone of voice which is not very different from their usual conversational one — but there is *some* difference.

In finding your hypnotic voice you will have to confront for yourself some of the performance aspects of the hypnotic task. It will take some trial and error as well as practice to find the vocal style that feels right and works best for you. Listening to a tape recording of your own voice as you read or speak the hand-separation test or the B.H.E. induction can be an embarrassing but highly instructive learning method. It is the *only* way to really do anything about this important dimension of the hypnotic task.

I have two specific suggestions based on the experiences of many students. First, remember that the patient must hear what you are saying in order to respond; be sure that your voice does not gradually trail off or sink into a dramatic but inaudible whisper. Keep in mind that in these forms of communication there are no visual cues to fall back on. Second, don't rush the process of arriving at your own hypnotic voice. Many beginners take some time to get used to the actual content of the preliminary procedures or induction, and have all they can do to read them to their patients in a clear and audible voice without losing their place. Once the words themselves are familiar, and even a little boring, you will find it much easier to add some dramatic inflections and pauses. When this time comes, let yourself go a little. Your hypnotic voice should have *some* differences from your conversational one. You can always use a tape recorder or a trusted friend to make sure that you are not sounding too mechanical or too phony.

Now you are ready to move on to the actual procedures.

The Hand-Separation Test

To administer the test, have the patient extend both arms straight in front of him at shoulder height with palms facing. Demonstrate the correct position yourself — the first instance where you will be modeling parts of the hypnotic task for your patient. Have the patient look at his hands briefly and note their position, and then close his eyes. Emphasize that you will be providing the thoughts and images in this procedure, and that all the patient has to do is to concentrate actively on what you say and let whatever happens happen. The hand-separation test is considerably shorter than the B.H.E. induction, so that you will be able to do it on your own without a script after a relatively brief time. While you are getting the knack, use this script or at least read it over before you administer the test. Remember to shift into your hypnotic voice as your begin the actual test procedure:

"Look at your hands and note their position. . . . Now, close your eyes and listen to what I say. I will be providing the thoughts and images in this exercise, and all you need to do is to concentrate actively on what I say and let whatever happens happen. . . . Now, focus your attention on the feelings in your arms and hands and imagine that your right arm is growing heavy and at the same time your left arm is growing light . . . Your right arm is growing heavy . . . heavier and heavier

. . . heavier and heavier . . . *very* heavy. At the same time your left arm is growing light . . . lighter and lighter . . . lighter and lighter . . . *very* light."

WAIT FIVE SECONDS AT THIS POINT AND WATCH FOR A RESPONSE. IF THERE IS NO DEFINITE RESPONSE, CONTINUE AS FOLLOWS:

"Concentrate on your hands and arms, just listen and concentrate. You may want to imagine a huge buoyant balloon attached by a soft string or ribbon to your left wrist, gently pulling it up into the air . . . up and up . . . lighter and lighter . . . higher and higher. . . .Now shift your attention to your right hand and arm and imagine that several heavy, boring books are attached by a bookstrap to your right wrist, pulling it down . . . down . . . further and further down . . . heavier and heavier."

* * *

AT THIS POINT NOTE THE VERTICAL SEPARATION OF THE PATIENT'S HANDS (CENTER TO CENTER) IN INCHES. THE BASIC RATING IS A SEPARATION OF SIX INCHES OR MORE (POSITIVE) VS. A SEPARATION OF LESS THAN SIX INCHES (NEGATIVE). AFTER YOU HAVE RATED THE HAND-SEPARATION, CONCLUDE THE PROCEDURE:

"Now, without moving your hands or arms, open your eyes and note the relative positions of your two hands. . . . Now open and close your hands a few times to restore your usual sensation and control."

* * *

This is the end of the usual hand-separation test. If you have read or spoken it at an appropriately slow and deliberate pace, the whole procedure should have taken between two and a half and three minutes. You have your own behavioral rating of the actual hand-separation, and are now ready to proceed to an inquiry about the patient's subjective experiences with the test. Before we go on to this phase, however, let's consider some of the alternative results during the actual test that can cause problems for beginners.

The most common result that causes problems for beginners is the absence of any behavioral response from the patient. You read or talk away, watching his hands carefully, and they just stay there. About two minutes into the procedure, you're usually thinking something to yourself like, "Why did I ever try this stuff in the first place!" If your first patient is a complete nonresponder, nothing that I say will remove the inevitable disappointment that this brings. Let me assure you, however, that this disappointment and its negative effect on your use of hypnosis are nothing compared with what happens to a beginning hypnotist when his first formal induction produces no response. Console yourself with this point — this is exactly why I have built in this preliminary test procedure. As you will see soon, the absence of hand movement may or may not mean that your patient is a complete nonresponder.

From a practical point of view, what should you do under these circumstances? If you cannot see *any* movement at the end of the balloon/book phase, don't end the procedure right then. A sensible course is to repeat the test once omitting the introductory statement (the sentence that ends with "let whatever happens happen"). Start with the next sentence, omitting the "now": "Focus your attention on the feelings in your arms and hands" . . . etc. This time, continue on to the end of the test even if there is no movement at all.

For your first few cases, this is about as far as you should go at this point: you want to speak with the patient about his experiences of the test before you do anything else. After you have gained some experience, you may want to push a little further. What I usually do under these circumstances is drop the two arm procedure and focus for about a minute (a surprisingly long time) only on suggestions of heaviness in the right hand and arm. I continue with the book suggestion for a while, and then try some other images:

"You may want to imagine that your arm is made of stone, or holding a heavy bowling ball, or that it is made of steel and that a strong magnet is pulling it down. . . . Choose whatever image helps you get the feeling of heaviness. Heavier and heavier . . . heavier and heavier . . . more and more down."

There is a trick to giving ideomotor suggestions the second time around because of nonresponse to the first set. You need to let your pace and tone communicate persistence and patience without any traces of rushing or anger. You have all the time in the world, and the patient is going to respond. In this case time (fatigue) and gravity are working with you. Obviously, you want to eliminate what you can of the "yes you will; no I won't" parent/child struggle. Don't be surprised if this does not come easy while you are still mastering basic hypnotic skills: inner quietness and patience are difficult and rare.

Somewhat less common than nonresponse are patterns of partial or unusual responses, such as only one hand moving, or (most upsetting to beginners) the left (light) hand going down and/or the right (heavy) hand going up. These less common response patterns call for no modification of the procedure itself — just continue on once through to the end. They are best dealt with during the inquiry phase and do not necessarily mean that your patient will be a poor candidate for self-hypnosis.

One rather rare response pattern to this test *is* cause for concern for a beginner: the patient opens his eyes before the test has been completed with a question or a frank report of anxiety. I would take this response quite seriously and consider it a signal that hypnosis may not be the right treatment for that patient at that time with you as the hypnotist. I say this because the test procedure itself is rather innocuous and, if you have followed my suggestions, you have led up to it carefully. I would feel quite differently about questions or even reports of some anxiety after the test during the inquiry phase; it is the inability to get through with the test that is the problem. If you are working with a patient whom you see in ongoing therapy, you may want to try the test later; if this is a consultation, I would consider some other treatment option.

Now let's return to the procedure. When your patient opens and closes his hands a few times at the end of the hand-separation test, you are ready to begin your inquiry. Note that opening and closing the hands is linked to the restoration of "usual sensation and control." This illustrates a general principle that applies to all hypnotic suggestions: the cancellation of any suggested distortions in experience after they have served their purpose for the patient.

Try to be looking cheerfully and approvingly at your patient when his eyes actually open. I usually smile, give a nod, and say "fine," even if there has been no overt hand movement; after all, the patient has done his part. You may want to pause for a few seconds to let the patient digest the experience and the hand-separation that he has noted. Some first-time subjects are frankly amazed at substantial hand-separation and/or at the sensations they experienced during the test. Give your patient the time to say, "That's incredible," or "Wow!" if he wants.

Begin your actual inquiry nondirectively with a phrase such as, "Well . . . can you tell me what that was like for you?" Then sit back, listen, and nod approvingly whether the response is "It *did* feel *a little* light," or "That was absolutely incredible!" For that particular patient, the response reflects the experiences that you will have to build on and work with. In addition to understanding the general response pattern, you may learn the reasons for partial or unusual responses without further inquiry. If you noted these and they are not explained, ask about them (e.g.: "I noticed that your right hand went down but you left hand didn't move. Do you have any ideas about that?"). One patient explained that she had been frightened as a small child by a balloon blowing up in her face, and had found the balloon image mildly upsetting because of this. This was a real gain from the test, since the balloon image is also used in the B.H.E. induction. The problem was solved by substituting an image of a feather floating on the breeze (also in the B.H.E.) for the levitation of the left arm. I repeated a modified version of the hand-separation test using only left arm levitation with the feather image; there was a response of several inches and the patient went on to a successful experience with the B.H.E. induction (minus references to balloons) and exercise.

Patients may also comment on your voice ("I couldn't really hear you very well near the end"), on the experience of having their eyes closed ("I got dizzy for a second when I shifted from thinking about one arm to the other"), or on any number of features of the experience. Whatever they say, spontaneously or in response to your questions, you accept it and try to make appropriate adjustments in the exercise to deal with problems (e.g, talking louder, using just one arm if there are problems with shifting back and forth, etc.).

The center of your inquiry should be the patient's experiences during the test. Did the arms feel light and/or heavy? Was the experience pleasant? Scary? Interesting? A dramatic or even moderate experience of lightness or heaviness is more important for hypnosis (which is basically an experiential process) than the actual arm movements. If you get such a report, you can feel free to move on to the induction. You will be more relaxed yourself when you administer it, since you will not be straining to watch for a dramatic levitation.

An emotionally negative or extremely bored response to the test is a signal that you should scale down your expectations from hypnosis for that particular subject. If there are significant negative experiences reported, then try to correct them by simple means like the balloon elimination described above. Even if the patient says that "it should be fine now" after an adjustment, make sure to test the modified procedure to confirm this before going on to the actual B.H.E. induction. If several attempts at adjustments do not produce an experience that you and the patient are comfortable with, let go of the idea of hypnosis for a while.

If you have gotten this far following my guidelines, you should be able to work out most problems satisfactorily. This is more a matter of your skill as a psychotherapist and knowledge about that particular patient than any special features of hypnosis. Issues of control, autonomy, and readiness to live without symptoms regularly express themselves at this stage. The reverse responders (light arm down and heavy arm up) that I mentioned earlier are often good hypnotic subjects (after all, they did respond even if in the wrong direction). The reversed response should simply alert you to make sure that the patient does not have trouble telling right from left, and to inquire into mixed feelings about hypnosis or about the specific situation that you are in.

The three necessary conditions for responding to hypnosis that I mentioned earlier (active concentration, willingness to respond, absence of interference) provide a useful framework for your inquiry about this or any other hypnotic experience. While you are starting out, you should probably review each of these conditions explicitly with your patient to make sure that they are optimal before going on to the induction. This systematic process of review and adjustment firmly establishes the role model that you are looking for: a friendly, non-coercive collaboration between you (the teacher) and your patient (the student) as he or she learns and masters a new skill. Since you are teaching this skill individually, there is no reason that the procedure (and the induction) cannot be modified to best meet *his* or *her* needs. Together, you experiment and find the images and pace that work best for the patient. This may not be the usual style for him (or for you), and the hand-separation test is an ideal setting for trying it on. Don't get into too somber a frame of mind about all this. The hand-separation test is often an enjoyable and fascinating experience for patients. This and other ideomotor phenomena *do* have an almost magical quality the first time they are seen or experienced. Try to share some of your own fascination and enthusiasm with your patient; the treatment will benefit thereby.

I usually end my first session at this point and send the patient home to practice the hand-separation procedure three or four times before the next session. I encourage him to experiment with different images or different elements within the same image. He might find it useful to imagine my voice, or another voice, giving the images. Or he might find visualizing a balloon especially effective as compared with simply imagining the feeling of lightness. Either the lightness or the heaviness might prove significantly easier to imagine or to experience.

I review his reports of his experience and behavior carefully at the next session before beginning the B.H.E. induction. If one type of image or response seems *much* more pleasant or effective, I will sometimes modify the induction accordingly (e.g., change levitation to lowering for a patient who gets a strong and pleasant response to one but not to the other). More usually, I incorporate what I have learned into small adjustments in my delivery and in my practice instructions. You may have learned, for instance, about a distraction at home that interfered significantly with the practice of the hand-separation procedure and is sure to do the same with the self-hypnosis exercise if it is not dealt with.

All this has been time well spent. Basically, you are ahead of the game because you have gotten a small sample of hypnosis-related behavior before attempting a formal induction. The actual Brief Hypnotic Experience induction will build explicitly on the ideomotor response as a pathway into hypnosis.

The Chevreul Pendulum

The Chevreul pendulum is as close to a foolproof procedure as you can get in clinical hypnosis. With few enough exceptions so that you don't have to worry about them, everyone who sincerely tries to work with the pendulum can get it to move. The movement has its origins in ideomotor action, which is the basic principle that you will be using in the hand-separation test and in the first phase of the Brief Hypnotic Experience induction. As I mentioned earlier, this is the preferred introduction to the hypnotic task for patients in ongoing therapy for whom time pressures are not crucial and for those who have been identified in advance as likely to have hesitations or other problems with hypnosis.

The use of a relatively foolproof procedure to begin the hypnotic task is an example of a principle with more general applicability in the clinical use of hypnosis and elsewhere: leading from strength or building on success. The patient who has had a pleasant and successful experience with the pendulum is going to approach the hand-separation test with some of the emotional overflow from the earlier experience operating to enhance the later one. In practical terms this means a small but definite increase in the patient's active involvement with subsequent procedures and (since active involvement is one of the crucial factors in hypnosis) an accompanying increase in your chances of overall success with that particular patient. By using a procedure that virtually never fails, you are at least assuring the first element of this sequence as much as you can. This same principle is utilized heavily in the wording of all hypnotic inductions and other procedures. Its signature is the word "as" used to chain one event or experience that has already occurred to a subsequent and usually more challenging one (e.g., " . . . as the sensation of lightness spreads, the fingers begin to lift, bit by bit . . . ").

On the negative side, you are learning relatively little about your patient's level of hypnotic talent when you use an extremely easy test like this — the Chevreul pendulum is *not* one of the more valid brief tests of hypnotic responsivity, since almost everyone responds. Another negative aspect for a small number of clinicians is the mildly exotic and definitely mechanical nature of the procedure itself: somewhere between a pocket magic trick and a high school science project. If these elements still bother you a good deal after experimenting with the pendulum yourself, leave this test alone. For most clinicians, however, the ease and fascination of the demonstration make up for these shortcomings and give the pendulum a secure place in their hypnotic repertoires.

Now let's get down to the specifics of the Chevreul pendulum procedure. I am going to go into considerable detail here for a reason, and you may wonder why I am bothering to tell you about kinds of thread, different visual targets, and other seeming trivia. I have included this information to come as close as I can to giving you an expertise transplant that will function long enough for your own expertise to develop and take over. Remember that expertise is both an objective quality of the practitioner and a perception of the patient. If you are following the guidelines proposed here, the patient with whom you are using the Chevreul pendulum will benefit especially from a reassuring perception that you know what you are doing.

Since you *are* a beginner at hypnosis and should not deny this fact if asked, it is particularly important to send your patient some reassuring messages about your knowledge and competence in this area. "Don't worry, I know what I'm doing," or any explicit statement with the same content, is hardly reassuring. What, then, can you do? The most reassuring communications in this situation are probably indirect and/ or nonverbal; a detailed, hands-on familiarity with the procedure is one of the best ways to get this message across. If you are having trouble getting the point of all this, think back to the last time you visited your dentist. You probably didn't even notice the many things he or she did "routinely"—drawing up the Novocain, testing out the drill, etc. But just imagine how you would have reacted if your dentist couldn't get the needle to stay on the syringe, or seemed unsure about how the drill worked. These little details may not be at the heart of professional expertise, but they communicate much of it in day-to-day clinical transactions.

The equipment you will need is simple, but deserves some preparation and practice before you use it with patients. My favorite pendulum consists of a spherical button about one-half inch in diameter attached by a neatly trimmed knot to a ten-inch length of black button or carpet thread (thicker than usual sewing thread). The only other piece of equipment you need is a visual target. I use a circle four to seven inches in diameter centered on a standard sheet of white typing paper and divided into ninety degree quadrants by two straight lines that intersect at the center of the circle. I have provided a 4½-inch diameter visual target in Appendix C that you can photocopy, if you wish, for your own use and to give to patients.

The particular equipment has nothing to do with the effect itself, which depends on the physical characteristics of the pendulum and ideomotor action. It does, however, convey the impression that you have put some time and preparation into the procedure, and that you do things carefully and neatly; such an impression often serves to encourage the patient to work harder or concentrate more on trying to achieve the effect. If circumstances preclude using a carefully prepared pendulum, the same process can be demonstrated with a short length of thread tied to a paper clip and a freehand drawing of the target.

It is important to demonstrate this procedure yourself before asking a patient to try it. I present the demonstration in an upbeat but matter of fact way in my usual (nonhypnotic) tone of voice. I do not use, or advise you to use, a scripted approach to this demonstration. You should try it a few times yourself, and then demonstrate and explain it to your patients using your own words and style of presentation. As you can see, the pendulum as presented here is even more nonhypnotic than the hand-separation test and thus can be used to ease a cautious patient into hypnosis.

Now put this book down and make yourself a pendulum and a visual target. When you have them in hand, choose an appropriate time and physical setting to try the test yourself. The preferred position is sitting at a desk or table with the elbow of the hand you write with resting on the table and the pendulum string held between the tips of the thumb and forefinger. (If no desk or table is available, you can do the procedure using an improvised lap-board or even resting the target in your lap.) The most important characteristic of the physical position is firm support for your elbow, such as that provided by a table or the arm of a chair. This allows maximum freedom for the muscles of the forearm and hand that are actually responsible for moving the pendulum.

In the ideal situation, your wrist should be flexed slightly so that your palm is facing and roughly parallel to the desk. The visual target rests flat on the desk, which should have been cleared of distracting stimuli. Adjust the position of your arm and the point at which you hold the string so that the bottom of the button is just touching the center of the target with your arm at an angle of 45 to 60 degrees with the table top.

If you (or your patient) have never experienced ideomotor action before, prepare for a surprise. When you are ready, just lift the button barely off the target (an eighth of an inch or so) and *think* of movement back and forth along either one of the intersecting lines. Don't consciously move your hand or the button, *just think of movement*. If you have followed my instructions, the button will begin to move along the path you have thought of. Amazing!

Now spend some time playing or experimenting with the equipment to explore the phenomenon. You should be able to get one-half to one inch of total movement easily in a straight line. When you have done this, touch the button to the center of the target to damp the motion

Position for Holding Pendulum

and try movement in the line perpendicular to the one you used first. Depending on how you positioned your elbow and hand, one direction is usually slightly easier than the other. Once you have experimented with straight motion, stop the pendulum and think of a circle. Decide in advance whether it will be clockwise or counterclockwise, and use the circle around the edge of the target as a model if you have trouble thinking in circles. After you have gotten the button circling in one direction, stop the pendulum and try the other.

This is about as far as I usually go in terms of the physical characteristics of the Chevreul pendulum phenomenon. There is little to be gained clinically by trying to obtain larger excursions, different or larger patterns of movement, etc. My further work with the pendulum is devoted to exploring the specific kinds of thoughts and/or images that are most effective for that particular patient in getting the pendulum to move. By doing this I am able to get an idea of the patient's cognitive and imagery style. I use this information to make small adjustments in the wording of the hand-separation test and the B.H.E. induction so that they incorporate sensory modalities or types of imagery that are especially effective for that particular patient. This kind of custom tailoring of suggestions is noticed and appreciated by patients, especially when you are using a script for some parts of the procedure.

Here are three types of imagery as applied to the Chevreul pendulum.

Obviously, the type and direction of movement should be held constant when exploring different imagery styles:

a) verbal: say to yourself, aloud or mentally, "back and forth . . . back and forth."
b) visual: imagine you can see the pendulum swinging back and forth; concentrate on the line.
c) kinesthetic: imagine that the pendulum is made of a magnetic material and that a strong electromagnet has been turned on with alternating polarities, pulling the pendulum first one way, then the other . . . one way, then the other.

Observe the differences in response to these or similar variations in thinking and imagery, and compare your observations with your patient's. These modalities can be combined into a procedure for the pendulum that is maximally effective for that particular patient. This specialized, collaborative hands-on tinkering is a good way of easing into some of the less conventional elements of the therapeutic relationship that are involved in teaching and learning a self-hypnosis exercise.

Now let's review some common questions and problems that beginners have concerning the pendulum. First, how should it be introduced? As mentioned earlier, I usually begin with a simple introductory statement defining ideomotor action: "the fact that thinking about a movement or about an image associated with that movement causes a tendency to make it."

I then continue something like this: "You will have a chance to experience ideomotor action for yourself now with a simple device called the Chevreul pendulum. This procedure will give us a good idea of your readiness for hypnosis." (Notice that you are implicitly reminding the patient that this is not real hypnosis, but that he is approaching it. Learn how to spell Chevreul in case your patient asks you to write down the name of the procedure later.) "When the pendulum is held like this" (demonstrate proper position) "the pendulum acts as an amplifier of tiny movements in the muscles of your arm and hand. We could measure these movements electrically, amplify the signal, and record it visually — but it is simpler to use this mechanical amplifier and this visual target to make our measurements."

Spend as much time as you need to get the correct position and to explain to the patient that you want him to simply *think of movement* back and forth along one of the intersecting lines, not try to move the pendulum consciously. You may want to move one of your own fingers back and forth along the line the patient chooses to give a nonverbal suggestion, but this is not usually necessary and can detract from the patient's perception that it is *his* thoughts and images that make the pendulum move. If you use this nonverbal suggestion, use it only once to clearly communicate what is wanted and to get the process going. While the patient concentrates on movement, you should be looking expectantly at the pendulum; you *know* it is going to move! If the movement does not start right away, you may want to make comments such as "just concentrate on movement . . . don't actually move your hand . . . just let it happen." The moment you note the slightest motion, you can reinforce it with a statement like "that's right; *very* good!"

If things go well and you get movement along with the characteristic emotional response ("Weird!" or "Amazing!"), you can then go on to explore the several varieties of motion and types of imagery that have just been discussed. I usually conclude with a brief review of the necessary conditions for responding to hypnosis (active concentration, willingness to respond, absence of interference) and have the patient practice with the pendulum at home if the session is ending at this point. Having the patient practice with the pendulum at home has the advantage of setting up a framework for later home practice of the self-hypnosis exercise.

When he comes for his next session I review the results of the practice in detail: Were there any problems? Any new images that seem to make the pendulum move better? Differences between using the pendulum in the office and at home?, etc. Once these issues have been explored and if the movement response has persisted and the patient feels positive about the experience, he is ready to go on to the hand-separation test.

If I know the patient, or know about him, I usually give some thought in advance as to whether I want to give him a pendulum and target to take home with him or have him make a set of his own. The psychotherapeutic issues here are clear and not insignificant: giving a gift to a patient; providing a physical product of your interaction that he can show to others; testing his ability to work on therapy away from the office in a concrete way, etc. If I do decide to give the patient a set, I usually let him take home the target that he used in the office. As a beginner, you may want to use your own "well-worn" pendulum to teach the patient (and nonverbally imply your expertise) and then give him a new one similar to yours to take home with him.

Whatever you give your patient, make it neat and professional looking. Buttons should be unworn and conservative. Regular thread breaks too easily, and string does not bend at the hinge point where you hold it easily enough. If you use the suggested button and carpet thread, run it through your thumbnail held to your fingertip a few times to soften it a bit and make it more flexible right before you give it to the patient.

If you have decided to assign the construction of a pendulum and/or target as a homework project, discuss the materials and techniques with your patient in detail before he leaves your office. At one extreme, some patients get a surprising amount of pleasure out of making their own Chevreul pendulum equipment and come up with some nice-looking and creative variations on the theme. At the other extreme are patients who see it as a dumb and pointless chore ("I'm not paying this kind of money to be assigned a stupid grade-school homework project! I expect you to give me, or give me a prescription for, whatever I need!"). If you know nothing of your patient in advance, you should have a pendulum set ready to give him. You can always decide during your session that it would be more helpful and/or appropriate to have him make a set for himself at home.

What should you do if the movement is very small or if there is no movement at all? These two alternatives are actually quite different from each other. If you get only slight, even barely noticeable movement, simply reinforce it just as if it were substantial and go on to explore the different types of imagery. One of these may produce a considerably more dramatic response. Even if it does not, there is no reason to feel or to signal any disappointment. You have a response you can observe, compare, and build on and you are ready to move on to the hand-separation test.

After trying the hand-separation test, you may discover that your patient *feels* the suggestions with considerable intensity even though his hands (and the pendulum) barely move. Or he may continue the pattern of a small but observable response. It is still worth your (and his) while to go on to the Brief Hypnotic Experience induction and exercise as a means of helping the patient with his particular target symptom or problem. The chances of a significant clinical benefit are great enough, and the additional risk and expense small enough, to justify continuing.

The situation is quite different if you get *no* — absolutely *no* — response. I would advise you not to go on beyond this point with any hypnotic tasks until this absolute blockage is overcome. An obvious first step is to try again and watch carefully: there may be a very small, but clearly noticeable movement pattern, or the patient may not have understood the instructions. If there is still no movement, demonstrate the pendulum yourself once again.

If there is still no movement, I would consider abandoning self-hypnosis as a therapeutic modality that you are ready to teach that particular patient at that particular time. This is not a case for a beginner, and beginners should not be or feel trapped with new techniques. If you have valid special reasons for wanting to persist, go over the three necessary conditions for responding to hypnosis with the patient in detail:

1) Is he focusing all his attention on the movement of the pendulum? Perhaps he should say "back and forth . . . back and forth" out loud.

2) Does he feel comfortable with the idea that the pendulum might move? Does he really want to be where he is right now? Unwillingness blocks the process.

3) Is the air conditioner so loud in your office that he can't hear himself think? Or is there something worrying him so much that he can't concentrate on the pendulum task?

If you are lucky, this kind of inquiry will reveal a simple, easily correctable interfering factor. But don't blame yourself if there is no such help forthcoming. The test has served its purpose: screening out a patient who is not a good candidate for self-hypnosis. Because complete nonresponse to the Chevreul pendulum is rare, I can make a truthful reassuring statement: your next candidate will probably be much more responsive!

I'll conclude with a few questions that can throw beginners and that you should be prepared to answer promptly and matter-of-factly:

"Can the pendulum be used as a lie-detector or to predict the future?"
"Is the pendulum like a ouija board?"

This group of questions refers to some parlor game applications of the ideomotor action principle that your patients or their relatives may very well have encountered. While each of these subjects may be fascinating, this is not the time to be drawn into a discussion of them with your patient. In fact, you should use your reply to quietly distance yourself from these and similar exotic/controversial topics. Hypnosis itself can have enough exotic and/or controversial implications in many people's minds to keep you busy.

I usually acknowledge whatever obvious common elements are present, and then add a distancing comment. Here is an example: "Yes the ouija board does probably move through ideomotor action. That does not mean, though, that it can detect lies or predict the future. We are going to be working together on your anxiety problem, and the pendulum is merely a means of measuring your readiness for hypnosis and giving you some practice with one element of the procedure that we will be using. It's important for you to concentrate on this goal and not get detoured."

"I've got to show this to my brother!"

Another common point that patients bring up is their desire to show off or share the Chevreul pendulum (and later the self-hypnosis exercise itself) with family and/or friends. This subject is discussed in Chapter 9. The actual B.H.E. exercise *should not* be shared with others, and the earlier you make this clear to the patient the less likely it will be to cause problems related to later specific requests. I am more flexible in my approach to the pendulum and the hand-separation test — as long as they are presented as interesting scientific phenomena rather than as hypnosis. This may be a relatively harmless and enjoyable way of satisfying the curious, and of sharing a small element of the care that the patient has received and which others may want and/or resent.

"Can I (or someone else) become hypnotized by watching the pendulum?"

There are two answers here: an accurate, complicated one and the one you want to give your patient. Let's start with the practical response: "No, you cannot be hypnotized against your will by a pendulum or by any other mechanical gadget. Later on you will be learning a self-hypnosis exercise that you can do on your own, but the exercise that we will be using does not involve a pendulum."

If your patient seems satisfied with this, leave well enough alone.

If he shows evidence of a strongly held belief that pendulums can hypnotize people, he may be highly primed for a dramatic response to hypnosis or he may be expressing a resistance — subsequent events will tell you which is the case. Under these unusual circumstances, don't bother to argue. Tell the patient that if he is concerned, you will use the pendulum only in your office and not ask him to practice it at home. Make a note of this exaggerated concern and be sure to work it through before you get to the actual induction of hypnosis. Remember that your goal is to provide the patient with a helping tool that he can use himself at home. To do that he needs to feel more comfortable with the phenomenon of hypnosis than this kind of concern indicates.

Now for the more complicated actual situation. In fact, pendulums and metronomes are used regularly by some stage and clinical hypnotists as part of their induction procedures. Any rhythmic, monotonous stimulus may serve a similar function, and such stimuli are prominent in religious rituals and in some meditative techniques. Both pieces of equipment may have a considerable placebo effect through prior public exposure.

If your interest in hypnosis continues, you may want to try using these techniques for hetero- or self-hypnotic inductions in the future; they are both described in the classic book by Andre Weitzenhoffer (*General Techniques of Hypnotism*) referenced in Appendix B. As a beginner you are better off to learn, and to teach, one relatively simple technique. The less emphasis on gadgets, the better.

FIVE

First Induction and Introduction to the Exercise

Preparations

You are now ready to begin a formal hypnotic induction. All the interactions that have taken place previously — the explanations of hypnosis, the inquiries about prior experiences, the therapeutic contract, the hand-separation test — have led up to this point. They have helped to set the tone that you want: one of voluntary collaboration between an expert (you) and a beginner (your patient), as the beginner learns a new skill. Psychologically, some of the most important parts of the induction of hypnosis have already been completed. Nevertheless, the next step is a crucial one, the "real thing," and nothing will or should prevent both you and the patient from realizing this. You should therefore ask if the patient has any additional questions and make sure that he is committed to participating at that particular time and place, with you as the hypnotist. If the setting you are working in requires a written consent form, this is the time to review it with the patient and make sure that it has been properly signed and witnessed. A question such as, "Are you ready to begin now?" should conclude this inquiry.

When the patient has indicated his readiness, begin by making sure that he is seated or lying in a position appropriate for hypnosis. An ideal position would be seated in a reclining easy chair or comfortable high-backed chair that provides support for the arms, hands, neck, and head. This support allows the patient to relax some of the larger muscle groups without falling over or having to keep various muscles active in order to maintain postural balance. Support for the arms and

hands also helps with the hand levitation part of the induction by free-
ing the arm muscles to respond to the ideomotor action suggestions.
For this purpose the arms of the chair should be broad enough to ac-
commodate the hands, forearms, and elbows easily. (Some modernistic
chair designs with very thin arms offer either precarious or painful
perches for the patient's elbows and do more harm than good; under
these circumstances, or if the chair has no arms, the elbows can hang
down free with the patient's forearm resting along his thigh or in his
lap.) Once you have arrived at what you think is the optimal position
for the patient's forearms, test this out by gently grasping the patient's
left wrist and moving the forearm through about a 40 to 60 degree
levitation arc. This procedure not only acts as a warning of positional
problems before they complicate the induction, but also serves as a
subtle nonverbal suggestion as to what is to come.

If a reclining or high-backed chair is not available, you will have
to give some thought to the issue of head and neck support. Relaxation of the neck muscles causes the head to droop. If the head goes
forward, there is usually no problem; but a patient who has rested for
some time with his head back or, even worse, to either side, may emerge
from hypnosis with a crick in his neck that cancels out any positive
effects of the hypnotic experience. The best solution to the problem
is to let the patient choose the most comfortable among several alternatives: letting the head droop forward, keeping the head erect and
straight on the spine, moving to another chair, or placing a pillow,
towel, sweater, etc., behind the head or neck with the chair moved so
that its back is against the wall. If you or the patient forget these cautions, the neck discomfort will usually respond quite well to gentle
massage, rotation of the head, and positive suggestions for relief; one
episode of discomfort will usually cure the tendency to forget this aspect
of preparation.

The other aspects of position and location should be handled similarly. Keep in mind the basic question, "Will this be conducive to a
pleasant, private hypnotic experience during which profound muscular
relaxation may occur?" For reasons similar to those for head and neck
positioning, feet should generally be flat on the floor with legs un-
crossed (crossed legs can lead to post-hypnotic "pins and needles" or
numbness if relaxation has been deep and movement limited). Tight
or restrictive clothing should be loosened enough so that relaxation
or deep breathing would not put undue pressure on the neck or chest;

Ideal Position for BHE Induction

this applies especially to men's neckties. Make sure that physical position or clothing (a short skirt, for example) is not likely to leave the patient wondering afterward what was visible during the hypnotic session while their eyes were closed and they were relaxed. Some discreet preventive interventions at this point are justified by the embarrassment that they may avoid.

Glasses, jewelry, and wallets should usually be handled according to the patient's personal preference; some people do not like to part with these items at all. Contact lenses that are worn during the day only should be removed for hypnosis, as they have a tendency to become misplaced in the eye; contact lenses that are worn 24 hours a day may be left in if the patient prefers and there are no special reasons to the contrary.

Before beginning, check to make sure that the space and time that you have cleared for this hypnosis session are likely to be left uninterrupted while you work. Interruptions that can easily be handled by both therapist and patient in a conventional psychotherapy session are much more intrusive during hypnosis. Is the telephone disconnected, or is there a provision to have it answered quickly and/or silently by a person or a machine? Have you left a "do not disturb" sign on your door; if not, are you sure no one will knock or enter? If there are unavoidable limitations on your privacy, they should be discussed in advance with the patient so that he will not be unpleasantly surprised. You may even want to incorporate this issue into your hypnotic induction (e.g., " . . . you will not be disturbed if the phone rings and I have to answer it briefly . . . "). This same approach may be used with other stimuli that might intrude during the hypnotic session (people talking in a corridor, train noises, etc.).

If the session is to be recorded on video or audiotape, consent forms should be in order and equipment working and in place before you begin. Even if you are already familiar with the equipment from recording other therapy sessions, there are a few factors special to hypnosis. When subjects relax during an induction, camera and microphone angles often change; be sure that you will get adequate recording even if the patient's head droops or if he speaks softly. Although they are not always available, individual lavalier microphones for both you and the patient are ideal. A brief rehearsal session with the equipment before the actual session is usually a worthwhile investment of your time. If you are making a recording, it is best to record the entire session with the patient from the time your interaction begins. For a beginner using a scripted induction, much of the initial improvement in technique involves the preparatory phase before the formal induction. Starting the tape when your interaction begins may also reduce the risk of forgetting to turn it on—a common and frustrating omission.

Special considerations apply to patients who are bedridden, in wheelchairs, or in other special circumstances. A common sense approach will usually allow a simple and effective modification of the standard setup. For patients who have intravenous medication or feeding arrangements in place (or are likely to have them when they use the hypnosis—post-operatively, for example) you may want to modify the hand levitation part of the induction or exercise to limit or relocate the motion. The exercise instructions have been worded with this in mind, and intentionally do not focus on actual hand movement (" . . . allow it to become light and experience the feeling of it floating upwards").

Before you begin reading the induction script, make sure that your own personal situation is in order. Is the script visible and can you move from page to page with a minimum of hesitation and noise? Are you seated near enough to the patient to have your voice audible and to observe what happens? Are you comfortable? It is normal to be nervous under these circumstances when you are first learning how to use hypnosis. If you have practiced the exercise yourself, now may be a good time to use the cue phrase (e.g. "clear and calm") to bring some of the personal benefits of hypnosis into your interaction with the patient.

Using the Brief Hypnotic Experience Script

The hypnotic induction you will be using (Brief Hypnotic Experience) has been written out word for word as a script. Appendix C contains a version of this script that you can cut out or photocopy for your personal use. Accompanying this induction script is a self-hypnosis exercise and an evaluation form for the initial induction experience, also included in Appendix C.

If you have never worked in a research setting or used a similar instrument you may be uncomfortable at first with the idea of a scripted induction that you read to the patient word for word. That is certainly not the way that you usually communicate with the people you work with. The whole idea may remind you of "canned" self-help tapes or telephone answering machines. I have chosen this approach for several reasons, and in specific comparison with a number of alternatives (e.g., giving you the principles of a successful induction and letting you make up your own, a semi-structured approach, and various points in between). The most important reason for my choice is that the script approach is the one most likely to lead to your actually *doing* hypnosis with patients.

In introducing hundreds of beginners to the use of hypnosis with their patients, I have found that all other approaches frequently get lost somewhere between good intentions and actual practice. All of us are less fluent than usual in an unfamiliar situation and prone to omit one or two details of a new procedure. A clinician who is used to being articulate and in charge will usually abandon a new technique that makes him feel uncertain or uncomfortable. Hypnotic inductions and suggestions involve a sustained "patter" that is different from the usual "uh huh" and "that must have been very upsetting" that maintain long periods of nondirective psychotherapy. Most able therapists have no trouble mastering this mode of speech, but it does not come automatically. A script lets you learn by doing and devote your attention to the specifics of the patient's clinical situation that can never be standardized. By reducing the initial performance anxiety through eliminating the need to improvise, the script makes it more likely that you and your patient will enjoy his initial experience with hypnosis.

If you believe in and are comfortable with the script, you will have no problems explaining it to your patient. I usually comment in a matter-of-fact way that the particular induction we will be using is in a standardized form that has been used successfully with many people. This prepares the patient for the distinctive cadence of the script, which is clearly different from spontaneous speech. I rarely get any questions on this, but a patient may occasionally ask, "Does that mean anyone could read it and do hypnosis?" I use this opportunity to reinforce an important point that we have already discussed: "That's right. Hypnosis isn't hard to learn or to do. You will be doing it yourself, for yourself, in a very short time."

After you have used the script a dozen times or so you may want to make modifications to suit your own personal style and practice situation. When you know the script well, these may come to you in the process of the actual induction and may be accurate responses to verbal or nonverbal communications that are clinically significant for that particular patient. An obvious case can be made for matching the ideomotor and relaxation suggestions to what you are observing as you sit with the patient. You might abbreviate hand levitation suggestions if the hand rises immediately, or prolong them for a few minutes if you note no movement at all. For a patient with an amputation, the suggestion to relax that part of the body should, of course, be modified so that it is not dissonant. The use of a script does not mean that you have to abandon sensitivity or common sense.

One modification of the standard induction and exercise is particularly useful and should be used even by beginners, if needed, with their first patients, and routinely after they are familiar with the Brief Hypnotic Experience induction, exercise, and evaluation form. I have chosen a beach scene as the pleasant, relaxing experience that acts as a therapeutic escape from anxiety and/or pain. The scene is described in some detail in the induction, and its experience is examined later in the evaluation form. I chose this particular scene because it, or one like it, figures in the pleasant memories of many people.

For a small minority of patients, however, a beach scene either has never been part of their lives or elicits unpleasant memories and associations. One patient's young daughter had just received several painful jellyfish stings while swimming at a beach—she jokingly, but appropriately, remarked that the beach was not the place for her to relax for a while. Another patient had witnessed an unsuccessful attempt to resuscitate a drowning victim and named this as his first association to the idea of a beach scene. For both of these patients, and for anyone with similar experiences, it is clearly best to construct a substitute scene—either based on past experiences or on a fantasy—that can provide the qualities of pleasantness and relaxation. One patient constructed a scene in which he was pausing at a bend in a favorite skiing trail. He was alone—a condition he associated strongly with relaxation and that he did not get to enjoy much in his busy life. He enjoyed the view out over the snow-covered pine trees on the slope, the swishing noise of the wind-blown snow, the feeling of warmth in his ski clothing in contrast to the cold outside.

The same procedure used to construct a substitute scene can also serve to fine-tune the beach scene in the Brief Hypnotic Experience material so that it serves the patient's needs best. Ask the patient to describe in his own words the beach scene that he would find most pleasant and relaxing. Perhaps it is a lakefront beach he describes, without waves and with pebbles rather than sand. The "sailboats out in the distance" may be canoes for him, or a view of an island shrouded in fog. Whatever the broad outlines of the scene, be sure that you and the patient fill in the details for each sensory modality: sight, sound, touch, taste, smell, temperature. The Brief Hypnotic Experience induction will give you an example of how this is done. When the process is complete, the patient will have a custom-made exercise that he can literally own.

Although there are many advantages to modifying the Brief Hypnotic Experience to suit your or the patient's personal style, modifications do cut into the advantages of the standardized format. These advantages have to do with fostering your own sense of comfort and "feel" for the procedure over a range of different patients rather than anything uniquely effective about this particular approach to hypnosis. Until you are familiar with the procedure through having used it with a number of patients, it is probably best to stick fairly closely to the standard format and to introduce modifications only if they are clearly indicated.

Your preparations are complete, and have created the conditions for a pleasant and clinically useful experience. You and your patient are now ready to begin the induction of hypnosis. The Brief Hypnotic Experience induction script begins on the next page, and is also printed in *Appendix C* in a form that is easy to read from and that you can cut out or photocopy for your personal use. Read it slowly and clearly to your patient, using your "hypnotic voice" as appropriate. Have the pages arranged so that you can go from one to another smoothly. *Appendix C* is designed with this in mind, so that the transition from one page to another comes at a natural pause.

The script has been punctuated to give you a feeling for the best cadence and timing. Paragraph breaks and series of three dots (. . .) indicate pauses to allow the patient either to decide or imagine in response to a complex suggestion or to experience an ideomotor or other response. If you vary your pace slightly to correspond to the responses you observe, you will increase the rapport between yourself and your patient.

The Brief Hypnotic Experience evaluation form and the self-hypnosis exercise instructions follow the script, and are also included in *Appendix C* in a form that you can photocopy for your personal use.

Brief Hypnotic Experience Induction

Just sit comfortably and close your eyes. . . . Listen to what I say and try to think along with and imagine the things I mention. . . . Don't try to force anything; just let things happen as they occur. . . . In this session, I will act as a coach and guide you, so that you will be able later to learn to enter hypnosis yourself. . . . Now focus your attention on your left hand. . . . Become aware of all the sensations in your hand and of any movements that occur. . . . These sensations and movements are always present, but we are not usually aware of them. You may notice a mild tingling sensation, or feel some small twitches in the muscles of your hand . . . or the feeling of weight as your hand rests on the chair (your leg, bed), or perhaps the sensation of your pulse beating in one of your fingers. You are curious about what will happen and open to the experience.

Now, as you continue to focus on your left hand, you will notice a sensation of lightness developing. First in the fingers and then spreading to the entire hand. As the lightness spreads, your hand will gradually float off the arm of the chair (your leg, the bed) and up into the air as your wrist or elbow bends to allow the hand to float upwards. Pay close attention and see which finger will move first. . . . A pleasant sensation of lightness . . . lighter and lighter, floating upward effortlessly . . . lighter and lighter. . . . As the sensation of lightness spreads, the fingers begin to lift, bit by bit . . . bit by bit . . . up into the air . . . floating . . . floating . . . higher . . . higher.

If you like, you can imagine that a huge buoyant balloon is attached by a soft string or ribbon to your left wrist. Imagine the balloon tugging gently at your hand. Gently lifting it up . . . higher . . . higher . . . gently lifting. Or, you may want to imagine some other image that is more comfortable for you, such as a magnetic force, or a gentle breeze with your hand light as a feather. Just let it float upwards gradually . . . higher and higher . . . lighter and lighter . . . higher and higher.

Now, take three deep, relaxing breaths and let the floating feeling in your left hand spread throughout your body as the left hand settles back down. As it does, your usual sensation and control in your left hand return.

Now, I'm going to begin counting slowly from one to ten. As I count, you will feel your body relaxing more and more, as you feel yourself floating into a deeper and deeper state of hypnosis, until at the count of ten you will be deeply relaxed and in a pleasant, comfortable hypnotic state:

> ONE—Let your hands and forearms relax. . . .
> TWO—Let the relaxation spread to your upper arms. . . .
> THREE—Let all the muscles in your shoulders and neck relax . . . more and more relaxed . . . deeper and deeper. . . .
> FOUR—Your scalp and your forehead. . . .
> FIVE—Now, let the relaxation spread to the muscles of your face . . . to your eyes, your nose and mouth, to your jaw. . . .

SIX — Let your chest and your upper back relax, deeply and com-
    fortably. . . .
SEVEN — Your lower back and abdomen . . . deeper and deep-
    er. . . .
EIGHT — Let the relaxation spread down through your upper legs
    to your knees. . . .
NINE — To your lower legs, all the way down to your feet. . . .
TEN — If there are any areas of tension remaining anywhere in
    your body, just let the relaxation extend to these areas now as
    well . . . to your whole body, now deeply, evenly, completely
    relaxed. . . .

You are now in a relaxed, pleasant hypnotic state. You can hear what
I say clearly, and respond to ideas and images that I will present that
are acceptable to you. You are in complete control and will always be
able to respond appropriately in any emergency. Deeply relaxed, and
in a calm, pleasant hypnotic state. You will be able to remember the
feeling that you have now and return to it when you want to.

Now, you are going to be able to use hypnosis to experience a very
pleasant scene. Just let yourself travel in your imagination to a warm,
pleasant beach. Perhaps it is a beach that you have actually visited in
the past, or it may be an imaginary beach that your construct for
yourself. . . . It's very pleasant, safe and warm.

You are sitting or lying comfortably. Above you, the sky is clear
and blue with a few fluffy white clouds floating overhead. . . . Out
in front of you is the water. You watch the waves coming in and
perhaps some sailboats out in the distance. You can hear the sound
of the waves . . . a very regular, soothing sound. The air smells and
tastes fresh and clean. . . . The sun is warm and comfortable. You can
feel it warming your body and warming the beach beneath you. . . . It's
a beautiful day — you're feeling at peace and relaxed. . . . Just enjoy
this scene now for a while on your own. . . .

(*Wait one minute while the patient enjoys the beach scene, then continue:*)

You will be able to return to this pleasant scene in hypnosis whenever
you want to. Remember how you feel right now. . . . You may want
to think of one or two words that express how you feel . . . words like

"clear and calm" or "warm and relaxed" . . . (or [*the patient's key phrase, if you are using one*]) . . . whatever words are best for you. . . .

Next, I am going to teach you a simple self-hypnosis exercise that will allow you on your own to do and experience all the things we have just done now. Just listen as I describe the exercise and let it enter your mind. Don't worry about responding or about remembering the details; I will give you the exercise later in written form to take with you.

The exercise I am going to teach you now follows directly and naturally from what you have just experienced and done. To do the exercise, find a time of day when you can have ten minutes without interruptions. Get into a comfortable position in a location as free as possible from noise and distractions; make sure that your left hand can move freely. If you are using a timer, set it for ten minutes.

When you are ready, close your eyes and let yourself remember the feeling of hypnosis. Direct your attention to your left hand. Allow it to become light and experience the feeling of it floating upwards. If you are in a public place, you can allow just your left forefinger to float up, or merely experience the feeling without any actual movement.

When you have the feeling of floating in your left hand, that will be a signal for you to take three breaths. When you do the exercise on your own, say to yourself: "I'm taking three deep, relaxing breaths and letting the floating feeling spread throughout my body." As the floating feeling spreads, your left hand will settle back down, with its usual sensation and control.

You then continue to yourself: "Now, I'm deepening the experience by counting slowly from one to ten." As you count, you let your body relax more and more, until at the count of ten you are in a deeply relaxed, pleasant, comfortable hypnotic state.

At *one*, you let your hands and forearms relax. . . . *Two*: let the relaxation spread to your upper arms. . . . *Three*: let all the muscles in your shoulders and neck relax. . . . *Four*: your scalp and your forehead. . . . *Five*: let the relaxation spread to the muscles of your face . . . to your eyes, your nose and mouth, to your jaw. . . . *Six*: let your chest and your upper back relax. . . . *Seven*: your lower back and abdomen. . . . *Eight*: let the relaxation spread down through your upper legs to your knees. . . . *Nine*: to your lower legs, all the way down to your feet. . . . And — *ten*: if there are any areas of tension remaining anywhere in your body, just let the relaxation extend to those areas as well, so that your whole body is deeply, evenly, completely relaxed.

You can then use the hypnotic state to help yourself achieve whatever goals you have chosen. You can say to yourself: "Now I'm experiencing a pleasant, peaceful, relaxing time, just as when I was at the beach. I can even see the clear blue sky with the fluffy white clouds; I can hear the soothing sounds of the waves and feel the warm sun. I feel clear and calm (*or key phrase, if using one*); . . . I am at peace." Let yourself enjoy this experience while you remain comfortably relaxed until you hear the sound of the timer or decide that the time is up.

When you are ready, you can end the exercise and come out of hypnosis by counting backward to yourself slowly from five to one, just as I will be counting for you in a little while. At the count of two your eyes will open; and at the count of one you will be fully awake, alert, feeling pleasantly refreshed, and with your usual sensation and control. You should flex and relax your muscles a few times before standing up.

The more you practice this exercise, the easier it will become to do and the more effective it will be to help you achieve your goals.

([*If using key phrase*:] Even when you are not doing the exercise, you will be able to use your key phrase to bring back some of the feeling of being _____ and _____ , . . . _____ and _____ .)

Now, I am going to count backward from five to one, just as you will do when you do the exercise by yourself. At the count of two your eyes will open, and at the count of one your hypnotic experience will be over and you will be fully awake, alert and refreshed. Ready now . . .

> FIVE — You are beginning to become more alert. . . .
> FOUR — Coming out now. . . .
> THREE — Feeling good. . . .
> TWO — Eyes open. . . .
> ONE — Alert and refreshed!

* * *

(*Make sure the patient flexes and relaxes his muscles a few times before standing up, and that you take time to inquire about his experience and answer any questions he may have. This is the time to have the patient fill out the Brief Hypnotic Experience evaluation form if you will be using it. The self-hypnosis exercise instructions should be given to the patient before he leaves.*)

Brief Hypnotic Experience Evaluation Form

Please choose the response option that best describes your experience, and circle the appropriate number to the left of the option (1-4).

Hand Lightness and Rising:

A. To an outside observer, my hand would have appeared
   1. not to have moved at all.
   2. to have moved a little but not really risen.
   3. to have risen less than 6 inches.
   4. to have risen 6 inches or more.

B. My hand
   1. did not feel light at all.
   2. felt a little light.
   3. felt moderately light.
   4. felt very light.

C. When my hand felt light and/or floated up,
   1. I felt like I was helping it along.
   2. though I felt like I was helping it along, there was some movement on its own.
   3. my hand seemed to move by itself, but I felt like I was helping it along somewhat.
   4. my hand seemed to move up by itself, without effort on my part.

Experience of the Beach Scene:

D. For me, the sensory experiences of the scene (sights, sounds, body feelings, smells, temperatures, tastes) were
   1. absent.
   2. faint.
   3. moderately vivid.
   4. very vivid.

E. During the beach scene
   1. I had no feeling of actual participation.
   2. I was mostly an observer with a slight sense of participating.
   3. I had some sense of actually participating in the experience.
   4. I felt like I was really there.

General Evaluation:

F. I found the experience of hypnosis
   1. unpleasant.
   2. neutral.
   3. moderately pleasant.
   4. quite pleasant.

Self-Hypnosis Exercise Instructions

   1) Find a time of day when you can have ten minutes without interruptions.
   2) Get into a comfortable position in a location as free as possible from noise and distractions. If you are using a timer, set it for ten minutes.
   3) Close your eyes and let yourself remember the feeling of hypnosis.
   4) Direct your attention to your left hand. Allow it become light and experience the feeling of it floating upwards.
   5) Say to yourself, "I'm taking three deep, relaxing breaths and letting the floating feeling spread throughout my body."
   6) Continue, "Now, I'm deepening the experience by counting slowly from one to ten. As I say *one*, I begin by relaxing my hands and forearms. . . . *Two*, I let the relaxation spread to my upper arms. . . . *Three*, I let my shoulders and neck relax . . . more and more relaxed, deeper and deeper. . . . *Four*, my scalp and my forehead. . . . *Five*, now I let the relaxation spread to the muscles of my face, to my eyes, my mouth, and my jaw. . . . *Six*, I let my chest and my upper back relax, deeply and comfortably. . . . *Seven*, my lower back and abdomen. . . . *Eight*, I let the relaxation spread down through my upper legs to my knees. . . . *Nine*, to my lower legs, all the way down to my feet. . . . *Ten*, to my whole body, now deeply, evenly, completely relaxed."
   7) Say to yourself, "Now I'm experiencing a pleasant, peaceful, relaxing time, just as when I was at the beach. I can even see the clear blue sky with the fluffy white clouds; I can hear the soothing sounds of the waves and feel the warm sun. I feel clear and calm; I am at peace."
   (Key Phrase: _____)

8) Let yourself enjoy the experience, remaining comfortably relaxed, until you hear the sound of the timer or decide that the time is up.

9) Say to yourself, "Now, I'm going to end the exercise by counting backward slowly from five to one. As I say *five*, I begin to become more alert . . . *four*, coming out now . . . *three*, I feel good . . . *two*, eyes open . . . *one*, alert and refreshed!"

10) Flex and relax your muscles a few times before standing up.

* * *

Review of the Hypnotic Experience and The B.H.E. Evaluation Form

You should be looking cheerful, and at your patient, when he opens his eyes at the conclusion of the B.H.E. induction. It sometimes takes people a few minutes to get reoriented after they have experienced hypnosis, especially if they are talented subjects. You will regularly get spontaneous comments from patients at this point, such as, "That was amazing!" or "I thought it would be more like being asleep." If there are no spontaneous comments, you might want to give an approving smile or an encouraging "That was fine" to reassure your patient that the process went as expected. Patients are highly responsive to suggestions during the immediate post-hypnotic period and you should adjust your communication with your patient with this in mind. This enhanced responsibility is actually utilized for deepening the level of hypnosis in an advanced technique called the fractionation method: the subject is immediately rehypnotized after emerging from the initial hypnotic experience.

At this point you are most interested in learning what your patient's experience of hypnosis has been like, and in offering reassurance and modification of future hypnotic experiences based on this information. You can use an unstructured, open-ended inquiry to gather this information if you prefer, starting with a question such as, "Now, could you tell me what that was like for you?" You can also supplement this with a more structured inquiry, and the B.H.E. evaluation form has been provided for this purpose.

The form consists of six questions that cover what I feel are the most clinically relevant dimensions of the B.H.E. induction. Three concern hand levitation, covering the behavioral (A), experiential (B), and involuntary (C) aspects. The next two questions evaluate the experience of the beach scene as to vividness (D) and sense of participation (E). The final question (F) concerns how pleasant the patient found the experience of hypnosis. Each question is accompanied by four graded response options which are numbered 1 through 4.

You can use the form as an outline for your post-hypnosis inquiry, simply making sure that you cover some or all of the areas that the questions explore. Alternatively, you could rephrase the questions in a more open-ended way. If the patient's hand had risen, question C might be asked as, "When your hand floated up, did it seem to move up by itself, or did you feel like you were helping it along?" My own preference, and practice, is to have the patient fill out the form before he leaves the first session and to then go over his responses one by one. This ensures that all the areas that I consider important have been covered, and lets me compare the responses of that particular patient to others.

For example, you would use a review of the form to note that the patient's hand only moved slightly but that it felt quite light. This would allow you to focus your subsequent work with the B.H.E. exercise on sensations rather than on movement and to provide needed reassurance that the movement was an index, not the desired process. Specific sensory elements of the beach scene could be reviewed one by one, and fine-tuned for subsequent presentations. One patient, for example, wanted to include the calls of gulls with the sound of the waves, since he associated this particular auditory stimulus with relaxing memories. I modified subsequent inductions accordingly, and the patient included the gulls in his own version of the B.H.E. exercise. Obviously, the question on whether the experience of hypnosis has been pleasant or not gives you a chance to catch potentially serious problems and to find out what is behind them.

The response options for each item in the evaluation form are graded in intensity, and it is possible to add the numbers that accompany them to produce a total score (from 6 to 24) that roughly reflects the intensity of the patient's hypnotic experience. You should not confuse this numerical score with the score on one of the carefully constructed comprehensive scales (e.g., Stanford Scales or Harvard Scale) that are used in legitimate hypnosis research and that are described in Appendix B. If you are doing clinical research with the B.H.E., I would definitely advise you to include one of these scales in your patient assessment.

Appendix B also refers to the April 1979 issue of *The International Journal of Clinical and Experimental Hypnosis*, and to the October 1978/January 1979 issue of the *American Journal of Clinical Hypnosis*, both of which contain helpful articles on the nature and use of the standard scales.

Despite these limitations, the B.H.E. evaluation form may be quite useful for clinicians and as a rough or screening measure in certain research settings. Because it is scripted and administered with subjects' eyes closed, the B.H.E. induction with its evaluation form can be, and has been, used for group administration. In a group of 29 non-patients, the means and standard deviations for each of the items and for the total score were: A, m = 2.72, s.d. = 1.13; B, m = 2.66, s.d. = 0.90; C, m = 2.62, s.d. = 1.08; D, m = 2.97, s.d. = 1.76; E, m = 2.72, s.d. = 0.84; F, m = 3.21, s.d. = 0.86; TOTAL, m = 16.55, s.d. = 4.42.

For a different group of 22 clinicians participating in one of my workshops who completed both the B.H.E. evaluation form and the well-validated Harvard Group Scale of Hypnotic Susceptibility, the correlation coefficient between B.H.E. total score and HGSHS: A total score was r = 0.54, which is modest but statistically significant (df = 20, p < .01, 2-tailed). Thus the B.H.E. evaluation form total score probably does measure roughly the same dimension of hypnotic talent or responsivity that is assessed much more precisely by the established scales.

After you have evaluated your patient's responses to the B.H.E. induction in the post-hypnotic discussion, you must make an on-the-spot decision about whether or not to proceed with self-hypnosis. Unless the problems are severe and seem resistant to intervention, I would tend to go on at this point. Some patients with unimpressive responses still benefit clinically from the B.H.E. You will have much more information and be in a much better position to decide when and if your patient returns for his next session.

Before the patient leaves, give him your own version of the B.H.E. self-hypnosis exercise instructions. I would suggest that you start out by using the model that I have given you typed or photocopied onto your own professional letterhead. After you have worked with a number of patients, you will probably want to modify the instructions to reflect your own way of putting things and include any procedures that apply to your own practice. Whatever you do, remember not to make the sheet too long. It should never require more than one side of one sheet of paper if you want to motivate patients to practice regularly.

I usually encourage the patient to practice the exercise twice daily, five days a week for two weeks. Depending on your practice setting, the patient might return at the end of two weeks or at one week. Ideally, the purpose of this practice is to acquire *skill at self-hypnosis*, not to apply the technique to the patient's target symptoms. Sometimes the realities of the patient's clinical problem or of your own practice setting prevent a defined practice period of this length (20 trials over two weeks), but even if the time or number has to be abbreviated, make sure that there is a defined period of practice devoted to fixing and fine-tuning the patient's self-hypnotic skill.

In most practice settings work on self-hypnosis will be going on at the same time as other work on defining and dealing with the patient's problems. Thus the definition and assignment of time for self-hypnosis skill development will be within as well as between individual sessions. For this reason, the material on practice and follow-up is in Chapter 9, which concludes this book. The next three chapters cover the clinical applications of self-hypnosis that are the raison d'être of learning self-hypnosis yourself and teaching it to patients. The issues you emphasize in practice and follow-up will depend a great deal on the specifics of who your patient is and what are his current needs.

SIX

Applications to Anxiety, Tension, and Stress

Evaluation and Diagnosis

If your patient's target symptom is anxiety, tension, or stress, you have an ideal application for the Brief Hypnotic Experience exercise. You should know yourself, and you can tell your patient, that there is an excellent chance that he will get significant relief from using this self-hypnosis exercise. That will make him feel better — and when your first few self-hypnosis patients feel better, you will feel great. There is even more good news. If you have followed the recommended procedures up to this point in selecting your patient and target symptom, devising a recording system, and introducing your patient to the B.H.E. exercise, you are just about home-free! From here on, when we are dealing with anxiety, tension and stress, the system pretty much works by itself. For a change, I am telling you that you can relax.

Your enviable position is no accident, however, and you should understand how it came about. As I mentioned in the Introduction, this book focuses intentionally on a narrow range of initial applications. My goal has been to give you the best chances of having an initial clinical experience with hypnosis that both you and your patient rate as a success. To this end, I have chosen anxiety, tension, and stress as the ideal clinical application for the exercise. My reasons for this choice are relatively simple and straightforward: these symptoms are common and are not restricted to any occupational or social group, and they respond well to treatment with self-hypnosis compared to other currently available treatments.

This choice itself played a large role in determining the structure and even the wording of the Brief Hypnotic Experience exercise. Put most directly, the exercise has been custom-built for anxiety, tension, and stress relief. That's what I meant when I said earlier that with these patients the system pretty much works by itself. As with the choice of a limited range of initial applications, I have opted to introduce you to hypnosis through one specific hypnotic technique among the many in valid clinical use today: a brief self-hypnosis exercise.

There are many ways to structure such an exercise, however (e.g., relaxed vs. alert, eyes open vs. closed, etc.), each with its own advantages in dealing with certain conditions. For the Brief Hypnotic Experience exercise, all of these choices have been made with the relief of anxiety, tension, and stress in mind. The exercise even contains some features (e.g., a muscle relaxation sequence) that are neither necessary nor sufficient for hypnosis but are useful in treating these conditions. Every clinical procedure needs to have some "character" of its own, and this is the character I have chosen for the B.H.E.

In this particular application, there are relatively few pitfalls in the evaluation and diagnosis phase. That is not to say that either anxiety or stress is a simple subject where we have all the answers; both areas are the current focus of many trendy treatments and legitimate scholarly disputes. Rather, the B.H.E. exercise is so simple to learn and to do and has so few risks that it is easy to justify its role in the treatment approach. Before we discuss the specifics of treatment, let's go over a few definitions and diagnostic points that are important.

The terms anxiety, tension, and stress are clearly related, but the distinctions among them are worth making. I use *anxiety* in its usual psychiatric sense to refer to the feeling of apprehension and uneasiness that accompanies the anticipation of internal or external danger ("I feel as if something terrible is about to happen"). Although it is not crucial for the application of self-hypnosis, I like to hold on to the distinction between anxiety and fear: in anxiety, the object of the fear is unknown or its extent is unrealistic; in fear, the danger is real and the response is appropriate. To the person undergoing them, anxiety and fear feel the same. In addition to the cognitive and emotional elements, both feature autonomic and motor arousal expressed by such phenomena as rapid pulse, tremulousness, light-headedness, fidgeting, easy startle, and initial insomnia.

A number of well-known psychiatric syndromes have anxiety as one of their central features. Most of these have been gathered together under the heading of "Anxiety Disorders" in DSM-III.* The Anxiety Disorders are:

1) Agoraphobia with panic attacks;
2) Agoraphobia without panic attacks;
3) Social Phobia;
4) Simple Phobia;
5) Panic Disorder;
6) Generalized Anxiety Disorder;
7) Obsessive-Compulsive Disorder;
8) Post-traumatic Stress Disorder (Acute and Chronic or Delayed)
9) Atypical Anxiety Disorder.

Along with this core group of Anxiety Disorders, there are a number of other disorders described in DSM-III where anxiety may be prominent and which should be kept in mind in formulating a differential diagnosis. These include:

1) Organic Mental Disorders and psychological effects of physical disorders (e.g., substance intoxication or withdrawal, hyperthyroidism);
2) Adjustment Disorder with Anxious Mood;
3) Hypochondriasis;
4) early phases of Schizophrenic or Affective Disorders;
5) Personality Disorders (Axis II), especially Avoidant, Borderline, Compulsive, and Schizotypal.

If you are not familiar with this diagnostic system, I would recommend that you at least read through the sections in DSM-III on the diagnoses I have listed above. Even where we have little understanding of etiology and are basically describing a clinical syndrome, it is helpful in planning and evaluating treatment to know the features that group together and something of the expected course.

Tension refers to the feelings, especially physical sensations, and the overt behaviors associated with anticipation. The physical metaphor of being stretched is apt: you can be ready to fly forward or to snap. Although prolonged tension is uncomfortable and may be unhealthy,

*American Psychiatric Association, Washington, DC, 1980.

a certain amount of tension is part of many good things in life, from reading a mystery to sports to the structure of a symphony to sexual intercourse. Thus, tension has fewer pathological implications than anxiety.

In the DSM-III system, tension is often part of Anxiety Disorders and related mental disorders, or one of the "psychological factors affecting physical conditions," the current term for many of the problems that used to be known as psychosomatic. Because the clearest kinds of tension are muscular, the most obvious connections with physical conditions are with problems such as tension headache and backaches related to muscle spasm; not surprisingly, these are excellent target symptoms for self-hypnosis, even in patients who have no evidence of psychological anxiety or apprehension.

Finally, I am using the term *stress* mostly to describe stressful events or experiences ("stressors"). Careful researchers in this area have correctly noted that one term ("stress") is used indiscriminately to describe the cause, the effect, and various points in between. The organism's response is sometimes called "the stress response" and the negative effects of that response "strain." This is clearly an area where more precise and standardized terminology is needed, but none of the various specific proposals for such a terminology has been adopted widely enough to end the confusion.

Stress and its management are popular concerns these days and are often discussed free of any of the negative implications that still attach to most psychological problems or treatments. This is especially true when the stress originates in a work setting or social role that does not totally define the person involved. Self-hypnosis, meditation, and related techniques are often a part of the stress-management programs offered by the large variety of practitioners in this field.

As a clinician, you try with each patient to arrive at as accurate and precise a diagnostic formulation as possible so that treatment can be planned and evaluated sensibly. For these general purposes you should use whatever diagnostic system is currently recognized by your own profession. Once you have arrived at a diagnosis and decided on self-hypnosis as an appropriate treatment technique for any particular patient, more specialized evaluations become relevant.

The Brief Hypnotic Experience exercise can be used effectively to treat all of the conditions and problems that I have just reviewed, whether they are best described as anxiety, tension, or stress. Within this rather broad spectrum, the factors that make the biggest difference for self-hypnosis have already been described in Chapters 2 and 3. There is, however, a kind of diagnostic scheme that does play an important role in *how* the B.H.E. exercise is used clinically. I will give you an outline of this system here, and then use it to structure the discussion of the clinical applications of the B.H.E. exercise to anxiety, tension, and stress. The system involves the *timing* of target symptoms rather than their content.

Steady vs. Predictable vs. Unpredictable Symptoms

Target symptoms for self-hypnosis can be divided into three broad groups: *those that are relatively constant or steady, those that are episodic but predictable, and those that are episodic and unpredictable.* Many patients with anxiety, tension, and stress problems have symptoms that combine two or even three of these descriptions. However, for the purposes of treatment with self-hypnosis it is worthwhile separating out these components because the optimal use of the B.H.E. or of a similar self-hypnosis exercise is different for each of them.

Constant or steady target symptoms are always present, or are present continuously for long periods of time (e.g., a full day or more). An obvious psychiatric example is Generalized Anxiety Disorder. Relatively continuous tension and/or stress lasting over a defined period of time would also fall in this category, such as that accompanying cramming for a bar examination and awaiting the results or trying to deal with the diagnosis of a life-threatening illness in oneself or in a family member. When the target symptom is relatively constant, most active people can still suppress it for brief periods of time by getting involved in work, family, or recreational activities. Even when they are involved in these activities, however, they are often aware at the time or later that they feel different (and worse) than they usually do.

Episodic but predictable symptoms last for brief periods of time compared to the symptom-free intervals, and are associated with some identifiable stimulus or set of circumstances that allow the patient to have a good idea when and where the symptoms will occur. Simple or Social Phobias are the most obvious examples of these types of symptoms within the group of Anxiety Disorders. A patient may become anxious and tense whenever he is in a high building or on a bridge, or whenever he has to give what most people would consider a non-stressful talk in public. Some stresses of normal work or family life, such as teacher conferences for certain parents, have this episodic but predictable character. For all of the patients in this group, the problem and its treatment are clearly related to a specific situation; out of the situation they feel and function well enough so that more generalized treatments with hypnosis or any other technique are not needed and/or accepted.

Episodic and unpredictable symptoms are usually limited in duration from a few minutes to an hour, but the patient is unable to identify and/or control a specific stimulus or situation that reliably brings them on. Panic Disorder provides the best example of genuinely unpredictable, episodic symptoms. For the patient suffering from Panic Disorder the distress caused by the symptoms of overwhelming terror, a sense of impending doom and various frightening physical sensations such as dizziness and trembling are compounded by the knowledge that the attacks may occur at any time without warning.

Some stress-related target symptoms in this group have easily identifiable precipitants that in their nature cannot be effectively predicted or controlled. Professionals in medicine, law enforcement, and the clergy, for example, must react efficiently and helpfully in a variety of life-threatening situations for themselves and the people they serve. People in these professions know that they must face such situations and are trained to deal with them. But that does not prevent them from experiencing anxiety and tension, especially when the situations come on suddenly and without warning.

You should be able to use these three broad groups to categorize your patient's target symptoms and to adjust your initial application of the B.H.E. exercise so that it is as likely as possible to affect that particular pattern. This is often a matter of appropriate "dosing" of the exercise so that it matches the timing of the patient's symptoms. Often more than one of these categories will apply, as in a patient with Panic Disorder who is always tense in anticipation of an attack. The system is still useful in such cases, however, because it will permit you to break down the total symptom picture into more manageable segments that can be addressed one by one. Not infrequently self-hypnosis may be an effective treatment for one component of the patient's problem even if it does not work with others.

The Key Phrase

The Brief Hypnotic Experience exercise incorporates a "key phrase" that summarizes the positive aspects of the hypnotic experience and can be very useful in the treatment of anxiety, tension, or stress symptoms both within and outside of hypnosis. In the exercise itself, the phrase is introduced at the end of the patient's first experience of the beach scene in this way: "You will be able to return to this pleasant scene in hypnosis whenever you want to. Remember how you feel right now. You may want to think of one or two words that express how you feel . . . words like 'clear and calm' or 'warm and relaxed.' Whatever words are best for you."

In using the exercise for anxiety, tension, or for any other symptom, the key phrase provides an opportunity to anchor your treatment somewhere near the patient's actual problem. Your patient does this with your help by constructing his own key phrase that is linked as an *opposite, healer or escape* from whatever his problem may be. Your patient should decide on this phrase before the first B.H.E. induction, so that his own personal phrase may be substituted for or at least added on to the phrases "clear and calm" and "warm and relaxed" in the exercise script.

Choosing a key phrase may seem like a minor chore, but it is actually a key juncture in the clinical use of hypnosis. Since I do not usually administer the induction during the patient's first session, the choice of a key phrase is most often discussed during the first session and then given to the patient as one of a number of "homework" assignments for the second session.

The choice of a key phrase is crucial because it goes beyond the recording of target symptoms to at least the description of what it would feel like to be without them. Words and names have a certain magic of their own, and for many patients coming up with a key phrase marks the real beginning of their symptom-related treatment. Naturally, if resistances to treatment are going to appear (as opposed to resistances to experiencing hypnosis) this is one of the places they frequently show up.

The actual construction of the phrase is simple enough, but I usually go over the concept in some detail with patients to be sure they know what is entailed. I start by asking the patient to give me a list of five to ten words that describe the way he feels when he is experiencing his target symptom. One patient with anxiety and tension symptoms presented this typical list: "tense, uptight, scared, frozen, like I'm going to fall apart, stomach in a knot, wound-up, terrible."

I don't ask for a detailed explanation of the phrases that the patient comes up with, but instead ask him to go on and give me opposites of each of the terms he has used. I write the opposites, or have the patient write them, next to the descriptive words. For the list just presented, the patient came up with the following opposites:

> tense — relaxed
> uptight — also relaxed
> scared — not scared
> frozen — loose
> like I'm going to fall apart — OK
> stomach in a knot — don't notice my stomach when I'm OK
> wound-up — loose
> terrible — great

This is the point where you want to clarify what the terms he has used mean for your patient. Remember that meanings of terms like this can be quite idiosyncratic, and control your tendency to share your patient's use of language to be like your own. The more the key phrase reflects your patient's own personal style, the more effective it will be.

What you are looking for in a key phrase are two words connected by the conjunction "and" that express the opposites of central components of the patient's target symptoms. A longer key phrase than this is cumbersome for use outside of hypnosis. Using only one word, especially a relatively common one, can lead to the patient using this stimulus so often that it loses all uniqueness or conditioning to the pleasant hypnotic experience.

As we look over the list, it is clear that some of the terms are more promising than others. "Relaxed," "loose," and "OK" both appear twice. "Not scared," as a negative, is a poor candidate. "Great" is certainly a desirable way to feel, but it may be asking too much even from a well-taught self-hypnosis exercise, especially when the phrase is to be used outside of hypnosis to control anxiety in a stressful situation.

I sent the patient home with the three terms that had appeared twice (relaxed, loose, and OK) and the assignment to choose a combination of two of them joined by "and" that was best as a preliminary key phrase. I had already discussed the beach scene with him and knew that he found this setting pleasant and relaxing; any of the three might conceivably describe ways you would feel lying on a warm, pleasant beach. Obviously, working on the key phrase is a good check point for evaluating the beach scene for the patient you are working with. The scene is useful only if it is pleasant for the patient and serves in some way to counteract his symptoms. This is usually the case with anxiety, tension and stress symptoms, but beaches are negative for some patients and a different type of scene may have to be used.

This particular patient ended up with the key phrase "relaxed and OK." He found that the term "loose" served well as an opposite for "frozen," but he did not like its sound or feel as a positive sensation itself. "OK" for him had a more positive implication than usual, and signified a confident sense of wellness that was right on target for the negative feelings and thoughts that formed his own symptom picture. He tried repeating "OK and relaxed" and "relaxed and OK" to himself, and preferred the latter.

This example should give you a feeling for the therapeutic potency of this process: for the patient, it is a novel way of experiencing the target symptoms with implications, at least, of liberation and mastery. Selecting or modifying key phrases is a knack that comes with practice, but it is not difficult and your patients will help you make needed modifications as they work with the phrase in learning the exercise and using it in their daily lives.

The key phrase is used in several different ways depending on the type of target symptom and on the patient's circumstances and personality. It can be repeated subvocally during the B.H.E. exercise itself as a way of reinforcing therapeutic aspects of the beach scene or of the hypnotic experience itself. The phrase, if used often enough, becomes a kind of conditioned stimulus to the pleasant experience of the exercise. After this has occurred, patients can repeat it softly or subvocally to themselves when it would be impossible or inconvenient to do the entire exercise.

Repetition of the key phrase outside of hypnosis can be particularly useful for episodic unpredictable target symptoms. For some patients this repetition brings *some* of the relaxed, pleasant feelings associated with the exercise. Patients usually rate this effect as being only 20-25% of what they get from the exercise itself, but this can be genuinely helpful and is not a bad yield for two words. Specific instances of how the key phrase can be used outside of hypnosis will be given in the case examples.

Constant or Steady Symptoms

Patients with constant symptoms are helped in a number of ways by the Brief Hypnotic Experience exercise. The process of learning the exercise and the exercise itself once it has been learned serve as times out from the uninterrupted tension of their problem. That this time out is prescribed by a sanctioned healer makes it acceptable to a number of dutiful patients who would otherwise feel guilty about doing anything enjoyable (such as visiting a real beach). In some ways, this is similar to the role of Sabbath observance in punctuating the weekly work cycle. Where the stress is very severe, just this factor independent of the hypnotic aspects of the B.H.E. may be enough to produce significant clinical improvement.

Whether these patients experience the emotion of fear/anxiety or not, they often have the physical sensation of tension in one or several muscle groups, or a generalized sense of being "uptight." The wording of the B.H.E. incorporates a number of terms designed to counter these feelings: "comfortable," "relaxed," "floating," "pleasant." The deepening part of the induction uses a count of one to ten to structure the progressive relaxation of all major muscle groups. The beach scene that comes next in the exercise is a multisensory stimulus that is relaxing to most people; to "get into" this scene is almost by definition to feel warm, comfortable, at peace, and relaxed.

This review should make clear that the Brief Hypnotic Experience exercise is *loaded* with specific thoughts and images that relieve or are the natural opposites of anxiety, tension, and stress. In general, therefore, you do not need to make any modification to the exercise as I have presented it for use in the treatment of this group of patients. The process of tailoring the exercise to patients in this group consists almost entirely of adjusting the dosing of the exercise and working out the nature and usage of their key phrase.

The Brief Hypnotic Experience exercise takes about ten minutes from start to finish in its unmodified form — its brevity is intentional and part of its basic character. Even if your patient learns the exercise well and is quite talented hypnotically, there is going to be a gross disproportion between the time he spends in hypnosis and out of it.

Thus, whatever therapeutic effect the self-hypnosis exercise is going to have is *not* going to be a direct manifestation of the hypnotic state. How, then, do you dose this brief exercise for symptoms that are always there?

For steady target symptoms, the dosing of the exercise ends up being based on practicality more than on anything else. Like an antianxiety drug, the ten-minute B.H.E. exercise does have a kind of dose-response curve with an almost immediate therapeutic effect falling off fairly rapidly in the first few hours after the exercise is actually done. There is some individual variation in this pattern which you will get a feeling for quickly as you work with patients.

In your initial work with self-hypnosis, I would recommend the practice schedule you and your patient have arrived at for learning the exercise as a practical starting point for its therapeutic application in these cases. The basic schedule that I use is twice daily, five days per week. The details of setting up and modifying this practice schedule are covered in Chapter 9.

Because it is tailored to the actual conditions that the patient is living with, an individualized patient schedule is more likely to last through the long haul of persistent symptoms than an intensive treatment program that eventually falls prey to fatigue and/or boredom. As with a practice schedule, the actual timing of when and where the patient does the exercise may depend more on when he can be alone and undisturbed than on any other factor.

Since the B.H.E. exercise is so brief, you should not be surprised if one repetition provides only a few hours or less of symptom relief. This is, in fact, a considerable accomplishment for a patient-initiated risk-free treatment procedure. It can have a real impact by enabling the patient to do more and also by overcoming the oppressive sense of demoralization that is often part of chronic or steady problems. If your own perspective is realistic you are in a position to be realistically pleased when you should be and disappointed when you should expect more.

In some cases, I have found it useful to increase either the frequency of the exercise, up to five times daily, or (more rarely) the length of time spent in self-hypnosis. The extra time is usually devoted to enjoying the beach scene or whatever pleasant, relaxing dream-like experience the patient and you have constructed. Some patients describe and experience the scene as a "mini vacation" that interrupts relatively unrelenting symptoms or stress.

Most patients who are helped by an exercise that lasts longer than 15 minutes find the use of a timer, as described in Chapter 9, frees the timekeeping part of their minds and lets them relax more in the scene or fantasy that they have developed. For beginners in the clinical use of self-hypnosis, I would not encourage you or your patients extending the individual sessions with the B.H.E. exercise beyond 30 minutes. Other systems of self-hypnosis (and many of meditation) use longer intervals, but it is best to start out by using the B.H.E. pretty much as it was designed. You will find several alternative approaches to this issue suggested in the readings mentioned in Appendix B.

Another aspect of dosing the B.H.E. exercise is expressed by the old medical maxim: "use a new drug quickly, while it works!" New treatments (or new packagings of old ones) introduced into a population of clinicians and patients always have an enhanced therapeutic value for a short time simply because they are new and different. Clinicians want to try them and are interested in whether and how they will work. This interest spills over to the patients who are the first recipients of the new technique, and can add new and sometimes needed life to the treatment relationship. Patients too are curious, perhaps a little apprehensive, and sometimes flattered to be chosen for these trials.

As long as the new treatment is inherently as good as or better than the available ones, it will come out ahead during this honeymoon phase. As the use of the new treatment spreads, side effects, treatment failures, and controlled research studies begin to appear. The new entry then settles, usually down, to its place in the clinician's regular treatment spectrum.

Hypnosis can hardly be called a new treatment, since it has been used clinically since ancient times. For you as a beginner, however, it *is* new. Moreover, it is likely to be novel, exciting, and perhaps more than a little scary for the first patients you use it with. Even if these patients have had previous experiences with hypnosis, this will be the first time they experience it with you. All this should alert you to the fact that the "honeymoon factor" is likely to be a significant one in your use of self-hypnosis.

The honeymoon analogy is especially apt for steady or persistent anxiety or stress symptoms, or for any chronic problem for that matter. Many relationships do very well as brief romances but wear thin rather quickly when you actually have to live with that particular partner. Astute (and perhaps lucky) people are able to know which is which and have the opportunities to make these choices. There is a valid role for brief, dramatic treatments whose effect has a large honeymoon component in acute syndromes of various kinds.

Unfortunately, this is not the case with steady and/or chronic conditions. In these situations it is performance over the long haul, living with both the symptoms and the treatment, that counts. It is especially important to anticipate and control the disillusionment and demoralization that accompany a patient's realization that self-hypnosis, or any other new treatment, is not going to make it all better permanently. In my own experience supervising beginners in the use of self-hypnosis, realization that this honeymoon factor is operating helps them identify it for what it is and use it constructively to fuel the initial practice phase. Like transference, it can be a tool for healing if you know how to use it.

The other protective factor against post-honeymoon disillusionment is a system of recordkeeping as described in Chapter 3. Such a system, even a very simple one, can allow you to accumulate the data that will lead to an informed and reasonable decision by the patient about whether and how much self-hypnosis has helped him both in the honeymoon period and beyond. This in turn is the best starting place for a sound decision as to whether he wants to continue to use self-hypnosis on an ongoing basis to help control his symptoms. Let's pull some of these factors together now with a case example of the use of self-hypnosis to treat persistent anxiety and stress.

Hilda B. was just getting ready to start enjoying life when her world fell apart. She and her husband Albert had both worked in the public school system of a large city for many years. When they retired in their mid-sixties within a year of each other, Hilda was the long-time principal of a junior high school and Albert was the director of training for the system, a system that had educated them as immigrant children from Europe and which they had served well. Their last ten years of work had been difficult as they tried to cope with disciplinary problems in their students and concerns of younger teachers that were alien to the way of life they had known. They supported each other through these tough times and drew strength from the knowledge that they had a good pension, adequate savings, and grown children who were doing well on their own. They especially looked forward to a series of trips to parts of the world they had never seen or had left as children.

It was on the first of these trips, a Caribbean cruise, that Hilda first realized that something was wrong with Albert. He had a great deal of trouble adjusting to any changes in the printed itinerary that had been sent to them in advance. Once, he was literally almost left behind because he lost his way in a shopping area. Although the people they were traveling with affectionately dubbed him "the absentminded professor," Hilda was frightened and could see that Albert was upset by his lapses of memory.

Hilda tried unsuccessfully to discuss these episodes with Albert when they got home, but she soon realized that he couldn't or wouldn't talk with her about them. Things were OK for a few months in the predictable routine that they had settled into since retirement, but then Albert's memory problems began getting worse. Things came to a head after he made several serious errors in balancing their checkbook, and Albert finally agreed to visit his internist. After evaluation by a neurologist, psychological testing, and a battery of laboratory procedures, Hilda and Albert were brought face to face with the diagnosis they had both suspected and feared — Alzheimer's Disease (Primary Degenerative Dementia).

Two years after the diagnosis was made Hilda began seeing Ann, a clinical social worker who specialized in counseling family members of Alzheimer's victims. Albert, Hilda, and their children had handled this severe stress well, as they had the other stresses in their lives. They had even managed to arrange and enjoy together a trip to Albert's childhood homeland in Europe, where Albert's retention of and interest in childhood memories brought them pleasure instead of sadness. But taking care of Albert on the trip, and in day-to-day life around the house, was a constant drain on Hilda. Her internist, who also cared for Albert, suggested she see Ann when Hilda complained of a constant feeling of anxiety and tension and fears that she might "fall apart" and be unable to care for Albert.

Ann first helped Hilda to make sensible plans for Albert's future and for her own, including opportunities for respite and home health care. She then helped Hilda work through as much as she could of her grief and anger at Albert's illness and at what it had done to their retirement. She also taught Hilda the Brief Hypnotic Experience exercise as a way of relieving both the physical tension she was experiencing and the feelings of fear.

Hilda was not a highly talented hypnotic subject, but she practiced the exercise diligently and settled down into a twice daily schedule coordinated with Albert's naps. Hilda described the exercise itself as a "perfect antidote" for the feelings of anxiety and tension that had become almost constant. The feelings returned a few hours after she did the exercise. Hilda said that she would prefer to do the exercise three or four times daily, but she soon discovered that this was impractical in her routine with Albert, and trying to do it was stressful in itself. Instead, she found that looking forward to her late afternoon exercise "helps me to get through the day." The fears that she would fall apart decreased and gradually disappeared over a few months even though Albert's condition continued to worsen.

Going over her records of target symptoms (feelings of anxiety and tension, fears that she would fall apart) with Ann helped Hilda to justify taking the time for herself to do the exercise and gave her a chance to experience positive progress and mastery in one area of her life. She developed a trusting collaborative relationship with Ann that helped her and her family through the final phases of Albert's illness.

Hilda had chosen to use a real beach scene from the early days of her marriage to Albert as part of her exercise. For her it was associated with an island of romantic and pleasant time in their lives together before they had children at home or weighty administrative responsibilities at work. She chose "free and easy" as her key phrase, and found that her only moderate ability to experience the sensory aspects of the scene was enhanced by repeating it to herself while she did the exercise.

Hilda would repeat "free and easy" to herself outside of hypnosis when she found herself becoming frustrated with some task or snapping unproductively at Albert. When Ann cautiously explored what the actual words meant to her, Hilda's only conscious associations were to her memories from the beach. Once, she mentioned to Ann that she had begun crying immediately after ending the exercise as she realized that her carefree days with Albert were irrevocably in the past. She cried briefly in the office, and Ann found her own eyes filled with tears as well. Hilda said at their next session that she had noticed and been moved by Ann's feeling for her.

Episodic But Predictable Symptoms

When symptoms are episodic but predictable, your therapeutic efforts must be more focused than for constant symptoms. A good starting point is to have the patient try doing the B.H.E. exercise as close as possible to the time he is to enter the situation that produces symptoms. The case of Walter P. in Chapter 2 is a good example of this technique. Walter learned the exercise and then used it right before the sales presentations that were bothering him. The antianxiety effects of the exercise itself lasted long enough to suppress his symptoms, and his anticipatory and social anxiety soon faded. As often occurs with such patients, he stopped doing the exercise regularly as soon as his symptomatic distress was gone, and used it only on an as-needed basis.

An important aspect of these cases is helping patients either find the time and place to do the exercise right before the anxiety-provoking event, or realize that such an effort will not succeed and adopt some alternative strategy. The B.H.E. exercise is about as brief and unobtrusive as a self-hypnosis exercise can get. I have had patients use it at their desks in open office spaces, or in airplanes preparing for a parachute jump. But there *are* limits. A ringing telephone, or even the expectation that one might ring at any moment, can make it very difficult to do the exercise or to experience it as relaxing. When you are worried about a specific situation, the last thing you need is the added burden of finding a quiet place alone in a noisy, crowded environment.

Under these circumstances, you can work along two different dimensions with your patient; one or both may produce what you need. First, you can move the exercise back in time to a situation in the patient's day when he is able to do it undisturbed. Cynthia V., for example, always knew she was in for a bad headache and/or anxiety attack when her mother-in-law came to visit. She had a good marriage and a good sense of humor, but she and her husband's mother were just too different. After a few hours together, they began to get on each other's nerves and the situation got worse from there on. One of their major areas of disagreement was rules for her children, and she spent much of her time during the visits exerting a much tighter control on their behavior than she or they were used to.

Cynthia was taught a self-hypnosis exercise similar to the B.H.E. by her family physician, who used it himself to relax in the rare breaks between office cases. She soon found that the exercise was impractical when used during the day after she was interacting with the family; it was one more demand on her time, which she didn't have to give. We suggested instead that she set her alarm 15 minutes early on visit days and do the exercise in bed before she got up. This modification turned the exercise from a burden to "somewhat of a help," as she expressed it to her physician. "At least it gives me a good morning and puts the headache and nerves off till the afternoon." For people with crowded lives, this may be as much of a positive outcome as you are going to get.

The other direction in which the exercise may be modified is to place a heavier reliance on the key phrase, much as you do when the symptoms are episodic and unpredictable. Mark R. was a graduate student who worked weekends as a waiter in a luxurious restaurant to help support himself. On the very long Saturday night shift, the demands of his finicky customers and his maitre d' began to get to him around 10 o'clock, just when the largest group of diners were getting ready to pay their checks. His neck muscles would knot up painfully and he almost dropped his tray several times.

Mark got only a brief direct effect from the exercise, which he had learned as part of a class, and there was no way he could do the exercise or anything like it at the restaurant. I worked with him to find a key phrase appropriate to the situation, and he came up with "loose goose." The phrase had nothing to do with the beach scene, but made him smile on Saturday night, which was no mean feat. Mark did the exercise several times a week as he was going to sleep at night. At the end of the beach scene, he would repeat "loose goose" to himself five times or so and imagine a fat goose emerging from the surf and waddling up the beach. Mark used the phrase, repeated subvocally and sometimes in a soft whisper to himself, when he felt his neck getting tight at the restaurant. He reported that it "broke the cycle of tension" enough so that he could get through Saturday nights without mishap. As is frequently the case, Mark found that the introduction of humor into a tense situation — even one silly phrase — magnified his relaxation.

Episodic and Unpredictable Symptoms

To apply the Brief Hypnotic Experience exercise directly to episodic and unpredictable symptoms the patient must use the exercise or the key phrase derived from it after the symptoms have begun. While this may not seem like much of a problem, in practice it places severe limits on treatment of these patients with self-hypnosis. A case example (one of my own treatment failures) will make this clear.

Fred F. was an officer of a large corporation who had succeeded admirably in a demanding work setting. Although he was not married, he had a number of close friends of both sexes and was loyal and supportive of them and of his colleagues and employees. Fred got my name from a friend who had been helped by self-hypnosis, and came with positive expectations of me and of the procedure. His problem was what he called "gas," a distressing sense of abdominal fullness that had been investigated thoroughly by his gastroenterologist with no specific organic findings.

The physical nature of Fred's complaint did not bother me. The B.H.E. exercise is quite body-oriented and is a good treatment match for problematic physical sensations. The gas came on rather unpredictably, and a large variety of dietary and meal-timing manipulations had failed to eliminate it. When he had a bad attack, Fred would feel anxious, dizzy, and would often leave the room to lie down by himself for ten minutes or so. With the attacks coming on several times a week, this was becoming a real problem at work and in social situations.

Fred proved a highly talented student of self-hypnosis and soon became expert at the exercise. Like many talented students he modified the exercise creatively so that it was just right for his own style and circumstances. Fred reported that he had a sense of actually participating in the beach scene experience, and found the phrase "sound and relaxed" both expressed the positive aspects of the scene and the opposite of the sick and scared feelings he had during his "attacks." The stage seemed to be set for a successful therapeutic application of self-hypnosis.

Our initial plan was for Fred to do the exercise twice daily and use the key phrase to lessen the negative impact of the attacks. Because the attacks never troubled him when he was alone at home, he did the exercise before breakfast and around 2:00 p.m. in his office (he had no problems having his secretary take calls and being undisturbed for ten minutes). After the first week, Fred reported that doing the exercise regularly made him feel slightly more relaxed, but that the key phrase "just wasn't working" for the attacks.

During the second week we tried having him do the exercise instead of just lying down for a few minutes when he had the attacks. The attacks themselves were becoming more frequent and severe, and Fred had to walk out of an important meeting when he felt like he "was about to pass out." Although he was able to repeat the key phrase "sound and relaxed" during the attacks, he got no real relief from this repetition. When he tried to do the actual exercise, he found himself unable to concentrate. By the time he was able to do the exercise, the attack had passed.

Sometime during Fred's next weekly appointment, I realized that Fred's "gas" attacks were really manifestations of a steadily worsening Panic Disorder. He had stayed home from work two days that week, a pattern very unusual for him. That evening he began taking a small dose of doxepin (Sinequan or Adapin), and within another week his panic attacks were beginning to lessen. They subsided gradually over the next month to the point where he described himself as "not really aware of my stomach," and he remained symptom free. After several months we tried tapering the doxepin, but his symptoms reappeared and he preferred to continue taking it with periodic reviews and attempts to taper and discontinue. A year and a half later, Fred was still taking the doxepin. He used the B.H.E. exercise occasionally for relaxation, but we both knew its limits for him.

In Fred's case I made a diagnostic error in not considering Panic Disorder as part of my original differential diagnosis. In general, I find that patients with moderate to severe Panic Disorder are too upset during the attacks themselves to do a self-hypnosis exercise or even to use a key phrase very effectively. In such cases, the treatment just does not "grab" the disorder with any leverage. Fred was not harmed by learning and using the B.H.E. exercise, but I could have saved us both some distress by having the medication in more ready reserve and using it sooner.

In mild cases of Panic Disorder and in many unexpected stressful situations the key phrase can be useful to produce a small decrease in tension and anxiety/fear and to give the patient an active coping technique. A number of people who work in law enforcement and military fields have used it right before or during a dangerous confrontation in the same way that some people use a prayer or a comforting family image. Like the other skills that help people survive in such situations, the exercise from which the key phrase comes must be learned and practiced well before the crisis occurs.

After the actual crisis is over, participants often find themselves "keyed up" and unable to sleep that night even if the next day is going to be just as difficult. Under these circumstances, the Brief Hypnotic Experience exercise itself can often produce enough relaxation to allow some sleep. Even if the person is unable to sleep, the muscular relaxation and chance to "get away" to the beach scene are often quite helpful.

Integration of the B.H.E. with
Pharmacologic, Behavioral, and
Psychodynamic Interventions

As a specialized treatment technique, self-hypnosis should be integrated into a broader framework of evaluation and treatment tailored to the needs of the individual patient. The Brief Hypnotic Experience exercise can form part of a wide variety of treatment approaches to anxiety, tension and stress. Here are some approaches to this integration for the most widely used treatment techniques.

Antianxiety medications such as the benzodiazepines and related drugs like sedating antidepressants or beta-adrenergic blocking agents are often used to treat these symptoms. Since the mechanism of action of these drugs is far from clear, it is much too soon to be precise about whether they exert their antianxiety effects through the same pathways as hypnosis. To make the situation even less clear in the case of the B.H.E. and most other self-hypnosis exercises, we have already seen that the exercise contains many nonhypnotic elements that act to relieve anxiety symptoms.

Patients who are both using the B.H.E. exercise and taking medications can usually describe a subjective difference in their effects, but I have found that these described differences are highly individual and resist easy categorization. The case of Fred F. highlights the importance of not using self-hypnosis for a problem like severe Panic Disorder where the nature of the symptoms interfere with the application of the treatment and where specific drug effects may be helpful. We will encounter this situation again in Chapter 8 ("More Advanced Applications") when we consider the limited role of self-hypnosis in the treatment of depression.

From a practical point of view the only direct interaction that you should be prepared to deal with is that between the B.H.E. exercise and as-needed (prn) drugs used in the treatment of episodic symptoms. These are usually drugs with a relatively short half-life, such as oxazepam (Serax) or lorazepam (Ativan), or drugs such as diazepam (Valium) which have a relatively quick onset of action. An obvious approach in such cases is to try the self-hypnosis exercise first for a week or two and then compare its results to the prn drug. Such situations highlight the need for a system of quantitative recordkeeping, however simple.

If clinical considerations dictate using the self-hypnosis exercise and the prn drug at the same time, you will need a method of sequencing or combining them. Let me describe the protocol that I typically use in such cases; you can then modify it to suit your own needs or develop one of your own. I usually present the protocol to the patient in written form when he leaves my office. A typical protocol would be:

1) Look at your watch when you have _____ (the symptom) and note the time.
2) Wait ten minutes.
3) If the symptom is not gone or diminishing, repeat your key phrase five times or do the self-hypnosis exercise, if you are able.
4) Wait ten minutes after repeating the key phrase or finishing the exercise.
5) If the symptom is not gone or diminishing, take _____ (the appropriate dose of the prn medication).
6) If the symptom is not gone or diminishing an hour after you take the medication, take _____ (the second prn dose, if you are using one).
7) If the symptom is not gone or diminishing two hours after you take the second dose, call _____ (if this is appropriate in your treatment relationship—make sure the patient has your telephone number if you want him to call under these circumstances, and be specific about calls after hours or to your home).
8) Do not take more than _____ (maximum daily dose you recommend) in one day.

This protocol gives the patient a sequence of coping behaviors to use for his anxiety, tension, or stress symptoms. Simply having such a sequence may be reassuring in the same way as a single diazepam (Valium) tablet carried in a wallet or purse for years "just in case." The sequence includes a limited waiting period, during which some anxiety symptoms will begin to diminish spontaneously. The intermittent experience of this spontaneous symptom relief may have some protective value against the excessive ritualization of the self-hypnosis exercise or the development of psychological and/or physical drug dependence. In the context of the protocol both taking the medication and calling the therapist are prescribed actions to be used in sequence as needed. For some patients this may lessen the likelihood of excessive use of these options or inappropriate guilt concerning them if they are used.

Behavioral approaches to anxiety and stress often call for some antianxiety condition to be paired with the anxiety-provoking stimulus. This may be part of systematic desensitization, as developed by Dr. Joseph Wolpe, or of a number of related procedures. The B.H.E. exercise can be used in such approaches in the same way as Jacobsonian muscle relaxation or various imagery techniques. For therapists concerned that the learning in hypnosis may be relatively state-dependent and therefore not transfer well to the patient's life situation, the key phrase may be substituted for the exercise itself. A number of patients have used the ten-count muscle relaxation sequence from the B.H.E. exercise by itself with good results. In general, behavioral therapists are comfortable with the exercise and with the approach to target symptom specification and recordkeeping presented here.

Although self-hypnosis has a less obvious role in *cognitive therapy* approaches to anxiety, cognitive therapists are also often familiar with and open to the appropriate use of self-hypnosis with their patients. In most cases, the cognitive therapist has already accumulated considerable data on target-symptom occurrence. For some patients, the B.H.E. exercise and/or a particular key phrase may help gain useful distance from troubling automatic thoughts.

Therapists who use a predominantly *psychodynamic approach* to the treatment of anxiety, tension, or stress symptoms may be more familiar with hypnosis as an uncovering or dream-inducing technique than with an exercise like the B.H.E. The B.H.E. exercise is *not* designed for these uses; its brevity and highly structured nature make it a poor choice for the job. Psychoanalysts will recognize the many differences between the relationship with the therapist fostered by the B.H.E. (collaborative student-teacher focused on an activity mainly done outside the treatment hour) and the one fostered by psychoanalysis. These differences may dictate referral of a patient engaged in psychoanalysis or in intensive psychoanalytically-oriented psychotherapy to another therapist for training in self-hypnosis even if the psychoanalyst can and does use this treatment with other patients.

These cautions should not obscure the crucial role of an understanding of psychodynamics in the interpretation of how patients react to self-hypnosis, and in solving problems within the treatment relationship. Several excellent examples of how this process works in the treatment of anxiety, tension, and stress symptoms are presented by Fred Frankel in his book *Hypnosis: Trance as a Coping Mechanism* (see Appendix B).

SEVEN

Applications to
Dysfunctional Pain

Hypnosis and Pain

I know of no experience involving the clinical use of hypnosis more gratifying to both the clinician and to the patient than the relief of pain. When successful, it leads to the kind of genuine, uncomplicated gratitude that has become unfortunately rare in the world of hi-tech medicine. A few cases of this kind can keep you going through some less responsive and/or thankful patients. Compared to the standard surgical and medical treatments for pain relief, self-hypnosis is relatively inexpensive and risk-free; that is why I have included it along with anxiety as one of the two initial clinical applications for beginners.

The history of hypnosis has shown a persistent interpenetration and alternation of activity in these two clinical categories: anxiety and pain. Mesmer in the 18th century and Freud in the 20th concentrated on what were then called hysterical and neurasthenic disorders. But it was a group of English physicians and surgeons (John Elliotson, James Esdaile and James Braid) working in the mid-19th century on surgical anesthesia and clinical pain relief who kept the interest in the practice of hypnosis alive in the interval.

Their work also served to anchor hypnosis in a part of the healing arts that provided a healthy contrast with its more psychological developments. It is interesting to note that each of these waves of interest in hypnosis was terminated by a scientific discovery that took investigators and clinicians off in a different, nonhypnotic direction. Mesmer's animal magnetism was not really magnetism, but imagination. Ether and chloroform worked even with the unhypnotizable. Memories retrieved through hypnosis were not factually accurate, and the emotional complexes behind them could also be explored through the nonhypnotic technique of free association. And yet, through three centuries of modern medical and scientific history, interest in and use of hypnosis keep coming back—perhaps because the phenomena of hypnosis embody so much of what we still do not fully understand about how the mind works and heals.

Another reason I have chosen pain relief as one of the two initial clinical applications for self-hypnosis has to do with the nature of pain itself. Put most simply, powerful subjective experiences are at the core of both pain and hypnosis, and what you learn about one can enrich and deepen your understanding of the other. Remember the working definition of hypnosis from Chapter 1: "Hypnosis is a process that allows us to experience thoughts and images as real." This common core has more than educational value for you as a student, however. It underlies the therapeutic leverage that hypnosis gives you to deal with pain. If you can help a patient learn how to create and modify vivid thoughts and images that he experiences as real, you can teach him to relieve his pain.

The interrelationship of hypnosis and pain has been explored extensively by a number of eminent researchers. From a clinical point of view, you should know that this is one of the areas where hypnotic talent or responsivity as measured by standard scales is often significantly related to clinical outcome—in this case, to pain relief. The laboratory research and relevant clinical studies in this area are covered in the book *Hypnosis in the Relief of Pain* by Ernest and Josephine Hilgard and in the chapter on hypnosis by Martin Orne and David Dinges in Wall and Melzack's *Textbook of Pain* (see Appendix B). The *Textbook* has many useful chapters on various aspects of this complex subject that go far beyond the scope of this book.

Since pain is such a complex subject from both a clinical and experimental standpoint, the commonalities with hypnosis cover only part of its territory. You yourself may be a dentist or family physician with extensive clinical experience treating patients whose major presenting problem is physical pain, or a social worker or psychologist who has had relatively little primary responsibility for this kind of diagnosis and treatment. If you are in the former group, the next few pages may seem relatively superficial and you might want to skim them rather lightly. If you are in the latter group, these paragraphs will give you some helpful guidelines but will obviously not equip you to diagnose and treat painful physical conditions yourself. The basic caution from

Chapter 2 that you should never treat any patient using hypnosis whom you would not treat without it applies particularly strongly here.

I have found it useful to understand my preliminary explorations with patients who have pain and for whom self-hypnosis is being considered as a treatment in terms of two statements. These statements are:

1) All pain is real.
2) Not all pain is useful.

When and if the patient and I understand and accept these two statements as they apply to him and to his particular pain, we are usually ready to begin with self hypnosis. Let's go over the statements and their implications now in detail.

Pain As an Experience

If pain is essentially a subjective experience and a patient tells you he has pain, then he has pain. Unless you have chosen to specialize in forensic work, in evaluations for compensation, or in the detection of deception, there is no reason for you as a clinician to qualify this sentence by adding the phrase "unless he is lying." This might expose you to the risk of being fooled by the rare patient who is intentionally deceptive, but the risk of misinterpreting and abandoning genuinely suffering patients is much greater, at least in my estimation.

Accepting all pain reports as real can have a significant therapeutic effect in itself aside from self-hypnosis or any other specific treatment techniques that you may use. It is not unusual for patients to present this problem rather explicitly themselves in the first interview: "They keep telling me on the orthopedic ward that it's not real, that the nerve isn't under pressure anymore, but it still hurts when I try to walk or drive!" Sometimes these patient reports are literally true and describe physicians who have confused pain experiences and changes in x-ray or nerve conduction studies. Just as often, however, they represent understandable distortions of unsatisfactory and frustrating doctor-patient interactions as experienced by the patient. In these cases, patients may be helped a great deal by clearing the lines of communication with the referring physician and arriving at some mutually satisfactory definitions: pain is an experience and is always real for the patient. Most physicians in any specialty can accept this easily, especially if they can get some help in dealing with their patient's pain.

Patients are almost always grateful for this kind of validation and clarification. It also allows you as a clinician to narrow the focus of your intervention to an area where you may be able to help and where self-hypnosis is very much to the point: what and how the patient feels. You may be able to be quite helpful in this area while not having any significant impact on a number of other facets of the patient's medical problem or life situation. As long as you and the patient accept this relatively narrow therapeutic focus, dysfunctional pain can be a rewarding application of self-hypnosis for both of you.

In the process of exploring and defining the focus of your intervention, you may encounter a number of other expectations and fantasies that are common in patients with pain and that can block your efforts to feel and to be helpful. These can be a serious problem if you are a beginner in the clinical use of self-hypnosis and have not had extensive prior experience in the treatment of patients with pain. You want to know at least something about them in advance so that you can bypass avoidable sources of anger and disappointment.

The two most frequent potential problem areas in my experience are: 1) fantasies of complete cure or relief from serious and/or chronic conditions; and 2) expectations that the major product of your work together will be a letter or document certifying some level of damage or disability or providing support in an ongoing conflict at work, in the family, or with another clinician. These are all real and valid issues for work with an attorney or with another clinician, but they are not direct products of the clinical use of self-hypnosis.

Although it rarely comes up in day-to-day clinical practice, you should be especially wary of requests to use self- or hetero-hypnosis to find out "what really happened" during an accident or other traumatic situation that may have contributed to a clinical pain problem. As explained in Chapter 2, hypnosis is not only unreliable as a way of getting at objective truth, but its use may also irretrievably alter the memories involved. This is true even when there are *not* clear self-interest issues involved in one or another version of the incident; it is even more so when there are.

Once you have done your best to clarify these issues and identify the patient's real pain experiences as your target symptom, you are ready to work out a recordkeeping system that will give you and your patient a baseline rate for the frequency and intensity of the pain and allow the impact of the self-hypnosis exercise to be evaluated. The process of quantification prepares the way for the possibility of a measurable though not necessarily spectacular therapeutic effect — no mean accomplishment considering the high benefit to risk and cost ratio of training in self-hypnosis.

Dysfunctional Pain

The term dysfunctional pain is a fancy way of saying that not all pain is useful. This second basic statement moves a little closer to the prospect of decreasing or eliminating the patient's pain. Clearly what is called for is an exploration of whether and how *this* pain, of *this* patient, is no longer useful or never was.

The concept that pain usually has a signal value is the one that I most often start with, using an example intentionally unrelated to that patient's personal situation. I might describe the value of a throbbing shoulder to a baseball pitcher: a signal to have a reliever called in during that particular game so that he will be able to pitch in others that season. Another example is the characteristic crushing chest pain radiating down the left arm that signals a heart attack and may allow a person to get life-saving medical attention if the signal is not denied or ignored. After presenting the example, I usually ask the patient to examine his own pain from this perspective and see if it has any valid signal value to him now.

By definition, dysfunctional pain has lost its signal value to the patient. A patient with severe back pain gave this typical response: "Sure, the pain tells me that there is something wrong with my back. But I know that already, and the doctors know that. They say they have done everything that they can with surgery, and the drugs make me too sleepy to work. I just want to get rid of it!" An answer like this can lead naturally to a trial of self-hypnosis for pain relief.

In contrast, another patient with a past history of ulcer disease recognized that something was different about her current episode of abdominal pain after I had asked her only a few questions. This pain was not related to meals and had a different qualitative feel and distribution. She decided to check with her gynecologist, who promptly diagnosed a potentially hazardous ectopic pregnancy. Here the pain had very real signal value, and any attempt to teach this patient self-hypnosis to relieve the pain would have been a serious mistake.

Even if patients are sure that their pain does not have any valid current signal value, you should always confirm this yourself with the physician who has primary responsibility for the diagnosis and treatment of the painful condition. Often a personal phone call is all that is necessary, and this usually leads to a go-ahead such as "Sure—give it a try. Right now that pain isn't doing her any good. I'll be following her regularly and I'll let you know if the situation changes." A less reassuring response, with or without the suggestion that the current episode of pain needs further diagnostic evaluation, should be your signal to hold off teaching the patient self-hypnosis until *you* are satisfied that the medical or dental situation has been adequately evaluated and that the pain does not have current signal value.

There is another, more psychological, sense of the idea that pain may or may not be useful to a patient. This has to do with the pain's value in terms of what it means or does for the patient intrapsychically (e.g., punishment for a perceived wrongdoing), interpersonally (e.g., keeping a spouse in a marriage who would otherwise leave), or socially (e.g., ensuring continued financial payments). You should certainly be as aware as possible of these dimensions of the patient's inner and outer life. The values involved are clearly potent and will contribute to any patient's motivational balance towards self-hypnosis. Their effect is likely to be at least as large as any of the factors I have already discussed that relate to previous experiences or expectations concerning hypnosis itself.

As a beginner in the use of self-hypnosis, you should obviously try to select your first patients so that these possibly confounding factors are minimized. Your chances are best with acute pain in an otherwise healthy individual whose family and financial situations would clearly be served by relieving the pain. This is why hypnosis works well with patients in burn centers, or with children who have cancer and who will have to undergo painful medical procedures that may prolong their lives and relieve their disabilities. Your chances are worst with a chronically ill patient for whom the painful condition has become a way of life, and where ongoing social or financial rewards are still at stake. I would advise you to pass by opportunities to try self-hypnosis with patients at this end of this spectrum until you have had some success with patients at the other end.

I am not suggesting that hypnosis, including self-hypnosis, has no role in the treatment of chronic or mixed-motivation pain patients. But this is not an area for beginners at hypnosis, or for clinicians without in-depth experiences in the long-term treatment of patients with pain.

If you are such a clinician (working in a pain clinic, for example) self-hypnosis can prove to be a useful technique and is certainly easy to justify on a benefit vs. risk/cost basis. In fact, the risk of using hypnosis under these circumstances is often greatest with the patients who have the *most* hypnotic talent and who respond dramatically with reduction in their felt pain. If their psychosocial situation has not been adequately explored and prepared for the possibility that the pain may decrease, a dramatic "cure" can upset their equilibrium and lead to otherwise rare symptom substitution or to a family crisis.

For clinicians experienced both in treating pain patients and in the clinical use of hypnosis who are working with a patient in this group, it may be useful to explore a third statement that is really a tentative and qualified extension of the second: "Life is usually better without too much pain." The exploration of this statement as it applies to that particular patient broadens the focus to the patient's entire life, and to what it would be like if the pain were lessened or gone. The phrase "better without too much pain" is a logical tautology, but it introduces the possibility that a safe first step might be a small reduction in felt pain that does not otherwise deprive the patient of any of the intra-psychic or interpersonal benefits that the pain now brings. Clearly, this is a group of patients where small, reversible changes are in order. In the context of this broader life picture, otherwise confounding factors may be seen to be central and the helpful role of self-hypnosis to be quite small.

Let's return now to the treatment of the more clearly dysfunctional pain that you should be working with as a beginner. Once you have determined that the patient's pain is clearly dysfunctional you are ready to begin teaching him self-hypnosis.

Adaptation of the B.H.E.
Exercise to Pain Relief

The Brief Hypnotic Experience exercise has been designed to treat anxiety and stress symptoms without any significant modification; its application to pain often requires some specific changes or additions. Let's start with the situations where the least modification is needed and move from there to the more advanced applications.

The unmodified B.H.E. exercise can have a significant therapeutic effect where *tension and/or anxiety form a significant part of the pain experience*. Such situations span a rather wide range of medical conditions ranging from mild to quite severe. I saw Carl Z., for example, at the request of his family physician on a "try this first before we go on to something more drastic" basis. Carl had injured his trapezius muscle (between the neck and shoulder) while playing touch football over a weekend. After a few days of rest at home, he tried returning to his job as an automobile mechanic, but found that he had moderate to severe pain when he used his arm to reach up and turn at the same time — something he frequently had to do. He began to worry about losing his job and being unable to support his wife and two young children, and this clearly made the pain worse. His family physician correctly identified a strong anxiety component in his pain that amplified the tension and spasm of the injured muscles.

Carl knew and trusted his family physician and came to see me with positive expectations. He requested an "extra long session" so that he could learn the exercise as quickly as possible and see if it would work for him. I taught him the B.H.E. exercise with only one modification: instead of lying on the beach, he was floating on his back in very shallow, warm water near the shore. I described the movement of the warm water as providing a feeling of pleasant, comfortable relaxation without any specific mention of his pain or its relief. Since Carl had pain only with specific movements, it was easy for him to learn and to practice the exercise in a pain-free state.

After practicing about a dozen times daily for two days, Carl returned to work and did the exercise before he began working and every hour during the first day. Because the garage was so crowded and noisy, he locked himself in the men's room and sat on the toilet with the seat cover down to do the exercise. His friends at work made a few crude jokes, but were mostly curious about hypnosis and asked Carl to describe and demonstrate the exercise for them, which he did. Carl described the exercise as reducing his pain "from 8 to 2" on a 10-point scale, and was able to continue working the first day and taper the frequency of doing the exercise at work over the next week. He knew he was out of the woods when he began forgetting to take time out to do the exercise. Carl called me to cancel his follow-up appointment, and said that he'd call me if he ever needed me again. Clearly the pain, hypnosis, and the relationship with me were no longer central in his life.

In Carl's case the pain occurred only when he moved, so he could learn the exercise pain-free simply by sitting still. If you have ever tried listening to someone or reading while your sinuses were throbbing, you know that significant pain is a powerful distractor. This creates a harmful paradox when patients are unable to learn and practice the self-hypnosis exercise because of the pain it is supposed to relieve.

This is a real limitation of the technique, one that cannot always be overcome. When pain can be anticipated, as in childbirth or elective surgery, the solution is obvious: do the self-hypnosis training and practice in advance. The exercise is then in place and ready to be used when needed; just having it available may have a significant effect in reducing apprehension and distress. I usually advise practicing the exercise in its unmodified form between 10 and 20 times before it is applied to pain relief. Where the pain has already begun, the exercise can be learned and practiced during spontaneous pain-free intervals, which often occur even in the most serious conditions. Even if there are no pain-free intervals, clinically significant results can often still be achieved by scheduling teaching and practice to correspond with periods when the pain is less severe and/or the patient is less exhausted.

Situations where hypnosis is being considered for an absolutely unremitting severe pain symptom are one of the few indications for hetero-hypnosis as opposed to self-hypnosis; a forceful, insistent hetero-hypnotic approach can sometimes bring relief where there would be no chance for the kind of collaborative learning and practice emphasized in this book. Once the crisis has passed it may be perfectly feasible to instruct the patient in a self-hypnosis exercise that can be used for any remaining pain, or for recurrences. Several standard hetero-hypnotic inductions, including a number of brief and/or highly directive ones, are described in the clinically oriented books referenced in Appendix B.

A very different clinical application of the unmodified B.H.E. exercise is its use as an *escape from pain*. Here the hypnotic state itself and the experiences included in the exercise (especially the beach scene or a similar pleasant, relaxing dream-like experience) are used as a peaceful and relatively pain-free respite from the patient's current situation. This approach can be especially effective where either or both of two conditions prevail: the patient is a highly talented hypnotic subject and/or the physical pain problem is part of or has caused a difficult life situation from which episodic escape or respite is particularly appropriate.

The B.H.E. evaluation form (see Chapter 5) contains a number of items that measure the kind of hypnotic talent involved in this application. The patient who responds to items D, E, and F by describing the sensory experiences of the beach scene as very vivid, felt like he was really there, and found the experience of hypnosis quite pleasant is more likely to benefit from this application than someone with low-end responses on these items. Several of the longer and more elaborate scales of hypnotic responsivity described in Appendix B explore these aspects of the hypnotic experience with much greater depth and precision.

The difficult life situations that go along with physical pain are well-known to all clinicians who work with these patients. Common realistic problems include loss of work, decrease in self-esteem, inability to look forward to a happy long-term future, and exhaustion of customary coping techniques. In prolonged or life-threatening conditions, patients often have to either keep their complaints and fears to themselves or risk abandonment by friends and family. When the illness is obviously terminal, even these social evasions are sometimes not enough to prevent abandonment.

Under these circumstances an *episodic* escape like the B.H.E. exercise can be healthy and can provide the patient with needed respite without mobilizing persistent and potentially maladaptive denial. From a clinical point of view it is often impossible and not particularly useful in these cases to tease out the effects of the self-hypnosis exercise on the sensory aspects of the pain and on the demoralization, existential despair, and interpersonal stress that accompany it. The families of seriously or chronically ill patients also need and benefit from this kind of respite, as illustrated by the case of Hilda B. described in Chapter 6.

Please do not confuse the indirectness of this approach with its potential ability to relieve pain and suffering. Patients have been able to use the B.H.E. and similar exercises to make major modifications in their perception of even very severe physical pain, including the pain associated with major surgical procedures—they simply are "at the beach" and not in the operating room. For some patients this can have an almost out-of-body or strongly dissociative aspect.

Finally, there is an advanced application of the unmodified B.H.E. exercise for pain patients that takes advantage of the fact that the exercise itself does *not* specifically address pain. For certain chronic and/or mixed-motivation patients, this feature may make the exercise, or one like it, relatively acceptable compared to more direct interventions. Taking a brief period of time out to become involved in the exercise may give the patient needed respite and/or perspective without unduly threatening his intrapsychic or social equilibrium.

For the average patient with clearly dysfunctional pain, however, the unmodified B.H.E. exercise is not the most appropriate therapeutic technique. A more direct approach to the pain experience is often called for, and it is time now to introduce you to two such techniques that you will be able to learn and to teach your patients who have pain: induced numbness and the "flowing and discarding" technique.

Induced Numbness

Inducing numbness in the area where the pain is felt is the next step along the continuum of increasingly direct application of the B.H.E. exercise to pain. Most people who are not actively suffering do not find the sensation of numbness particularly pleasant, but it is quite familiar to the average patient as a technique for controlling pain. The majority of patients you will deal with have had a local anesthetic such as Novocain for a dental procedure, minor surgery, or as a spinal or epidural anesthetic. If you and your patient are lucky, there may be a specific memory available of therapeutically induced numbing of the area that is now painful. Even patients who have never had a local anesthetic usually know what the sensation of numbness is like from experiences with cold, a limb "falling asleep," etc.

Induced numbness is somewhat easier for beginners to use than the "flowing and discarding" technique because it can be taught and practiced when the patient is pain-free. Moreover, it may have an advantage for certain patients in not specifically attempting to move or modify the pain sensations themselves. This can be a positive feature when the physician with primary responsibility for diagnosing and treating the condition responsible for the pain feels that it may have some slight or intermittent signal value. Under these circumstances it may be quite possible for the patient to retain some awareness of the pain and even of its intensity while inducing enough numbness so that he can work and enjoy himself. Alternatively, the patient might not induce numbness for part of each day or for one day each week to "keep track" of the pain signals.

There may be a psychological advantage to a different group of patients from the somewhat indirect approach offered by induced numbness. It may permit a rather gradual readjustment to the prospect or reality of being relatively pain-free. For some patients, this gradual approach may prevent the development of resistances or symptom substitutions.

The specifics of the technique are relatively straightforward. The first step involves introducing the patient to the unmodified B.H.E. exercise and having him practice it ten times or so on his own without any specific focus on numbness or pain. When these preliminaries have been completed, the induction of numbness is inserted in the exercise in place of the beach scene. Some patients resent the loss of the purely pleasurable part of the exercise and prefer to include the beach scene after the induction of numbness or to alternate relaxation and pain relief applications of the exercise. Patients who enjoy and value the exercise like this are likely to benefit from it and should be encouraged.

Before you use the B.H.E. exercise to induce numbness for the first time you should go over a numbness "menu" with your patient and allow him to select the method and/or image that he would like to try first. Often you will have to try several items on the menu to see which one works best or is most pleasant; it is hard for patients or therapists to make accurate predictions here. I would recommend that you use the following menu for your first patients and then modify it as your experience with self-hypnosis grows:

1) X (appropriate body part or area) growing numb.
2) X getting cool, then cold and numb, perhaps using the image of X being gradually packed in clean, white snow.
3) A doctor or dentist is giving me a shot of Novocain in X, and it begins to get numb.
4) My X is gradually changing to wood, stone, or some other inert substance; it becomes like the X of a statue.

Read off each of these images and review them with your patient. There are wide ranges of individual associations and responses here. One patient may find coldness or snow frightening but not be bothered by Novocain or needles; for another patient just the reverse may be true. In general, patients find it easier to induce numbness with the images used in items 2 through 4. The pure sensation of numbness used in item 1 may be relatively hard to imagine; nevertheless, it proves ideal for some patients.

Once the initial numbing technique has been chosen, you should use it to induce numbness in one the patient's hands at the point in the B.H.E. induction script where the beach scene would ordinarily begin. I usually use the right hand if I have used the left for levitation, but this is not crucial and any available body part can be used if you are restricted by amputations, casts, intravenous attachments, etc. Here are sample scripts for each of the items on the numbness menu. These scripts are also printed in Appendix C in a form that you can cut out or photocopy for your own use while you are gaining familiarity with how these images are worded.

1) *Pure numbness:* "Focus your attention now on your right hand . . . As you do, you will begin to notice that it is growing numb . . . growing numb. You may notice some tingling sensations at first, or feel some twitches, but soon feeling will gradually leave the hand so that it grows more and more numb . . . more and more numb. . . . The more you concentrate on the hand, the more numb it gets . . . numb and without feeling . . . numb and without feeling."

2) *Cold:* "Focus your attention now on your right hand. . . . As you do, you will begin to notice that it is gradually growing cooler and cooler . . . cooler and cooler. As the hand gets cooler, a not unpleasant sensation of numbness begins to envelop it . . . cooler and more numb . . . cooler and more numb. You might even want to imagine that pure white snow is falling on your hand, covering it up and making it cool and numb . . . cool and numb. Or you might prefer to imagine that you are immersing your hand in an icy mountain stream. . . . As the water flows over the hand it gets cooler and cooler . . . cooler and cooler . . . more and more numb . . . cool and numb."

3) *Injection of Novocain:* "Imagine now that you are in your doctor's office and that he is giving you an injection of Novocain in your right hand. You feel a slight prick from the needle, then a little pressure as the medication flows into your hand. . . . Now, as the Novocain begins to work, you feel a sensation of numbness gradually spreading through your hand from the point of the injection . . . more and more numb . . . gradually spreading . . . more and more numb. . . . Now your entire hand is growing numb . . . more and more numb . . . more and more numb."

4) *Change to inert substance:* "Focus your attention now on your right hand, and let yourself imagine that it is beginning to change gradually into a piece of wood . . . a piece of wood just like the arm of a department store mannequin. . . . You can feel the change taking place, and as it does, your hand gradually becomes numb — just like a piece of painted wood. . . . It may look the same on the outside, but on the inside it is becoming more and more numb and without feeling . . . more and more numb . . . just like an inert piece of wood . . . without feeling and numb . . . numb . . . more and more numb."

After you have used these scripts with a few patients, you should feel free to extend, amplify, or modify them to fit the needs of each particular situation. As with other hypnotic talk, there is a kind of insistent, steady flow of statements and images that gets the point across best. As you get more at ease with the hypnotic voice and style of talk you will be able to keep up this patter for longer and longer periods without either faltering or overdoing the necessary element of repetition. Some patients need several minutes of continuous presentation before they feel any numbness or other suggested sensory changes, and as you move beyond the beginner stage, you will be able to adjust your technique and timing to their needs.

Remember to always cancel a suggested numbness in any application of hetero-hypnosis with a statement like "Now, let the image of your hand as X fade gradually, as your usual sensation and control in your right hand return." Depending on the structure of your sessions with the patient, you may have him practice and compare these images at home in self-hypnosis, in which case he can self-administer a similar suggestion between images and at the end of the self-hypnosis session.

I do not routinely encourage patients to test their numbness, since voluntary movements such as pinching sometimes "lighten" the hypnotic state and the real test will come with their pain. For a few patients, however, such a preliminary test is reassuring and helpful. After the patient has learned to produce numbness in his hand, he is ready to use the numbness to relieve his pain either by making the painful body part numb directly instead of his hand, or by transferring the numbness from his hand to the painful area.

Which of these two methods to use is a purely empirical question and I usually encourage patients to try both. If the patient is having pain while he is with me, I will go over these applications in the office. This is not absolutely necessary, however, and it is possible for the patient to try them out when he has pain at home or on the job.

When you have arrived at the most effective image for inducing therapeutic numbness and gone over it with your patient in the office, you should add the following qualifying statement to the B.H.E. script right before the count from five to one that ends the exercise. The point is important enough to justify another hetero-hypnotic session even for a patient who is using self-hypnosis comfortably:

"As you practice the exercise more and more, it will become easier and easier for you to make your X as numb as it needs to be to relieve your pain. When the pain is gone and you no longer need the numbness, the numb feeling will gradually fade and your usual sensation and control will return. No matter how much you use the self-hypnosis exercise to make your X numb, you will still be able to be aware of any changes in the type or pattern of the pain so that you can report them to your doctor. Part of you will always be aware of the signals that your body is sending you, so that you can protect your health and still be able to do the things that you want."

This statement is not a substitute for regular doctor's visits and diagnostic studies. Its function is to introduce sensible limits and termination conditions to the suggested sensory change—a good general principle in any application of hypnosis.

While trials of these first applications are in progress, you should meet weekly or even more often if necessary to adjust the exercise as needed. Some of this adjustment and support can be provided by telephone contacts, but this is one of the times in my experience when the personal element is most important. As with the application of the B.H.E. exercise to anxiety, the duration of pain relief after each individual use can vary from a few minutes to a day or so. You should give this dose-response aspect of the exercise patient and respectful attention. One of the common problems of beginners is the premature abandonment of a technique that provides brief but effective relief. Before such a technique is abandoned, you and your patient should explore whether or not it permits him to feel better long enough to do or feel something that he had not been able to do or feel before. For patients with pain, a little relief can sometimes go a long way.

You should gradually increase the daily frequency of doing the exercise as much as the patient will tolerate and stop the increase only when the patient is satisfied with the pain relief or it becomes clear that the technique is not going to work. I have taught patients who used the exercise hourly while they were awake and even more frequently when their pain was severe. As with medications, electrical stimulation, or any other pain relief technique, you should taper the frequency of use gradually rather than quickly if you or the patient feel that the need for the treatment has diminished. This will avoid having to re-establish a needed routine and may spare both of you the demoralization that a relapse, even an induced one, often brings.

Let's consider a typical application of the induced numbness technique for severe pain. Angelo M. was a 54-year-old married liquor store clerk who suffered from advanced metastatic cancer that was no longer responding well to radiation or chemotherapy. He continued to work and had been pleasantly surprised by the willingness of his employers to make accommodations for his treatments and growing limitation in terms of heavy lifting and carrying. Angelo knew, however, that this could only go so far, and was particularly distressed by the pain from a hip metastasis that was making it hard for him to even sit on his stool or go to get a bottle. He was highly motivated to keep on working and readily consented to talk to the psychologist who worked with the oncology team about hypnosis.

Angelo described his health to the psychologist as "not so great," but immediately went on to brag about his children and his length of service at the liquor store. He had worked there for 29 years and very much wanted to make it to his thirtieth anniversary with them. His use of denial and his focus on the positive were long-standing coping styles that had served him well. On careful inquiry, he described a steady, boring pain with superimposed "hot jolts" associated with movement. He had a number of prejudices about hypnosis, but was "willing to give it a try if you think it'll work."

Angelo turned out to have a high level of hypnotic talent and quickly learned the B.H.E. exercise through frequent practice at home and during his breaks on the job. After trying the various numbness images, he chose the technique of imagining a plastic bag full of crushed ice (something he could easily picture) resting next to his hip and gradually cooling it until it felt "cold and numb." He could get about two hours of pain relief after doing the exercise with this image, which was enough to extend his work ability several months beyond his thirtieth anniversary at the store. A week before he left his job for what turned out to be a brief terminal illness at home, he sent his oncologist and the psychologist who had taught him self-hypnosis bottles of good whiskey with notes saying simply, "Thanks — drink to me." They did.

Flowing and Discarding

The technique of induced numbness uses hypnosis to produce a sensation antithetical to pain; the "flowing and discarding" technique works directly with the pain sensations themselves. This difference makes the flowing and discarding technique more advanced and means that resistances, if there are any, will appear earlier. Many clinicians have noted that once a patient is able to change a symptom in any way, he has exerted some control over it and is no longer acting only in the role of passive victim. This initial step appears to be crucial in a number of conditions. It remains unclear at present whether it acts by mobilizing dormant hope, cementing the therapeutic alliance, or by some other means. In any case, self-hypnosis is an ideal technique for bringing about change in a symptom and thereby granting the patient a first step towards control.

The best way to learn this technique is first to understand the general principle and then to see how it is applied in a specific case. Put most directly, you want to get the patient to experience his pain as a fluid, to move that fluid through his body to his hand, and then to discard it. The language you use should be tailored to the unique characteristics of your patient's pain experience. Unlike the induction procedure or the previous pain relief techniques, a scripted approach has little to offer here.

With this technique, you are utilizing the aspect of hypnosis that allows us to experience images as real. In doing so, you may find yourself working with metaphors in a more concrete way than you are used to. Thinking or speaking of pain as a fluid that flows is no more distant from reality than speaking of an object as being charged with libido; both are metaphors that can be useful in certain clinical situations. Yet beginning users of hypnosis often feel and communicate discomfort with a metaphorical technique that pictures pain as a concrete substance. Let me assure you that this discomfort is not shared by patients, who find these techniques helpful with their pain. I have personally seen them used effectively by physicians and other clinical specialists whose views of pain, when it was not their own, were as scientific and sophisticated as anyone could wish. As a beginner, you should do what you ask your patients to do: think and imagine along with the instructions, and then evaluate for yourself the effects of the procedure on the patient's target symptoms.

Here is how the technique sounds in a modified transcript of an actual session with a patient. Eleanor L. is a chemical engineer with disabling lower back and leg pain secondary to degenerative disc disease. Several surgical procedures have not relieved the pain, and scar tissue from the surgery may be contributing to some of the present difficulty. Her work and family life are interfered with significantly. She is unable to roughhouse with her four-year-old son, for example, and is hesitant to become pregnant again although she and her husband would both like to have another child. She has been able to respond well to the Brief Hypnotic Experience induction, and has practiced the exercise diligently at home. There is some pain relief through the pleasant scene, which for Eleanor is an outdoor swimming pool in which she is floating comfortably instead of a beach, but it is sufficient for only mild pain episodes. The sensation of numbness has unpleasant associations for her, involving past episodes of nerve compression that produced frightening motor and sensory symptoms.

Eleanor describes her pain as an "unbearable deep grinding sensation" when most severe that changes to a "shrill shrieking feeling" when it lessens. The following instructions were given after the induction and deepening procedure had been repeated in the office as in the initial Brief Hypnotic Experience induction script. The count from one to ten had been completed with the progressive relaxation of different parts of the body:

"Now that your body is feeling more relaxed, I would like you to concentrate on any sensations of discomfort or pain that you may be having. . . . As you concentrate on these sensations, you will be able to experience them as a fluid . . . a painful fluid that carries with it the deep, grinding sensations that you have experienced in the past, and the shrill, shrieking sensations that you have had earlier this week. . . . Your pain is a fluid, and as you concentrate on it the fluid is beginning to move . . . beginning to move. . . . The pain is beginning to move up your legs, to the lower spinal area . . . any pain that you have there you can also experience as a fluid, and this fluid is beginning to move too . . . the pain from your legs and lower back is beginning now to move up your back . . . moving upwards, towards your shoulder.

"As the pain flows up your back, it begins to move towards your right shoulder . . . flowing . . . more and more. . . . When the pain fluid reaches your right shoulder, it flows down your arm and into your right hand. . . . As the pain begins to enter your right hand, you can feel the fingers of your right hand closing gradually into a fist . . . tighter and tighter . . . tighter and tighter. . . . Soon this fist will be full of pain, full of pain from your legs and lower back. . . .

"As your right fist fills with the pain, it clenches tighter and tighter. . . . When you are ready, you can throw away the pain that is in your right hand. . . . Just open your hand, and throw the pain away. . . . As your hand opens, you can feel the pain leaving your body . . . being thrown away . . . thrown away. . . . And as the pain leaves you feel a sensation of relief in your right hand and in the rest of your body . . . a pleasant sensation of relief . . . relief.

"Now, pay attention and see if there is any pain remaining in your body—in your legs, your lower back, or anywhere else. . . . You will be able to experience that pain as a fluid too, and allow it to flow, along with any tension that you may be experiencing, through your body and down your right arm to your right hand. . . . As any remaining pain and tension flow into your right hand, it again begins to tighten into a fist . . . tighter and tighter . . . tighter and tighter. . . . When you are ready, you can discard the pain and tension in your right fist; you can throw them away. . . . Just throw the pain and tension away . . . that's right . . . and enjoy the sensation of relief . . . relief.

"From now on, you will be able to use the technique that you have just experienced here in the office when you practice your self-hypnosis exercise on your own. To use the technique, just enter self-hypnosis as you have been doing, and deepen the hypnotic state by counting from one to ten. When you are ready, concentrate on any pain or tension that you may be experiencing and allow it to become a fluid that flows through your body to your right shoulder and down your right arm. . . . As the pain flows into your right hand, allow the hand to clench into a tight fist. When you are ready, you will be able to open your right hand and throw the pain away. You can repeat this procedure to discard any pain or tension that may remain after you do it the first time. . . . The more you practice this technique, the better you will get and the easier it will become. You will be able to use it when you need it to deal with the pain.

"No matter how much you use the self-hypnosis exercise to get rid of the pain, you will still be able to be aware of any changes in the type or pattern of the pain so that you can report them to your doctor. Part of you will always be aware of the signals that your body is sending you, so that you can protect your health and still be able to do the things that you want."

I then ended the hypnotic session in the usual way by counting backward from five to one. Eleanor smiled broadly as she opened her eyes, and reported enthusiastically that she had experienced more pain relief using this technique than with any other that we had tried. In fact, she had to "search" to find any pain or tension in her body when I suggested that she try the technique a second time. To be this free of pain was quite unusual for her recently. She left the session feeling confident and optimistic, to try out the new technique at home and on the job.

At our next session, a week later, Eleanor reported good results with the flowing and discarding technique. Because she had initially practiced the self-hypnosis exercise without any particular focus on her pain problem, she was able to accept the differences between the hetero-hypnotic and the self-hypnotic experiences without becoming concerned or losing her sense of confidence and optimism. Eleanor noted that when she did the exercise on her own, her sense of relief from her leg and back pain started when the pain began to move, even before it had been gathered into the right hand and discarded. The ability to experience the pain as a flowing liquid made it feel "light and far away." Still, the most dramatic relief came when she opened her right hand with a tossing motion and threw the pain fluid away.

At this point, Eleanor expressed a concern not uncommon in patients who master and get relief from the flowing and discarding technique: where was the pain going when it left her body? She said that she imagined the pain as a dark fluid inside her, but could feel it changing into a kind of "black smoke" as it left her right hand. Would the pain smoke contaminate the atmosphere and hurt someone else? Would it build up around her right hand to such a concentration that she couldn't discard any more?

Although these concerns were expressed outside of the formal hypnotic state, they graphically express the active imaginative involvement that Eleanor had attained in the exercise and in this particular technique. The first step in dealing with these concerns was to explore them in a nondirective way. As she discussed them with me, Eleanor smiled somewhat sheepishly: after all, she was a chemical engineer who in fact dealt with issues of environmental contamination all the time in her work. Clearly, she realized that the smoke was a metaphor, yet she was able to experience it as real when she did the exercise and this experience carried over into some of the concerns that she was expressing in the office.

A metaphorical solution to the metaphorical problems emerged naturally from our conversation on the subject. The smoke was *her* pain and could not hurt anyone else. She could imagine a gentle breeze blowing it away as she tossed it from her hand, and actually enjoy watching it dissipate and disappear. Clearly, Eleanor's choice of metaphors and concerns was psychologically overdetermined. The exploration of these issues, however, was not part of our treatment contract and in her case they did not interfere with her efforts to control her pain using the self-hypnosis exercise. Similarly, the illogical features of the metaphor were not of concern; it did its job and allowed Eleanor to do hers.

Over a two-year period since she learned the self-hypnosis exercise and the flowing and discarding technique, it has served Eleanor well for pain relief. The only problem with the technique itself occurred during a flareup of *upper* back pain related to disc disease in her neck. During this episode, the pain was significantly *worsened* by tightening her right fist as part of the flowing and discarding technique (due to the contraction of arm and shoulder muscles entailed). The problem was partially solved by allowing the pain to simply flow "out through the pores of my skin" in the right hand, but Eleanor experienced this image as less potent in terms of pain relief than the clenching and throwing movement she had used so effectively for her lower back pain. She experimented on her own with variations on this technique, and found that she could sometimes get good relief from upper back pain by just squeezing her right thumb and forefinger together instead of tightening her whole hand into a fist. We continued to meet regularly on a monthly basis to review her use of the exercise and to deal with changes that occurred.

You can use Eleanor's case as a guide for how the flowing and discarding technique can be applied to dysfunctional pain. As you can see, I incorporated Eleanor's own descriptions of her pain in the exercise instructions (" . . . a painful fluid that carries with it the deep, grinding sensations that you have experienced in the past . . . ") and was open to the way she experienced the metaphor and to the concerns that she expressed. The initial instructions should be based on the location of the patient's pain; remember not to confuse this with your own hypotheses as to the anatomical site of the lesion that is causing the pain. Pain around the eye, for example, might flow downward and back to the neck, then to the right shoulder, down the right arm, etc. If you are hesitant to use this technique with your patients because metaphorical thinking does not come naturally to you, you might want to try it yourself with a tension headache or a minor muscle pull (these are applications I am able to use effectively myself with only average levels of hypnotic talent); the personal experience may be what is needed to overcome your hesitation and minimize its communication to your patient.

It is possible to identify a "key phrase" associated with the flowing and discarding technique (or with induced numbness) in the same way as with the application of the B.H.E. exercise to anxiety and tension. "Out and gone" or "pain away" would be examples for flowing and discarding; "cold and numb" or "feeling gone" would apply to induced numbness. In general, I have not found the use of a key phrase out of the hypnotic state as helpful in clinical pain control as it is with anxiety and tension. If you suggest that a patient try it for pain, it should be presented in a low-key way as an experiment that might or might not help with the pain in situations where the patient is unable for any reason to do the exercise.

There are many other effective hypnotic techniques for pain relief, but the ones that have been covered in this chapter will give you all that you need to get started in this area. Specialized workshops on pain control are offered regularly by the recognized hypnosis societies and by several medical centers (see Appendix A). In addition to the books and papers that I have mentioned already in this chapter, *Hypnotherapy of Pain in Children with Cancer* by Josephine Hilgard and Samuel LeBaron offers invaluable guidance about this highly specialized and worthwhile application of hypnosis (see Appendix B).

Integration of the B.H.E. Exercise with
Pharmacological, Surgical, and
Psychosocial Interventions

The B.H.E. exercise and similar self-hypnosis techniques can and have been used in conjunction with almost all currently prescribed treatments for pain. This integration is obviously smoother if one clinician is responsible for all of the diagnostic and therapeutic program.

Such situations are becoming less common, however, as subspecialization of both clinicians and treatment settings becomes more widespread. I have already emphasized the need to ensure that pain is indeed dysfunctional (without real signal value) before it is treated with self-hypnosis, and discussed some of the complexities involved in making this determination. As stated previously, the pain relief provided by the B.H.E. can and should be qualified to permit the patient to note significant changes in the type or pattern of pain.

The fact that hypnotic analgesia is not blocked by narcotic antagonists suggests a different neural mechanism for these two approaches to pain. As with its use in the treatment of anxiety, self-hypnosis can be combined with *pain medications* to good effect. Many patients and some clinicians make this combination less effective than it might be by overemphasizing the contrast between self-hypnosis and medications. The B.H.E. exercise or a similar procedure is perceived as a "natural," self-administered cure in contrast to the passive and potentially addicting use of analgesic drugs. Although I certainly favor the clinical use of self-hypnosis, I find that view has little positive to offer and often merely generates useless guilt. I have seldom encountered this kind of thinking in clinicians who specialize in treating severe pain. They are usually glad for any help they can get, and have no trouble mixing different approaches on an empirical, case-by-case basis.

When a patient is already taking pain medication, self-hypnosis may sometimes be used to reduce the dose or to provide relief between doses. This can be particularly helpful for patients with severe pain who experience unacceptable side-effects, such as sedation, from the medications they need. Supplementary use of self-hypnosis can sometimes allow reduction of the dose to levels where the patient can function again on the job or with family. The B.H.E. exercise is well-suited to these applications because it is brief and relatively simple. It can therefore be used prn (as needed) or on a regular basis in just those situations (e.g., before a family party) where even a brief reduction in pain can make the difference between a patient's participating or not in a work, family, or social event. Repeated involuntary nonparticipation in activities that the patient wants brings with it isolation and demoralization that sap hope and physical resistance and ultimately leave the patient alone with his pain.

Surgical treatments for pain may attempt to remove or modify its cause (as in the excision of a tumor) or to interrupt the nerve pathways that carry pain messages at any level from the peripheral nerve to the brain. Because many surgical interventions are irreversible, it may be appropriate to try self-hypnosis for pain relief before surgery even in situations where the prospects for success with hypnosis do not seem very promising. The knowledge that a number of nonsurgical interventions have been given a fair trial can help patients accept the inevitable risks and side-effects of surgery when and if it becomes necessary. A bonus of the presurgical trial of self-hypnosis for some patients is their ability to use the B.H.E. exercise or a similar procedure to relieve pre-operative apprehension and cope with post-operative discomfort or pain. After the results of the surgery on the pain symptom have had a chance to be adequately assessed, self-hypnosis may be reevaluated as a supplementary technique. For some patients, the pain relief provided by surgery allows them to practice and benefit from a self-hypnosis exercise that was not practical for them before.

There are documented cases where hypnosis has been used as the sole *anesthesia for major surgery*. Although these cases are fascinating in themselves and for what they teach us about the nature of pain, this is not a practical use of hypnosis for the average clinician. Its major limitation is inherent in the very connection with hypnotic talent that makes pain relief such an important clinical application of hypnosis. Unfortunately, those who need the surgery are not always the people with the high levels of hypnotic talent required for surgical anesthesia (about 5–10% of the population).

In the areas of *medical or dental minor surgery and uncomfortable or painful diagnostic procedures*, however, the B.H.E. exercise may be quite useful, especially if the patient has time to learn and practice the exercise in advance of the procedure. Pain control in these situations is often considerably enhanced by any technique that provides the patient with an active coping strategy and also works effectively on anxiety, fear, and tension. The B.H.E. exercise fills the bill here nicely. In these applications, try not to make the use of self-hypnosis an either-or matter or allow a moralistic tone to enter the treatment planning ("we know you want to get through this study without needing any drugs"). Local anesthesia or other nonhypnotic techniques for relieving pain should also be available. For both clinicians and patients, having them at hand may mean that they do not have to be used.

Anyone who has experienced or studied *natural childbirth* will have noticed the many similarities between the various relaxation, self-control, and imagery techniques that have a central role in these procedures and a self-hypnosis exercise such as the B.H.E. If your patients (or you yourself) are comfortable with it, the B.H.E. exercise can be useful in managing the discomfort associated with normal childbirth. For some couples, however, the similarities between the B.H.E. and natural childbirth techniques can be confusing and lead to a sense of divided loyalties. In these situations, especially where group support and learning are part of an organized natural childbirth program, it is usually better to avoid the introduction of an additional and potentially confusing technique.

Physical therapy, acupuncture, and transcutaneous electrical nerve stimulation (TENS) are all specialized pain control techniques that are not usually administered by general clinicians. All have relatively low risk levels, and can be used in sequence or together with self-hypnosis. If you have prescribed them for a patient or if you know that he is receiving them, it makes sense to give some thought to the timing on self-hypnosis training. Try to avoid a situation where it is *completely* impossible to tease apart the effect of two or more procedures, each of which may require continued application and monitoring. In deciding how to sequence therapeutic trials, the least intrusive and/or expensive therapy should usually be tried first, and this will often be self-hypnosis. In these situations, flexibility in scheduling is important, and you may have to condense teaching and practice into longer, intensive sessions. The effort is worthwhile, however, in terms of the opportunity to get a more precise idea of the relative role of self-hypnosis (and of the other techniques as well) in the total pain management program.

When comparison of treatments for pain is mentioned, many clinicians and researchers think of *placebos*. Placebos are potent drugs, and placebo effects contribute significantly to the healing associated with *all* treatments, including pain medications and surgery. Because the B.H.E. exercise is fundamentally a clinical technique, no effort has been made to eliminate nonspecific or placebo effects that might seriously confound a research design. On the contrary, these have been incorporated into the exercise wherever possible, as have several elements such as relaxation that are not inherently hypnotic. Nevertheless, there is some research evidence that, for highly hypnotizable patients, specifically hypnotic approaches to pain may contribute something to the pain relief beyond what is contributed by a placebo response.

Finally, you should be aware (if you are not already) of the specialized evaluation and treatment centers known generally as *pain clinics or pain evaluation and treatment teams*. They can be found at many medical schools and larger medical centers, either as free-standing clinics or affiliated with departments of anesthesia, neurosurgery, neurology, psychiatry or physical medicine. Most often they are staffed by members of one or more of the above medical specialties, along with psychologists, social workers, and nurses.

These clinics are important potential helping resources for any clinician who is trying to treat pain patients. In general, their staffs are intimately familiar with the problems and confounding factors that I have mentioned throughout this chapter, such as family dynamics, compensation issues and the full gamut of "pain behaviors." Chronic pain patients are a challenge to work with, and the people in these clinics work hard.

Because they see so many pain patients, these professionals are in a good position to distinguish uniquely worrisome problems from those that are more routine. One or more staff members are usually familiar with hypnosis or related procedures, and may be ideal people to supervise or consult on your use of hypnosis with one of your patients who has pain. The evaluation and testing protocol that is usually part of the clinic's program can help you and your patient put self-hypnosis in perspective along with the realistic risks and benefits of other treatments that may have been considered.

EIGHT

More Advanced Applications

Further Uses for the B.H.E.

The purpose of this book is to get you familiar with the B.H.E. exercise and to guide you through its use with several patients who have anxiety and/or dysfunctional pain problems. Once you have reached this point and have been successful in your clinical use of hypnosis, you will want to go further. Self-hypnosis, and the B.H.E. exercise in particular, represents only a small part of the broad range of hypnotic phenomena and treatment techniques. Probably the best pathway for further development is through attendance at one of the meeting and workshop sessions offered by the major legitimate hypnosis societies. Here you will have a chance to learn of other ways of understanding hypnosis and other approaches to using it in treatment. The societies are described and their addresses are given in Appendix A.

Another way of exploring the field further is through reading relevant books and journals; my own suggestions for further reading on hypnosis are given in Appendix B.

In this chapter, I will focus on specific applications of the B.H.E. exercise to a number of conditions that either are common, are commonly treated with hypnosis, or are especially suitable in my experience for an approach such as the B.H.E. If you have or develop the expertise necessary to treat these conditions, you may want to consider an application of the B.H.E. or have some understanding of the problems associated with this application if your patient should mention or request hypnotic treatment. I will not be presenting a detailed account either of the conditions themselves or of their treatment with other hypnotic and nonhypnotic techniques. Both subjects are well beyond the scope of this book and will vary depending on your own professional discipline, practice setting, and level of training.

For an excellent overview of several of the clinical areas covered in this chapter, I would highly recommend the review article by Thomas Wadden and Charles Anderton entitled "The Clinical Uses of Hypnosis" (see *Appendix B*). It offers scientifically valid and clinically sensible coverage of the applications of hypnosis to psychosomatic disorders, pain, and habit disorders. My own thinking and practice in these areas closely follow their approach. Contrasting discussions of hypnotic treatment of the clinical problems described in this chapter can be found in the books by Crasilneck and Hall and by Spiegel and Spiegel that are described in *Appendix B. Hypnosis: Trance As a Coping Mechanism* by Fred Frankel (also referenced in *Appendix B*) offers a clinical approach to which I am especially partial.

Psychosomatic Disorders

Although the term "psychosomatic disorders" is no longer a part of the official psychiatric nomenclature, the broad field that it encompasses does present a unified picture in terms of applying the B.H.E. exercise clinically. Whether the problem is diagnosed in DSM-III terms as a Somatoform Disorder or as Psychological Factors Affecting Physical Condition, there is always at least the possibility of a significant interaction between mental and physical phenomena. The mental side of this interaction may have its origin in life events, in focused neurotic conflicts, or in broad areas of personality dysfunction. The physical aspect may be expressed in terms of such "classical" psychosomatic conditions as peptic ulcer disease or asthma, or in the course and complications as a patient recovers from surgery following trauma. In all of these conditions there is at least a potential role for helpful or healing thoughts and images, and hence for the B.H.E. exercise.

One of my own first applications of hypnosis to psychosomatic conditions occurred in a setting where I had a more than usual interest in the outcome. I was an intern on night duty in the emergency room of a busy university hospital, and was getting very little sleep in general and almost none on heavy nights. One of our most frequent visitors was Dwight T., a 17-year-old boy with severe asthma whose attacks were difficult to break and who had required several recent admissions to the hospital. By the time I saw him, it was impossible to tease out purely allergic and psychosocial factors in his disease; both he and his family were fairly constantly upset and/or demoralized. It was uncertain whether he would be able to finish his senior year of high school on time.

I taught Dwight a simple self-hypnosis exercise while we were both waiting to see if one of his middle of the night attacks would subside in time for him to go to school the next day. The exercise involved eye closure and progressive relaxation with slow counting, but did not feature hand levitation or the beach scene. In hypnosis, I instructed Dwight to concentrate on his chest (he experienced and described his attacks as "a tight chest") and to allow all the muscles in it to gradually relax. He found that a repeated slow count from one to five made it easier for him to pace this relaxation, and we incorporated this into his exercise. He terminated the exercise by counting backwards from five to one.

The self-hypnosis exercise did not cure Dwight's asthma, but everyone involved in his care saw an immediate and marked reduction in the frequency of his attacks by about half. On more careful inquiry, it seemed that there were as many episodes of tight feelings in his chest, but that Dwight was able to neutralize about half of them using the self-hypnosis exercise before they got out of hand. The reduction of frequency of the severe attacks kept Dwight away from the hospital and gave him and his family some needed time to catch up with their lives.

Looking back at Dwight from my current perspective, I can see a number of factors that contributed to the relatively positive outcome. Although he had had it and lived with it for many years, Dwight was literally sick and tired of his asthma; I can remember how very much he wanted to finish high school with his classmates. He was an old-timer in the stressful, crazy world of the emergency room night shift, and shared zestfully in some of its grimmest humor. Dwight had seen many interns come and go, and our professional adolescence echoed his own personal turmoil. Finally, he took to the exercise easily and modified it himself to serve his needs. Not surprisingly, asthma is one of the relatively small number of conditions where clinical outcome has been related to hypnotic talent or susceptibility.

Notice that the exercise that helped Dwight focused on the tightness he felt in his chest muscles, rather than on the bronchoconstriction that was more physiologically central to his asthma. In applying the B.H.E. exercise to any psychosomatic condition, as in using it to relieve pain, you should take the cue for your helping/healing thoughts or images from the patient's subjective experience of his disorder rather than from your notions of its anatomical or physiological basis. If the patient experiences his disorder as tension, then the beach scene or a similar relaxing experience may be ideal. If the symptom is experienced as heat, then an image of coolness may help.

An even further extension of this dissociation between healing image and biological origin is the common and effective technique used to treat warts hypnotically. Although warts are most probably caused by a virus, the standard suggestions for healing warts ignore the viral aspects and instead involve the creation of a tingling sensation in the affected area.

The B.H.E. exercise adapts itself well to the treatment of psychosomatic problems for several reasons. It is structured to counter anxiety and tension, which are major factors in many conditions in this group. Furthermore, the multisensory experience of the beach scene contains a broad range of potentially helpful and healing images — so broad, in fact, that it may be a good idea to allow the patient to learn and practice the unmodified B.H.E. exercise for a while before you try a more symptom-focused intervention. I have had several patients discover helpful elements in the scene or modify it themselves in ways that I would never have thought of. For example, one patient with annoying and persistent tinnitus (buzzing or ringing in the ears) used the sound of the waves on the beach to mask her symptom temporarily. She found the episodic relief that this gave her significantly helpful.

If the unmodified exercise does not help the patient's target symptom, you can experiment with specific images or thoughts (as embodied in key phrases that accompany the images) that approach the problem more directly, as I did in Dwight's case. The physical symptoms that occur in psychosomatic conditions are sometimes easier to quantify than purely psychological ones, and this can be helpful in recordkeeping and in making decisions as to whether and how the treatment is working. Naturally, if you are not the patient's primary care physician or the dental or medical specialist treating the psychosomatic problem, regular liaison with that person is important. Anatomical and physiological indices of the condition should not be lost sight of in the midst of enthusiasm over subjective improvement. The issues of acute vs. chronic symptoms and of the psychosocial and financial consequences of illness that I discussed in Chapter 7 are also often relevant to psychosomatic conditions, but the ability to accept and integrate small positive changes is often greater than in chronic pain patients. As long as there are no unrealistic expectations of complete cure, instruction in self-hypnosis is often worth trying.

Mood Disorders

Mood disorders can range, in DSM-III terms, from relatively mild Cyclothymic or Dysthymic disorders (pronounced mood swings or periods of depression) to the full picture of a Bipolar Disorder or Major Depression. Although life events can often trigger or exacerbate these disorders, they characteristically have a certain life of their own once symptoms have started. When severe, patients may have suicidal thoughts or impulses. Family history is often positive for similar problems. This is the group of disorders usually treated with antidepressant medications, lithium carbonate, and focused, often cognitive psychotherapies.

Mood disorders per se are not usually treated with hypnosis, and this is entirely appropriate. *Self-hypnosis, in particular, can be dangerous for severely depressed patients because their inability to concentrate on and practice a self-hypnosis exercise feeds into an already lowered self-esteem and may precipitate or worsen feelings of hopelessness.* Manic patients are often interested in hypnosis and other unorthodox therapies, but are seldom able to summon the sustained attention needed to learn and practice an exercise. As with other conditions in which reality-testing can be impaired, a treatment that focuses on internal subjective experience is usually not what is called for.

Does hypnosis have *no* legitimate role in the treatment of mood disorders, then? My own experience with a number of patients and the confirming reports of a number of colleagues have left me in a position somewhat short of this absolute negative stance. But I would consider mood disorders a distinctly advanced application, well beyond the beginner's level and suitable only for those accustomed to treating these disorders with nonhypnotic techniques on a regular basis.

My first experiences with the use of self-hypnosis in depression were with patients who had learned the B.H.E. exercise for unrelated conditions and applied it on their own to a later depressive episode. Depression is such a common problem in the general population that these opportunities to try self-hypnosis are not unexpected. Since the exercise was so effective in alleviating pain or tension, they reasoned, might it not also succeed in lifting the heavy, painful, hopeless feelings of depression?

In summary, the B.H.E. exercise proved useful to some patients as a way of coping with mild feelings of depression, but had little or no effect on the thoughts and emotions associated with severe depressive symptoms. Once the full syndrome of a severe depression was established, the exercise just didn't take hold of the symptoms, exactly in the way it failed with Fred F.'s panic disorder as described in Chapter 6. As with Fred, the prescription of appropriate antidepressant medications brought relief.

With one patient the B.H.E. exercise did seem especially helpful in dealing with mild depressive symptoms that occurred as part of an episode of early morning awakening and difficulty falling back to sleep again. Under these circumstances, doing the exercise and experiencing the beach scene while repeating a soothing phrase such as "clear and calm" or "warm and relaxed" was regularly able to "break" the episode. When this happened, the patient was either able to fall back to sleep again or to get up feeling better than usual under those circumstances.

Another patient with recurrent depressive episodes that responded well to appropriate treatment with medications and psychotherapy felt that the exercise had allowed him to "short-circuit" several episodes just as they were starting that would in the past have developed into full-blown depressions. Because spouses or lovers are usually asleep when episodes of low mood and early morning awakening occur, having a private and silent coping mechanism does seem to help.

In my opinion the B.H.E. exercise and similar procedures have a very limited role in the management of depression, but may be worth trying in the very early phases of an episode. Ideally, the technique should be learned while the patient is in a nondepressed state so that it will be available when needed. In my own experience with the B.H.E., patients taking antidepressant medications have reported no adverse interactions with drug effects. Obviously, a patient who has just had ECT (electroconvulsive therapy) would be a poor candidate for any procedure that depended heavily on short-term memory. Several patients have used the key phrase from the B.H.E. to reinforce points learned in cognitive therapy (e.g., "don't take it personally"), but I know of no evidence that the specifically hypnotic aspects of the exercise are unique here.

Habit Disorders

In the current issue of the Philadephia Yellow Pages, the treatment of habit disorders is the most commonly advertised service offered under the category "Hypnotists" by a wide assortment of practitioners. The most frequently mentioned habits are smoking and overeating, but hypnosis has also been applied to alcohol abuse, nail biting, and other habit problems. Why, then, have I placed this important group of clinical problems in the advanced applications section of this book rather than as one of the recommended first applications? My reasons for this decision are a good introduciton to my perspectives on this subject. If they do not make sense to you in terms of your own clinical or research experience, then this section will probably have little to offer you.

In contrast to hypnotic pain relief, I do not believe that the *hypnotic* part of treatments for habit disorders that use hypnosis is uniquely effective for these problems. This is not unexpected, since, as I have pointed out repeatedly in this book, hypnosis works most directly on experience rather than on behavior. It comes as no surprise, then, that the large bulk of well conducted research studies has failed to show any consistent association between measured hypnotic responsivity and clinical outcome in these problems.

But I have a more specific reservation concerning hypnosis that applies to habit disorder patients. In contrast to patients experiencing hypnosis in the treatment of anxiety, tension, or stress (where nonhypnotic effects may also be central), many patients who seek hypnotic treatments for habit problems come with a *specific* expectation about how hypnosis will work that actively interferes with what I believe are effective treatments for these problems. This specific expectation is that treatment with hypnosis is essentially a passive, instantaneous process in which the desire for the harmful substance or the tendency to perform the harmful behavior is eliminated from the patient's mind by the hypnotist.

In my own practice, this expectation is usually evident early on in one of the telephone calls I regularly get from people who have learned that I use hypnosis. Her doctor has told her that she must quit smoking now, or his wife has made some particularly painful comment about his paunch. At that particular moment, she very much wants to stop smoking, but she also wants to do it as quickly and painlessly as possible and hypnosis seems to be ideal for this. In fact, the very elements of loss or delegation of consciousness and control to the hypnotist that need to be corrected as *negative* expectations in other applications of hypnosis have to be corrected as *positive* expectations for habit control.

When I am able to correct these misconceptions, and when the patient is able and willing to participate in a comprehensive behavioral program to control the habit problem, the B.H.E. exercise can serve a limited but positive role in treatment. A clinical example will make this clear.

Sandra W. was the owner of a successful catering business, who called me after talking to a friend. Her friend was a former patient who had learned the B.H.E. exercise as part of a treatment program for anxiety and who recommended it, and me, enthusiastically. Nevertheless, Sandra was skeptical about any treatment that proposed to help her with what she perceived as her problem: being about 60 pounds above her ideal body weight. She had tried a large assortment of special diets, visits to "fat farms," and popular group approaches to weight loss. When she was particularly well-motivated, she would lose some or all of the weight, only to gain it back within a month or less after the special program had ended. She claimed to be "always ready" to lose weight, but was calling at that particular time because her boyfriend had begun recently to make negative comments about his own unhealthy diet and excess poundage. Though not specifically addressed to her, the comments upset her usual equilibrium on this topic. Sandra had decided that that the timing was right for another try.

Before our first appointment I talked with Sandra's internist, who was open to a trial of hypnosis for weight reduction but doubted that it would work. She had investigated the problem appropriately with history, physical examination, and laboratory tests. At her first visit I reviewed Sandra's current eating patterns, past efforts to lose weight, and goals for our work together. Sandra was significantly overweight and wanted to lose 50 pounds. Based on her negative experiences with crash diets she had no trouble understanding that attaining a stable weight loss of this magnitude might take a year or more and ultimately depend upon her developing new eating habits and patterns of physical activity.

I also spent some time at our first session exploring Sandra's previous experiences with hypnosis and introducing her to the hand-separation test, to which she responded dramatically. At our second session I taught Sandra the B.H.E. exercise, which she enjoyed and was able to experience vividly. Sandra not only was an excellent hypnotic subject, but also enjoyed and flourished in a collaborative role and would often elaborate creatively on approaches that I suggested in ways that were useful for her. She had a good sense of humor — a uniquely valuable trait in dealing with chronic and challenging health problems — that she applied equally to herself, to me, and to the various approaches we tried.

Sandra weighed herself weekly, and it quickly became apparent that the B.H.E. exercise itself used as a relaxing interlude would have absolutely no effect on her weight. We had explored a number of relatively mild options for reducing her caloric intake to the point where she would begin losing weight steadily, but "just like an alcoholic bartender" she was unable to apply them amidst the profusion of high calorie foods she dealt with daily in her catering business. As we were both becoming somewhat discouraged, Sandra decided to try a popular low-fat, low-calorie diet that involved a radical change in her eating habits. I was skeptical myself about this approach, but Sandra's boyfriend decided to try the diet at the same time, and the question then became whether self-hypnosis might be used in any way to increase Sandra's chances of success.

The approach that I tried was one that has been developed most extensively by Herbert Spiegel for control of habit disorders, which is described fully in the book *Trance and Treatment: Clinical Uses of Hypnosis* by Herbert and David Spiegel (see Appendix B). Put most simply, it uses a self-hypnosis exercise to present a brief series of "self-talk" messages that lead the patient away from the unhealthy habit. This approach appealed to Sandra, and she constructed the following series of messages: " 1) I want to look good and be thinner. 2) I am in control of what I eat. 3) Eating smaller portions and passing by snacks will get me what I want."

Sandra would repeat these messages to herself in hypnosis instead of or after the beach scene. She did her self-hypnosis exercise regularly twice a day, and I met with her every two weeks or so for a little less than a year. During our meetings I would review her progress in losing weight and her use of the self-hypnosis exercise, making modifications as needed. From a hypnotic point of view, Sandra was a talented and enthusiastic practitioner of self-hypnosis. After about a month she described herself as "able to go into hypnosis just like that" as she snapped her fingers. She found the B.H.E. exercise "brief and to the point," but also noted that our office sessions every two weeks seemed to "juice it up" for her. It was clear to both of us that the steadiness of my concern for her progress and my encouragement and patience with the inevitable ups and downs were significant helpful factors.

Sandra began to lose weight at about two pounds per week as soon as she began her new diet. At about the same time she decided to "go all the way" and begin a regular exercise program of taking a walk in the morning and swimming in the afternoon. The schedule she adopted was to do her self-hypnosis exercise right after breakfast and then to walk two miles to a commuter train station where she caught the train to her office. When she left her office in the afternoon she went to a health club where she did her self-hypnosis exercise in a chair by the pool before swimming. She did the afternoon exercise using only the feeling of lightness in her left hand, without any actual motion, and simply repeated her three phrases to herself. The whole process took less than five minutes.

Sandra's weight loss continued fairly steadily except for two interruptions during which she put on a few pounds. The first occurred after about a month and involved strong feelings of hunger that would distract her at work and lead to snacking. We found that these feelings could be slightly diminished by imagining a numbing, anesthetic pill that Sandra would pretend to swallow during her self-hypnosis exercise after she had repeated her three phrases. Sandra herself discovered after about a week of this that she could get much better relief by using the image of a "neutralizing pill" based on TV antacid commercials she had seen. After about a week of using this more powerful image, the hunger pangs stopped on their own.

The second interruption in Sandra's weight loss occurred about halfway through her program, when she broke up with her boyfriend. He had been her partner in many ways, including in the diet, and we spent several sessions around this time devoted mostly to a review of the relationship and related issues. Not surprisingly, the "deal" in their relationship had been that Sandra was fat, and the major change in her appearance upset the equilibrium. Sandra was able to take this loss in stride and commented sardonically that now she "*really* needed to look good!" Her weight loss began to level off as she neared her goal, and our last sessions were spent dealing with termination issues and adjusting her exercise for the "long haul." At a six-month follow-up she had regained 10 of the 50 pounds (which she attributed to a return to a more normal diet) but had held stable at what she felt was an acceptable weight for the last three months. She did her self-hypnosis exercise about twice weekly, but had kept up her exercise routine almost daily.

I have presented Sandra's case in some detail because it illustrates the complex interaction of personality resources, behavioral factors, life events, and hypnotic interventions that seem to be present when self-hypnosis is successful in the treatment of habit disorders. Sandra herself was aware that it was the diet and exercise that made her lose weight. But she had tried them both before, both alone and in combination, and credited the hypnosis as an "enabler" that finally got her going. Although the balance of controlled research studies show that hypnosis *per se* is not effective for overeating, smoking, or alcoholism, most clinicians who work with hypnosis can point to a few cases like Sandra's where its effect seems to have been clearly positive.

Improving Performance

One of the questions that patients regularly ask involves the ability of hypnosis to enhance performance. This question is sometimes based on the patient's own success at overcoming a clinical problem using self-hypnosis. Just as often, however, the question is based on seeing one of the standard stunts of stage hypnosis (e.g., having a subject lie rigid with his head and feet on two chairs while a heavy audience member stands on his abdomen) or a story in the news about how a professional athlete used hypnosis to break out of a slump. At times these are merely reflections of appropriate curiosity, but in some cases a legitimate clinical issue may be involved.

As discussed in Chapter 2, hypnosis works on experience rather than on behavior, so that the enhancement of performance is not an optimal use. The case of David E., the middle distance runner trying to deal with "the wall," is an illustration of an improvement in performance based on the use of self-hypnosis to modify a negative experience.

One of the most commonly used hypnotic techniques to enhance performance involves a somewhat different approach, but one to which the B.H.E. exercise can be adapted with little or no modification. The heart of the technique involves experiencing in hypnosis an ideal performance of the chosen task. This performance fantasy can be inserted in place of, or even into, the beach scene of the B.H.E. exercise. One patient who played golf imagined himself getting up from the warm beach, sauntering over to the nearby course, and hitting a perfect drive that he had seen on any number of televised professional tournaments and that left his golfing partners slack-jawed. He claimed that this fantasy did improve his game.

More relevant to the usual clinical uses of hypnosis was Peter D., another golfer, who was suffering from "the yips," a slump that commonly afflicts high-level players. Peter dispensed with the beach scene and substituted an image of *his own* best performance in a putting situation. Peter was a more serious golfer than the first patient and kept exact records of his performance. After only a week of practicing the B.H.E. exercise using his "perfect putt" fantasy he "broke out of the yips" and returned to his usual excellent game.

When you are dealing with a slump, the potential for performance is there, and self-hypnosis can sometimes overcome the blockage. The chances are obviously better in these cases than when the technique is applied in a vague effort to raise the baseline level of performance. Best or ideal performance images and fantasies seem to be part of the preparatory rituals of a number of professional athletes and performers; in some cases they have invented preliminary procedures that bear a striking resemblance to self-hypnosis.

Sex Therapy and Sexual Applications

Clinicians who specialize in sex therapy frequently deal with problems that have many of the characteristics of performance slumps. Disorders of sexual performance and enjoyment often are determined by a complex interaction of physiological, relationship, and individual psychological factors. The B.H.E. exercise can be used to supplement several standard sex therapy procedures that address the psychosomatic and anxiety-based aspects of these problems. It is *not* an appropriate treatment for relationship problems, which usually require work with both members of a couple that focuses on the specifics of their relationship both in and out of bed.

The case of Ellen G. described in Chapter 2 presents an example of the pitfalls of applying self-hypnosis to a problem that is based in a current interpersonal relationship. Ellen discovered on her own a feature of the B.H.E. and other self-hypnosis exercises that brought her some pleasure but did not help with her problem: the ability of the exercise to allow the patient to experience thoughts and images as real can be applied to sexual thoughts and images, and can produce extremely vivid and arousing fantasies. Many patients without sexual problems will discover this on their own, and several hypnotically talented patients in my practice have found that they can bring themselves to orgasm with little physical contact using the B.H.E. exercise. The beach scene, for a number of people, has been modified in highly creative ways.

As an expression of healthy lust and play, these uses of the B.H.E. usually have no negative effects and provide a useful internal reinforcement for doing the exercise. A few patients discovered that the exercise itself became conditioned to sexual arousal after experiments like these, and found it hard subsequently to "get down to business." Although the problem can be a mild annoyance, it usually indicates a high level of creative participation and enjoyment, which is more of a help than a hindrance to clinical applications of hypnosis.

In formal individual sex therapy, the B.H.E. exercise may be used as an antianxiety condition as part of a program of systematic desensitization to anxiety-provoking sexual stimuli. This can sometimes be done as part of the exercise itself, as illustrated by the case of Keith H.:

Keith was a single, socially active young man who had developed partial erectile impotence after his steady girlfriend laughed at his penis in bed. A harmless anomaly caused his penis to deviate slightly but noticeably to the side when it became erect, and his girlfriend had lightheartedly commented "Hi there, Lefty!" during their foreplay. Keith had no problems that night, but he began to brood about the incident and about his penis, which had never troubled him before. He knew rationally that his girlfriend found him sexually attractive and adequate, and that her comment had been truly lighthearted, but this did not seem to help. He visited a urologist who reassured him, and decided that the cost and risks associated with correcting the problem were prohibitive.

Unfortunately, Keith then began to have trouble "getting the laughter out of my mind," and experienced increasingly frequent losses of his erection during foreplay. In a common sequence of events in these cases, worry about performance produced a spiral of performance and enjoyment problems so that sex became something that he "dreaded." He was referred to me by the urologist, who thought that hypnosis might help and commented that Keith "seemed pretty healthy psychologically, except for this problem." Several sessions devoted to a general psychiatric and sexual evaluation confirmed this impression.

Keith learned the B.H.E. exercise without any problems, and had a moderate level of hypnotic talent. On the B.H.E. evaluation form he indicated that he had "some sense of actually participating" in the beach scene — he was able to distinguish this clearly from what he experienced by just closing his eyes and imagining it. Once he was comfortable with the exercise, Keith modified the beach scene so that he was sure to be alone and unobserved ("I don't want any of those guys on the sailboats watching me with binoculars!"). He started where he was comfortable at that time in real life, with solitary masturbation, which had not been disturbed by his impotence problem.

Keith moved quickly through a series of images that increasingly resembled the situation he feared: one in which a sexual partner laughed at his penis. He stayed with each image until he could experience it without any sense of tension or decrease in sexual arousal, and would confirm this regularly by masturbating to orgasm during the exercise while experiencing the given scene. He found that masturbation made him "more aware of where I really am" but did not totally cancel his sense of actual participation in the modified beach scene. Within a month he was able to be aroused by a scene where his girlfriend pulled down his bathing suit, giggled "Hi there, Lefty!" and kissed his penis. His impotence in real life disappeared at this point, and had not recurred a year later.

Other applications of the B.H.E. exercise are possible in the individual therapy of sexual disorders. Two cautions are in order concerning these applications. First, when a patient uses self-hypnosis to create a therapeutic sexual fantasy, this action in itself can sometimes engender jealousy and/or mistrust in a sexual partner or spouse who knows about the technique ("Who are you fantasizing about? Is it me? How do I know?"). As with other private behaviors, there are no real answers or reassurances possible here. Most often, the tension around this issue must be resolved as part of a broader evaluation of how much is kept private in a relationship and whether there are such things as "white lies." Clinicians who use self-hypnosis for sex therapy should have this possibility in mind early in their treatment planning.

The second caution applies to sex therapy, but is also relevant to all clinical efforts to control habits, enhance performance, or eliminate symptoms. Simply suggesting to the patient in hypnosis that the problem will go away or incorporating such a direct suggestion in the key phrase of the B.H.E. or other self-talk format is generally not a useful treatment strategy. Hypnosis can be an effective adjunct to relatively rapid behavioral or cognitive treatments, but it does not work instantly or miraculously.

NINE

Practice
and Follow-up

The Short Run vs. The Long Haul

If you have read this far, you are genuinely interested in self-hypnosis and have perhaps tried it already yourself or with some patients. This chapter will take you to the end of this book and to the edges of what we know about where and how self-hypnosis works. Along with the Introduction through Chapter 3, which cover issues and interactions that precede the formally "hypnotic" task, this chapter and its application lie at the heart of successful clinical use of self-hypnosis. There are many systems and techniques of hypnosis, and no clear evidence (despite vocal claims) that any one of them is superior. The Brief Hypnotic Experience exercise and the accompanying forms and procedures represent my own judgment about a sensible starting place for the clinician beginning to use self-hypnosis. If you believe in this, or in any other hypnotic technique, you will have a healthy percentage of short-term successes with your patients. Self-hypnosis looks very good in the short run.

The long haul is another picture entirely. Part of the problem has to do with the "honeymoon effect" that was discussed in Chapter 6 and that applies to all dramatic new clinical interventions. Another less dramatic component is related to the difficulty people have in doing new things that are good for them, such as buckling up their seat belts or taking their high blood pressure pills. These factors combine to create a significant fall-off in use of self-hypnosis, or of any other self-help technique, in the period after it has been taught.

It is difficult to get a feeling for this phenomenon in an ongoing clinical interaction, since at the point when you become aware of it you usually initiate some efforts to bolster the practice or deal with the problem. Sometimes, the entire issue of self-hypnosis and its practice just fades away with neither patient nor clinician mentioning it out loud, like a theme in psychotherapy that neither was quite ready for. You can get some idea of the magnitude of what happens from a nonclinical study that I did with a group of executives who were taught the B.H.E. exercise as part of a stress management program. They returned to their home offices at the end of the seminar to practice and apply the exercise on their own, and my inquiries about their use of the exercise were as an interested observer rather than as a clinician who was trying to get them to practice or apply what I had taught. One month after learning the exercise, 90% of this group was using it. Over the next five months this percentage declined steadily to 50%.

Clinicians and researchers who work with self-help techniques will recognize that these are fairly typical statistics for this kind of an intervention — 50% use at six months is not a bad yield, when you think of it, for an afternoon's instruction. Nevertheless, there may very well be some among the 50% who were *not* using the technique who would have been if it had been better taught and/or followed up. My own current research is concerned with this issue, and the answers are far from in. What follows in the rest of this chapter are my own recommendations for clinicians using the B.H.E. exercise on helping patients with the practice and follow-up phases. I have specifically tried to avoid an easy, and useless, prescription to do everything often and well. The areas and details that I emphasize are the ones that I feel have the best chance of paying off clinically. I believe in self-hypnosis, and I am not satisfied — nor should you be — with average results.

The Practice Phase

The "self" part of self-hypnosis will be tested for the first time after you send your patient home with his B.H.E. exercise instruction sheet to practice the exercise on his own. The goal for this phase is to establish a basic level of familiarity and skill on the patient's part with the B.H.E. exercise, which will then be directed towards helping him with his problem. At the same time that he is practicing the exercise, he will usually also be recording symptoms, constructing a key phrase, or engaging in some other activities that remind him of the clinical context. Thus, the skill development and clinical application tasks proceed from this point simultaneously, although I have of necessity separated them in writing this book.

I usually recommend a two-week practice period during which the patient does the B.H.E. exercise twice daily, five days a week. This gives a total of 20 practice sessions, enough in my experience to both develop the skill needed for most clinical applications and uncover any serious problems that the patient may have with the exercise itself. The practice sessions consist of going through the exercise with the beach scene (or another scene, if one has been substituted) and the key phrase if one is being used. Sometimes the wording of the key phrase is being worked out during this practice period; in that case, the patient can use "clear and calm," "warm and relaxed" or any phrase appropriate to the scene he is using.

Under ideal conditions I meet with the patient at the end of the first week to go over his experiences and make needed adjustments. If a meeting at the end of the first week is impossible, you may want to arrange a telephone call to answer questions and make minor corrections. *Do not* expect the patient to simply go home, learn the exercise, and come back with everything fine and dandy. This almost never happens to me or to other clinicians experienced in this area; there are almost always problems, often significant ones. One of the major failure points for beginners in self-hypnosis is right here, as feelings of mutual disappointment between clinician and patient bring the enterprise to a halt.

Why, even for generally experienced clinicians, is this such a difficult transition? The reason is simple, but it does not suggest any simple solutions to the problems of this phase. When your patient leaves your office, he leaves the direct orbit of your influence and the world that you know better than he does. At home, *his* home, other demands on his time and other relationships exert themselves. Who you are and what you have to offer are put in a different, and often sobering, perspective. This happens, of course, with any outpatient treatment. But teaching a self-hypnosis exercise and making sure that it is being used shift the emphasis much more than usual away from the clinician's office setting.

There is a wide range of abilities and experience in this kind of interaction among clinicians who try to learn and teach self-hypnosis. At one extreme, practitioners of preventive dentistry or medicine are well-acquainted with these issues and have a good feeling for how they interact with patients around them. On the other extreme, some psychoanalytically oriented psychotherapists find it difficult to switch to an emphasis on what is going on *outside* the therapy hour. Most clinicians fall somewhere in between.

The next seven sections address specific aspects of home practice of the B.H.E. exercise. By becoming aware of the issues and problems that can arise, and of some possible solutions, you will be in a good position to prevent avoidable disappointments and to know which simply "come with the territory." Thus, your own enthusiasm for the new technique will have a chance to exert its positive effect on both you and your patient. This is about as much as you can expect from a book, since expertise here consists of knowing how to adapt the technique to patients' individual personalities and circumstances. More than with other aspects of the clinical use of self-hypnosis, you will get much better at this simply with the passage of time and the accumulation of your own experience.

Making a Time and Place

The B.H.E. exercise is intentionally designed to be brief. The entire exercise,including the beach scene or its equivalent and adequate repetition of a key phrase can be done in 10 minutes. The practical question in using the B.H.E. exercise outside the office setting then becomes whether and how the patient can devote 10 minutes twice daily, five days per week, to learning the exercise.

This section is headed "making a time and place" rather than "finding a time and place" because this seemingly simple task is far from easy. It is an active, creative job that requires considerable energy and ingenuity. As a clinician, you should expect to spend your own time and energy helping your patient with it. In my own practice, I usually spend a total of about one hour with each patient working on issues of when, where, and how the exercise is to be practiced at home or at work. The hour is broken up into segments in each of the early sessions after the exercise has been taught and brief inquiries and adjustments later on.

The best way to get a feeling for the challenge of making time is to try it yourself. Ideally, you have done this already as part of your own learning and practice of the B.H.E. exercise. If for any reason you have not, ask yourself how *you* would make the time and place to spend 10 minutes twice daily for five days a week practicing or doing the exercise. If your life is anything like mine, this endeavor will make you humbler and more understanding of the patients you teach — we are all busy, or feel we are, and work, family, recreational, and social obligations compete for our time. All too often, the healthy activities are put off or forgotten.

These problems apply to *all* self-help health-promoting techniques, including meditation, physical exercise, or monitoring blood pressure. Your first job as a clinician is to help your patient put himself or herself in perspective — as deserving *some* time and care. For excessively guilty and/or dutiful people, *all* of whose time and energy is consumed caring for others, this may take some doing. The goal here is best expressed in the statement attributed to the great Rabbi, Hillel: "If I am not for myself, who will be for me? And if I am for myself alone, what am I? And if not now, when?"

Once your patient is committed to making time for the exercise, he must decide when that time will be. To help make this decision, I generally go over how the patient usually spends his days during weekdays and on weekends (e.g., "When do you get up? What awakens you? What do you do when you get out of bed?", etc.) I am often surprised by how much I learn about the patient and his problems in the course of this seemingly pedestrian inquiry.

In general, your goal is to find the most private and predictable time and place in the early and late parts of your patient's day. Unless your patient lives or works alone, ideal conditions are very rare. The best times for practice are often transitional periods between other activities that are regularly scheduled and done, thus letting the exercise benefit from whatever planning and discipline are already in place. Not infrequently, separate practice schedules will apply on weekends or for different job assignments or shifts.

Below, I have compiled a listing of relatively scheduled times and convenient places that have been used by patients to practice and to apply the B.H.E. exercise. In addition to my own experiences, the list reflects the persistence and creativity of many patients and clinicians who have shared their techniques with me. I have included comments on each specific setting, so that you can begin to get a feeling for the attitudes and principles that facilitate this task:

1) *In the morning, after awakening and before getting out of bed.* For a significant number of patients, this is the only time and place where they can be sure of being able to practice self-hypnosis. I usually keep

it as my standard for comparison with other settings and my "fallback position" for other ideas that don't work out in practice. People are often relaxed and relatively free from demands in this situation, and a pleasant and successful experience with self-hypnosis will often positively influence mood and energy through the first part of the day or even longer.

The problem with this setting is the tendency to fall back to sleep while doing the exercise. Having a definite physical position (e.g., lying on one's back with the left arm outside of the covers) associated with the B.H.E. exercise that is different from the usual position on awakening from sleep sometimes helps. Some patients need to go to the bathroom or brush their teeth to "get in gear," but this can backfire if it is perceived by spouses or children as a signal of availability. Such communication can be a serious loss, since this is one of the limited number of settings where self-hypnosis can be practiced relatively covertly, if that becomes necessary.

2) *In the bathroom, as part of a morning (or other) washing/toilet routine.* Next to being asleep in bed, the bathroom is the setting where patients are most likely to be left alone and undisturbed for the brief period required to complete the B.H.E. exercise. Although many people find the setting unappetizing, it ranks high as a practical alternative. In some work settings, this is the *only* place where a patient can be by himself and be left alone.

A major issue is often where to sit, with the toilet as an obvious (and often the only) alternative. Since hand or arm rests are usually not available, the hand levitation is most often done from a starting position with the forearm resting on the thigh. Fortunate patients have a chair in the bathroom, or can introduce one. Although many people associate the bathtub with a relaxing bathing ritual, it is not a good place to practice self-hypnosis for obvious safety reasons.

3) *On public transportation to or from work or other regular travel.* A number of patients have found this setting ideal for doing the B.H.E. exercise. One executive did his own controlled experiment, comparing the exercise to a nap and to reading the paper during his daily half-hour ride home on a commuter train. He was able to appreciate the specific contribution of self-hypnosis to managing his stress, as well as the more general benefit of the other "time out" activities. He has

done the exercise daily in this setting for over two years. Other patients report that airplane travel provides both ideal seats for the exercise and a needed opportunity to benefit from its refreshing aspects, especially when sleep time is lost due to business or time zone changes.

This is probably the place to insert a seemingly obvious, but sometimes necessary caution: *Self-hypnosis should never be practiced while driving a vehicle.* It *is* possible to do the B.H.E. exercise with eyes open, but this does not change the unacceptable dangers of misdirected attention and possible sleep that such a practice would bring. Doing the exercise in a car pulled to the side of the road or in a safe parking spot *with the engine off* is also possible, but depending on the community may provoke highly disturbing inquiries from criminals and/or police.

4) *During a break at work.* Where the B.H.E. exercise is used to manage stress that is related to the work environment, this would at first glance appear to be the optimal timing. Both you and your patients should be prepared, however, for the fact that in all but a few work environments it is extremely difficult to create the uninterrupted privacy that fosters effective practice of the B.H.E.

This is especially true of eliminating phone interruptions, a problem that is only partially solved by using an answering machine or having a secretary, colleague, or child (in the case of a homemaker) take calls. Many patients report that hearing the sound of the phone, even if it is being answered, distracts them significantly from the exercise. Some phones with convenient modular plugs can be completely disconnected for the brief time it takes to do the exercise.Some patients adapt and can shut out the sound or shorten the distraction, but only rarely is it eliminated entirely. A number of patients have found that fairly radical approaches work best here, such as using a large closet, storeroom, library, conference room, or other area within their work environment where they are relatively likely to be undisturbed.

5) *In a meditation room, chapel, or house of worship.* A number of hospitals, universities, and even industrial plants have rooms set aside for quiet contemplation or prayer. Even well-attended churches, mosques, and synagogues have times when they are regularly both empty and accessible. If available to your patients, these are often excellent locations for practicing self-hypnosis. Religious patients who attend services or pray regularly are usually not bothered by this non-

religious use of these locations, or deal with it through an appropriate contribution to the helping institution. Nonreligious patients are sometimes uncomfortable in such places. Whether it is appropriate to examine or work through this discomfort will vary in different treatment settings. The relationship of the B.H.E. exercise to prayer is discussed later in this chapter.

6) *Before, after, or as a break during a regularly scheduled period of physical exercise.* This setting seems particularly useful for a number of patients who have responded to the current popularity of exercise programs. Whether the patient's particular exercise routine is self-initiated, part of a workplace program, or prescribed by a health-care professional, the B.H.E. exercise usually benefits from the work that has gone into carving out the necessary time and place. In general, patients seem to have less trouble being left alone in these settings than in other free-time activities. The brevity and unobtrusiveness of the B.H.E. exercise allow it to often go unnoticed at poolside or under a tree near a running area. The case of Sandra described in Chapter 8 gives an example of the integration of the B.H.E. into a physical exercise program.

In my own experience, there are no good general rules for whether the B.H.E. exercise is done before, after, or as a break from the physical exercise. The best method is to try each and chose the one that is most comfortable. A number of clinicians and patients have noted that when the B.H.E. exercise is used in this setting there are effects on the experience (and sometimes on the performance) of the physical exercise itself as well as on the clinical target symptoms. It is sometimes these interactions with the physical exercise that determine optimal timing of the B.H.E. Naturally, as physical training progresses, the interaction evolves and the optimal timing may change.

7) *As part of an end-of-day or coming home routine.* As with a number of the previously mentioned settings, the advantage of this timing is that something different from the usual work or family routine is already scheduled. Often, this is a time for changing out of work clothes, taking a shower, having a drink, or other behavior that "switches gears" into a more relaxed end-of-day mode. A significant proportion of patients perform this gear change less than perfectly and are often aware or are made aware that they are taking out problems of their work set-

ting on their family. In these cases, the B.H.E. exercise can be a useful adjunct to whatever routine is already in place. Some patients with alcoholism or tendencies in this direction particularly appreciate a non-pharmacological way to wind down and cheer up.

If it is effective in making the patient calmer and easier to live with, family members will seldom resent the additional 10 minutes during which their loved one is unavailable. Even when these benefits occur, however, young children may have trouble perceiving them. They often need and deserve special help (and some parental flexibility) in learning to be able to wait to have access to their parent or parents after a day apart from them.

8) *In bed, before going to sleep at night.* Where the B.H.E. exercise is being used to control symptoms of anxiety, tension, or stress, doing the exercise at night often significantly relieves the initial insomnia that is a regular part of these syndromes. Thus, the better the exercise works, the less of it may be done. I have regularly encountered patients who originally required over an hour to fall asleep who, after basic mastery of the B.H.E. exercise, never got through the 1 to 10 relaxation sequence because they were already alseep.

Where the relief of initial insomnia is not the main clinical goal, sleep onset can be a real problem for bedtime practice. Sometimes patients can keep from falling asleep by doing the exercise sitting in a chair or other location near their bed, but this technique does not always work. In any case, you should remember to reassure patients that falling asleep during the exercise has no harmful effects other than missing the exercise, and that they will not be stuck in a hypnotic trance.

9) *On weekends or holidays.* Practice of the B.H.E. exercise that is limited to weekends or holidays usually indicates either a low level of commitment to the procedure or problems with personal time management that may require some clinical attention. Some regular practice is better than none, however, and I have worked with a few patients who mastered the B.H.E. exercise using this kind of schedule and were able to benefit somewhat from its later applications.

When practice is limited to weekends or holidays, several special issues arise. First, it is often necessary under these circumstances to allow considerably greater than usual time for mastery of the B.H.E. exercise; often a month or more is required. In planning the schedule, I usually insist on 10 practice sessions as the minimum for consolidating the basic self-hypnotic skill.

Second, it is seldom useful in my experience to try to concentrate massive practice sessions in these time slots (e.g., 10 times or more daily) in an effort to correct for this slower pace. This is not because I feel that massed practice has no place. Rather, my reluctance stems from the massing of practice in a period specifically designated for rest and/or fun, which are thereby crowded out. The very patients for whom these issues come up are the ones for whom self-care is most needed and also the ones most likely to grasp any excuse for abandoning a self-care program. When these issues can be worked through reasonably, it is often possible to practice the exercise three or four times daily without having it dominate the weekend or holiday routine.

10) *In your office.* I mention this setting last because it is on the edge of what I will do before I abandon self-hypnosis as a therapeutic technique. It is a last-ditch fallback position for the patient who overwhelms you with excuses and sad stories whose bottom line is that he has not practiced the exercise. I refer here, of course, to the home practice that follows appropriate teaching, modeling (if necessary), and review in the first session or two. How you handle this situation will depend on your own psychological orientation and the amount of time you have to work with that particular patient on self-hypnosis.

If you do decide to go on, I have found that practice sessions in my office will either expose the relevant fear or other resistance and facilitate its resolution, or lead to a relatively quick decision to terminate therapy. Where I have had time to pursue the matter, I have occasionally been able to gradually shape the necessary behaviors of home practice away from me. I begin with practice in my office during the "official" therapy hour, and then move the patient to another location (e.g., unused seminar room) in my space, still during the regular hour. Gradually, I leave him alone more of the time to practice without me present. The next step is to keep the location constant but move the practice time outside the regular therapy hour so that the patient is no longer paying for it. When he is ready, the practice sessions can be transferred to the home or work setting.

These examples should give you an idea of the issues and processes involved in making the time and place needed to practice and use the B.H.E. exercise. Some of them may apply directly to your own patients, and you may also be able to use them as illustrations even where they do not. In the end, though, it comes down to creativity, persistence, and a sense of humor in turning good intentions into regular practice.

Keeping Time

In the part of the B.H.E. induction that introduces the patient to the self-hypnosis exercise, I mention, "If you are using a timer, set it for 10 minutes." A similar phrase is also included in the model self-hypnosis exercise instructions that I have provided. The use of an external timer frees up the part of the patient's mind that would have to keep time during the practice or application of the B.H.E., and allows him to relax and enjoy the beach scene or whatever similar experience is part of his own exercise.

Finding or buying an appropriate timer does take some investment of time and/or money. A common response of patients is to suggest or try the widely used wind-up kitchen timers that let you know in another room when the roast is done. You can save your patients, and yourself, some grief if you warn them *not* to use this type of timer for their exercise. Its strident jangle is enough to cancel out whatever relaxation or cognitive restructuring the patient may have attained and is the worst possible ending for the B.H.E. exercise. What is needed, then, is a gentle, easily set timer that can be heard.

My own personal choice (and recommendation) for this job is one of the small credit-card-size calculators that come with alarm clock and calendar functions. This makes them a little thicker (and more expensive) than the solar powered calculators which they resemble, but a reliable model can usually be obtained at an electronics or small appliance store for 15 to 20 dollars. The alarm on these clocks is a gentle beep that will not disturb roommates and is probably best heard from the distance of a chest level pocket or nearby table. Just as important, the time setting for the alarm function can be keyed in directly using the calculator keys (e.g., 4:15 p.m.). The alternative on some calculators and many alarm watches is much less desirable and much more time-consuming: you must push a button repeatedly to advance the minutes/hours to the time you want the alarm to ring. When you are in the greatest rush, it always seems as if the time is 23 hours away or you accidentally go one hour past by mistake. This last advantage is less important for patients who do the exercise at the same time each day; for them, a conventional alarm watch may be ideal.

You should be flexible about the length of individual practice sessions or applications as long as they occur regularly. For some patients, a five-minute exercise is ideal; others report that only by extending the exercise to 15 to 20 minutes can they fully experience the beach scene, attain adequate pain relief or relaxation, etc. The B.H.E. is not designed to be used for periods of longer than 30 minutes; for such applications, other techniques are more appropriate (see Appendix B).

Some patients genuinely feel that the use of an external timer is not worth the trouble. They either have the ability to estimate time with relative accuracy and economy of effort or are willing and able to accept the consequences of widely varying practice intervals. I usually adopt an attitude of watchful waiting in such cases, since I have found no good way to distinguish prospectively between patients who are giving me valuable information about what kind of timing works best for them and those whose resistance to an external timer is part of a more general lack of engagement with regular practice of the B.H.E. exercise.

Technique Issues

As your patient's use of the B.H.E. exercise moves out of your office and more into his own home or work setting, modifications of the exercise will, or should, present themselves. The highly structured way in which I have introduced you to the B.H.E. is an advantage in allaying the apprehension and uncertainty that are normal for beginners. The same structure, however, can occasionally stand in the way of effective application, and must always be seen for what it is: a means to a clinical end. I have summarized below some of the issues that regularly arise concerning modification of the basic B.H.E. exercise format.

In situations where a patient seems to be having trouble accepting and/or practicing the B.H.E. exercise, I regularly will *model* the exercise for the patient in my office. I actually go through the exercise myself, with a rather brief interval devoted to the beach or whatever pleasant, relaxing scene is most appropriate to my own needs at the time. Aside from the hand levitation, there is not much to watch in the B.H.E. exercise; nevertheless, patients regularly report that this modeling was helpful to them. The relevant factors in most cases are reassurance that the procedure is accepted and practiced by the therapist, and a chance to see and identify with the therapist in a more direct and physical way than usual. Although I have never experienced any problems with modeling or heard of any adverse consequences, the technique is not natural for a number of therapists and may resonate negatively with the dynamics of some patients.

There is a thriving industry in self-hypnosis *tapes*, and patients (and clinicians) often ask whether this might not be an ideal way to learn and apply the B.H.E. exercise. I have tried taping the B.H.E. myself, having patients or their family members tape it, and have concluded over the years that the benefit of the taped format does not make up for its inconvenience and, to a lesser extent, for its negative psychological implications. Neither problem, however, is insurmountable, and I have treated a number of patients who were able to adopt and to benefit from the use of tapes.

The inconvenience associated with the use of a tape is particularly visible with a self-hypnosis procedure like the B.H.E. exercise that places a premium on brevity, portability, and unobtrusiveness. I have seen this factor change over the last few years, however. One of the few health benefits of the "Walkman" phenomenon is the inexpensive availability of pocket or purse size playback units adapted for private listening. Such units frequently do not record, so that the patient must find another machine for creating the recording.

Whose voice to use for the recording is a matter of individual preference that, not surprisingly, has major transference implications. The very use of a tape detracts from the self-help and self-control thrust of the B.H.E. exercise and similar procedures, but I have seen a number of clinicians approach this issue too rigidly, as if the patient had to shape up to meet the clinician's standard of independent behavior. Although I do not routinely mention or encourage the use of a tape format, I am open to trying it as long as it increases the frequency and/or quality of practice. I generally suggest that the patient record his own voice, but will make a recording myself is the patient asks.

A more subtle technique issue involves the *mode of internal communication* that the patient uses when he does the B.H.E. exercise on his own. Both the B.H.E. induction script and the self-hypnosis exercise instructions provide a self-talk format expressed in phrases like, "Say to yourself, 'I'm taking three deep, relaxing breaths and letting the floating feeling spread throughout my body.'"

Patients vary widely in the extent to which they actually subvocalize (or even vocalize) this kind of self-talk, often reflecting their own particular style of "talking to themselves." For some, the self-talk mode is a comfortable form of internal communication. For others, it is extremely unnatural, and the internal communication that initiates and maintains the self-hypnotic process is more in the form of silent thoughts, visual images, or even affective memories that do not have a clearly specified verbal content. This other extreme is expressed in the phrase "let yourself remember the feeling of hypnosis" that is also included in the B.H.E. induction script and in the self-hypnosis exercise instructions. I have included a good deal of the self-talk format in the script and instructions because it is generally easier for patients to abandon or modify this format when it is not right for them than to adopt it later if it proves to be what they need.

Repeated Hetero-hypnotic Inductions

A final issue of technique is the decision concerning whether and how often to repeat a hetero-hypnotic induction after the patient has been taught the B.H.E. exercise and has begun to practice it away from the office. As with the issue of tape recording the exercise, change in the target symptoms that you and your patient have agreed upon should be your standard for this decision. My own preferred practice is to use office time to review the patient's home or work practice of the exercise and to modify the procedure accordingly. If a demonstration would help, I model the exercise myself and/or ask the patient to go through the exercise with me watching. A report on and discussion of his experiences both in and outside of the office, and of the effects of any modifications that we have made, form the substance of our work together in this phase.

Fairly regularly, patients will comment that they experience the B.H.E. exercise as practiced at home as "weaker" or less vivid than what they experienced during the first hetero-hypnotic induction in my office. I explain that this is to be expected, since I have had much more experience with hypnosis than they have and it will take some time to internalize and learn the exercise. Often this is enough to reassure the patient and facilitate further practice.

In some cases, however, patients explicitly ask to have the induction repeated. I decide on how to respond to such requests, and would advise you to decide, on an individual basis. The factors relevant to my decision are my knowledge of the patient's personality and current circumstances. Does he need support in a period of depleted resources or encouragement towards initiative and responsibility? Is the whole idea of self-hypnosis or any self-care technique foreign to his previously adaptive personal style? Are there good reasons for the patient to change this style?

Since the B.H.E. induction and exercise convey a fairly thoroughgoing self-hypnotic approach, you have plenty of room to maneuver before you find yourself practicing "old fashioned" hetero-hypnosis. Even if you do modify the procedure in the direction of hetero-hypnosis, there are worse things in therapy than an office procedure that is effective in reducing symptoms, but has to be repeated every month or so. That kind of schedule would seem just fine if you were talking about arthritis, lymphoma, or most other medical conditions and treatments.

I have regularly encountered patients who asked for and seemed to benefit from periodic hetero-hypnotic inductions, although it was clear to both of us that the major therapeutic work was going on in their continuing home practice of the B.H.E. exercise. A number were steady and successful in professions and/or family situations where they had to take care of many others. Unless we were also engaged in exploratory psychotherapy, the dependency issues raised by our interaction around self-hypnosis were not explored.

Religious Issues

The experience of hypnosis, like religious experience, is often a creative blend of the transcendent and the dependent aspects of human nature. Not surprisingly, religious patients or those who practice any systematic form of meditation feel and sometimes comment upon this kinship. As a clinician, I try to be respectful and open to these feelings and comments, as I would be to any interaction with an aspect of the patient's life that goes beyond what I can offer or control in the clinical setting. Beginners in the clinical use of self-hypnosis who are uncomfortable with religion or meditation sometimes feel compelled to respond in these situations with comments of their own that emphasize the uniqueness of self-hypnosis and/or attempt to explain the religious or meditative practice as "nothing but" X or Y. I have seldom found such comments accurate or helpful, and would advise silence as the best way to deal with these feelings of discomfort. You do not want to provoke an unnecessary contest between self-hypnosis and other helpful or comforting practices that the patient uses.

As described in Chapter 2, patients who have current problems with basic reality contact, especially interpersonal reality, will sometimes seek therapy with self-hypnosis or have it suggested by a family member or friend. A patient in this group will often raise the issue of religion and/or meditation as he reveals a long history of attempts to seek transcendent experience, self-knowledge, or spiritual enlightenment through various meditative or religious practices. Drug-induced altered states of consciousness have often also been explored by this group. For them, self-hypnosis is another technique to master inner and sometimes family turmoil. Clearly, this is an entirely different group from the patients with stable histories of strong religious or meditative identification and practice; those with reality problems are *not* good candidates for training in self-hypnosis, especially by clinicians new to the field.

Sometimes, however, a basically stable patient with good reality contact will bring up the issue of conflict between hypnosis and religious or meditative practices, and here a calm and reasoned response that deals squarely with the religious issues involved is indeed appropriate. I have found two common sources of conflict, stemming from very different roots. The first, and most superficial, is a simple issue of competition for time and/or emotional energy among two similar procedures that are being applied to reach the same goal.

The patient may be already practicing a meditation exercise twice daily for stress management or praying for healing and relief from pain. He is not particularly worried about any inherent conflict between what he is doing and self-hypnosis, but wonders whether they are redundant. Here the problem is one of sequencing and/or scheduling, and the patient needs help in deciding whether and how to compare self-hypnosis with the procedure that he is currently using. The crucial question, of course, is how well the target symptom is being relieved by what the patient is now doing. On occasion, the current procedures may be working quite well, and it may turn out that the patient was referred to you by someone who never thought to inquire about these other, but equally valid, kinds of healing procedures.

In other situations, the referral is appropriate. Whatever the patient is now doing leaves him with a significant residue of symptoms that are suitable for treatment with self-hypnosis. In these situations I will usually teach the patient the B.H.E. exercise and invite him to compare it with whatever he is currently doing. To do this practically, it usually means doing the B.H.E. exercise once daily rather than twice. This is not a problem if the timing of the procedures is rotated appropriately during the comparison period to prevent order or time-of-day effects from determining the comparison. Sometimes the patient will find the procedures are indeed redundant. Not infrequently, he will discover subjective differences in how they feel or in what they do that allow a widening of his self-help repertoire that proves helpful. Be open to coming out second in this kind of comparison, and resist the temptation to conclude that the patient "just hasn't practiced enough" or is unmotivated. You will have plenty of cases where self-hypnosis will be right on target.

The second common source of conflict usually is mentioned by patients with an orthodox or fundamentalist religious orientation. For them, self-hypnosis may be associated with deviant religious practices or forbidden forms of magic. Here, the conflict is perceived as being in principle rather than in practice, occasionally accompanied by inflated expectations concerning the nature and potency of hypnosis.

In my own personal and supervisory experience, these concerns can usually be resolved as long as the clinician is open to hearing about and transacting with the patient's religious world. A low-key exploration and correction of the patient's preconceptions and prior experiences with hypnosis, as described in Chapters 1 and 3 may be all that is required. If you are comfortable with it, a biblical quotation such as the one from Ecclesiastes 3 asserting, "To every thing there is a season, and a time to every purpose under heaven," may communicate to the religious patient both a respect for the Bible as a source and a sense that you are able to see hypnosis as only one of a number of valid options. For a minority of patients, the conflict is more serious and cannot be resolved within the therapist-patient interaction.

In these rare situations I will always offer to speak with the patient's minister, priest, or rabbi concerning his proposed treatment using self-hypnosis. I have never experienced or heard of a bad outcome from such an interaction. Most often, the clergyman or woman is open to my presentation and advises the patient to give it a try. In the few cases where the advice is to stay away from hypnosis, it is often, on reflection, well-given: some people are more comfortable, and better off, using the techniques they are familiar with. Most important, the communication is a friendly one that leaves the door open to future contacts and helping efforts. In situations where the religious objection is a conscious or unconscious screen for other reservations concerning self-hypnosis, the offer to communicate with a sanctioned religious leader usually initiates a more honest evaluation of the situation.

Family and Interpersonal Issues

Unless your patient lives and works entirely alone, learning and practicing self-hypnosis is likely to interest or involve more people than you expect. The private and self-initiated character of the B.H.E. exercise can be deceptive here, because it is balanced by the curiosity and other emotions that the subject of hypnosis always arouses. The issue frequently comes up in one of your first sessions, when your patient asks, "What should I tell my wife and kids about all this?"

I generally encourage patients to offer matter-of-fact explanations of the B.H.E. exercise appropriate to the age and education of the questioner. This is usually better than refusing to comment, since ideas about hypnosis are likely to be even stranger than those about other activities when distorted by the emotional currents that circulate in all families. An adult spouse or child might be given a condensed version of what the patient himself understands. A young child might be told, "Daddy is using this exercise to help him relax/help his back feel better," etc. For children who have heard the word hypnosis used, it often is worthwhile to explore what the term means to them and correct any glaring misconceptions—easily picked up from the portrayals current on TV programs many children watch.

This sharing of cognitive information will take care of some of the interpersonal problems precipitated by learning and applying self-hypnosis, but it is not unusual for some others to emerge that are not as simply corrected. In these cases, aspects of the patient's learning and/or practicing the B.H.E. exercise contradict or interfere with accustomed family or other interpersonal roles. The patient is thus left with the choice of concealing or abandoning the use of self-hypnosis, suffering conflict in important relationships, or questioning the pattern of things as they are. Joanne's case will illustrate a typical manifestation of this dilemma:

Joanne A's clinical problem was pain and spasm secondary to a whiplash injury. She had experienced good initial relief using the B.H.E. exercise, and seemed to be progressing well with twice daily practice in the early morning and evening. Her relationship problem arose around finding the time to practice the exercise at the end of the day after she came home from work.

Although her husband had initially been cooperative and helpful, after about a week he began to make unfriendly jokes about her practice, and failed to keep their two young children from bothering her during the 10 minutes it took to do the exercise. Joanne tried to switch the practice to her work setting, but found it almost impossible to get the privacy she needed. At the session following the appearance of the problem, Joanne was surprised to find how angry she was at her husband. They both held responsible jobs and thought of themselves as a couple who shared things. In particular, Joanne resented her husband's inability or unwillingness to give her 10 minutes a day when she regularly was called on to give him an hour or more undisturbed while he tinkered with his home computer. The whole issue, she half-joked, was "a real pain in the neck."

Joanne was not willing to abandon her home practice of self-hypnosis, and shared her feelings of anger and resentment with her husband later that week. They were both surprised at the explosion that ensued and, somewhat shaken, showed up together for Joanne's next session with me. They were a basically healthy and loving couple, and two conjoint sessions clarified the marital issues enough for Joanne to be able to resume her practice undisturbed. Her husband, it turned out, had been badly frightened by the auto accident that had caused Joanne's whiplash, although he had not been in the car when it occurred. He had experienced nightmares and disturbing daytime fantasies of her dying and of being left alone with their children, and these had only begun to diminish around the time they came to see me. Joanne was surprised by this glimpse of her husband's vulnerability, which he acknowledged in the sessions, and was able to integrate it into a more mature and realistic view of him and of their marriage. They both faced, but did not try to modify, the fact that Joanne was regularly called upon to give more, and do more, at home. When her pain was gone a few months later, she stopped her regular self-hypnosis practice.

Joanne's case illustrates a process that often occurs in less dramatic form whenever a change is made in family routines. In her case, a brief therapeutic intervention put things back on a healthy and mutually acceptable course. Sometimes more serious family or other interpersonal problems can surface in this clinical setting. The decision as to whether and how to intervene will depend in these situations on the nature of your training and practice and on the needs and resources of the patient and his family. The other alternatives for adaptation that I mentioned earlier are sometimes appropriate: concealing the practice of self-hypnosis or abandoning it if that is impossible.

Not all family or interpersonal side-effects of self-hypnosis are negative, however. For many patients who use self-hypnosis successfully for symptom relief, the physical and emotional energy freed up is channeled into improvements in a wide range of relationships. The beneficiaries of this improvement appreciate and support continued practice of the exercise. Friends and relatives who hear of symptom relief may call you directly or request referrals so that they too can benefit. Few communities are overloaded with able clinicians who also are skilled at applying hypnosis therapeutically.

Sometimes family or friends of a patient who has learned self-hypnosis will ask him to teach them the exercise himself. At one of our first sessions, I explicitly request that my patients *do not* teach anyone else the B.H.E. exercise. This ensures that subsequent discussion of this issue is not unrealistically focused on the particular friend or family member who made the request. I take this position for two reasons. First, I am teaching self-hypnosis in a therapeutic context that includes much more than the relatively simple exercise. Second, my position shifts the burden away from the patient for refusing to share with friends or family the substance of his therapeutic interaction with me.

When the requests are expressions of friendly contagious enthusiasm, I will often suggest that the patient teach a friend or family member the Chevreul pendulum or hand-separation procedures, as described in Chapter 4. I make clear in this setting that these are not hypnosis, but are interesting scientific phenomena that can give a person an idea of the kinds of processes and effects that are involved. This sometimes resolves the issue with good will and satisfaction all around. I don't want to take the fun out of hypnosis for the patient or for anyone else.

Staying With It, and Stopping

To the extent that an author and a reader share something in the experience of a book, we have come together to the last section of the last chapter. In the previous sections of this chapter, I have stressed both the problems and the opportunities that arise in the clinical use of self-hypnosis because the important work occurs outside of your office and beyond your direct control. So it is with you, and me, now. What your experience of hypnosis will be beyond this point and what you do with it are in your hands. That is fine with me, as it should be with someone who believes in and uses self-hypnosis. Let me finish with a few words on timing—when to stay with self-hypnosis, and when to stop.

I generally tell patients that they will have a good idea of whether and how self-hypnosis will be of benefit for their problem after about four sessions. This usually means an evaluation period of one or two months, and includes two sessions devoted to basic acquisition of the skill and two devoted primarily to application, with regular practice between sessions. If you have followed my basic guidelines in Chapter 3, you will have a baseline rate for the symptom against which to evaluate the effect of the B.H.E. exercise.

As described in Chapter 3, my bottom line question is: "Is your symptom better, worse, or the same, since you have been doing the exercise? If better (or worse), is it a little better or much better?" It is a tough question for any treatment, but the one that needs to be asked. If you have followed the guidelines in this book in selecting and teaching your patient, the answers will be positive frequently enough to keep you going. Until you and your patient can get a feeling for what the answer will be, you should both stay with it and persevere with practice and adjustment of the exercise.

If the symptom is improved at this initial evaluation point, I usually continue with scheduled sessions every two weeks to monthly until a) the improvement stops, b) the problem goes away, or c) the patient cannot or will not continue. The patient population that you deal with will have the most influence on what proportion of the people you treat using self-hypnosis falls into each of these three groups.

As a beginner, and for a general standard, it is not a bad idea to critically evaluate whether or not you should continue after about a dozen or so sessions with a given patient. Sometimes the self-hypnosis exercise has become an excuse, albeit a valid one, for ongoing and successful supportive or insight-oriented psychotherapy. In other cases, continued tinkering with and reinforcement of the exercise allow it to grow and change to deal with a changing symptom picture (not infrequent with serious and/or chronic illnesses). Remember that even slight improvement in a target symptom at acceptable cost and risk is OK, and is a good reason to stay with the treatment. It's not a bad idea to keep going, but both you and your patient should know why.

Learn how, and when, to stop. When the therapeutic relationship and/or the treatment with self-hypnosis doesn't work, there is usually little trouble deciding on termination. If you did your preliminary work well and did not encourage inflated expectations, this can usually be done calmly and cordially. The situation is a good deal more complicated when the treatment *does* work. I think this is one of the places where there is still a good deal of art and intuition involved in clinical hypnosis, because you want to stop treatment *just before* your patient and/or you lose confidence or interest in the process. Just as when you show friends your slides from Maine, your new magic trick, or your latest research project, you want to leave people wanting more, not looking for an excuse to leave.

If you have seen your patient for more than a few sessions, it is often a good idea to taper the sessions rather than discontinue abruptly, as with any significant counseling or psychotherapy relationship. I usually leave termination open-ended, assuring the patient that he can call me in the future if new problems arise or new issues need to be explored.

Now the time and place have come for me to stop. I wish you no more nor less from your use of self-hypnosis than I have had: the opportunity to turn a human talent into a healing skill, to explore qualities of the human mind that are often hidden or unused, to help, and to enjoy.

APPENDIX A

Resource Guide to Further Training

*Supervision, Consultation, and
Advanced Training*

The material presented in this book is meant to help you in your initial clinical experiences with using hypnosis. As explained in the section on "Your Personal Experience of Hypnosis" in Chapter 1, the ideal introductory learning experience is a well-conducted workshop, with group supervision or individual supervision by an experienced clinician as offering some, but not all, of the benefits of the workshop format. This same hierarchy applies, I believe, to more advanced training in hypnosis when you are trying to explore new areas of application or acquire new hypnotic skills. My recommendations concerning workshops are outlined in the next section of this appendix.

There is another kind of help needed by most clinicians that may not be provided best in a group or workshop setting: supervision and consultation about specific cases, especially those that present problems. Here the optimal setting may be a session with a supervisor or consultant whose role in that situation is to help you with specific cases and thereby improve your level of clinical skill. For supervision concerning cases where you are using hypnosis, the most important qualification is that the clinician be expert in the diagnosis and treatment of the problems presented by your patient; specific expertise in clinical hypnosis is *second* in importance to overall clinical wisdom and judgment. The phase of accumulating clinical experience with hypnosis after you have learned the basic technique and tried it with a few patients is a particularly good time to get this kind of supervision or consultation.

Hypnosis Societies and Workshops

There are a number of professional and lay organizations that offer workshops on hypnosis, publish bulletins or journals on the subject, or offer other benefits of membership. It can be difficult (and sometimes impossible) to distinguish among them substantively through their names — some of the least

189

professional have the most august titles. The field of hypnosis, unfortunately, has attracted more than its share of quacks, including some practitioners with absolutely no legitimate professional training. As you have already discovered, there is nothing particularly difficult about inducing hypnosis in cooperative subjects. In fact, a single-minded emphasis on hypnotic technique is very frequent among nonprofessional hypnotists who lack legitimate clinical training.

For these reasons, I take a very conservative position on hypnosis organizations; this position is an extension of the approach that I have presented in the rest of this book. Consequently, I would recommend only one group of hypnosis societies: those that are Constituent Societies of the International Society of Hypnosis (ISH), which is "dedicated to improving clinical practice and research, as well as both formal and informal communication pertinent to the scientific use of hypnosis. . . . Hypnosis is viewed not as an independent science but rather in the broader context of the psychological and neurological sciences" (p. v, ISH Directory, 1985). Fortunately, the ISH has constituent societies around the world.

In the United States, there is an additional scientific group which it may be helpful to know about:

American Psychological Association
Division 30, Psychological Hypnosis
1200 Seventeenth St., N.W.
Washington, DC 20036

Below, I have provided a listing of the ISH Constituent Societies, along with the current mailing address for correspondence concerning membership and workshops. More complete information, including membership requirements and telephone numbers, is provided for the two USA constituent societies:

AUSTRALIA

Australian Society of Hypnosis
P.O. Box 366
Glenelg, SA 5045,
Australia

AUSTRIA

Osterreichische Gesellschaft Für
  Autogenes Training und Allgemeine
  Psychotherapie
Dr. Siegfried Odehnal, Secretary
Schelleingasse 8
Wien A-1040, Austria

BRAZIL

Sociedade Brasileira de Hipnose
Dr. David Akstein, Correspondent
Av. Mem de Sa 197
Rio de Janeiro, 20230,
Brazil

Sociedade de Hipnose Medica de São
  Paulo
Dr. Jose Monteiro, Correspondent
Rua Cincinato Brago 184
São Paulo 01333,
Brazil

CANADA

Ontario Society of Clinical Hypnosis
Mrs. Lee Marks, Executive Secretary
200 St. Clair Avenue West, Ste. 402
Toronto, Ontario M4V 1R1
Canada

FINLAND

Tieteellinen Hypnoosi-Vetenskaplig
  Hypnos
Mr. Leo Hilden, Secretary
Ulvilantie 29E
Helsinki 00350,
Finland

GREAT BRITAIN

British Society of Experimental and
  Clinical Hypnosis
Dr. Michael Heap, Secretary
St. Augustine's Hospital
Canterbury, Kent CT4 7LL,
England

British Society of Medical and Dental
  Hypnosis
Mrs. M. Samuels, Executive Secretary
42 Links Road
Ashtead, Surrey, KT21 2HJ,
England

INDIA

Indian Society for Clinical and
  Experimental Hypnosis
Dr. H. Jana, Correspondent
Municipal Officers Quarters
Udyan Marg, Ellis Bridge
Ahmedabad, Gujarat 380006,
India

IRELAND

Irish Society for Clinical and
  Experimental Hypnosis
Dr. Dennis Baily, Secretary-Treasurer
6 The Lawn
Woodpark, Ballinteer, Dublin 16
Ireland

ISRAEL

Israel Society for Clinical and
  Experimental Hypnosis
Dr. Karl Fuchs, Correspondent
44 Hanassi Avenue
Haifa 34643,
Israel

ITALY

Centro Studi di Ipnosi Clinica e
  Psicoterapia "H. Bernheim"
Dr. Gualtiero Guantieri,
  Correspondent
Via Valverde 65
Verona 37122,
Italy

NETHERLANDS

Nederlandse Vereniging Voor
  Hypnotherapie
F. P. Bannink, drs., Secretary
Bachplein 47
Berkel en Rodenrijs 2651 TZ
Netherlands

NORWAY

Norwegian Society of Clinical and
  Experimental Hypnosis
Dr. Gunnar Rosen, Correspondent
University of Bergen
Bergen N-5000
Norway

SCOTLAND

Scottish Branch – British Society of
  Medical and Dental Hypnosis
Dr. M. S. Seltzer, Secretary
5 Arran Drive
Glasgow G46 7NL,
Scotland

SINGAPORE

Singapore Society of Clinical Hypnosis
Dr. Dominic Leung, Secretary
#05-03 Yen San Building

Orchard Road
Singapore 0923,
Singapore

REPUBLIC OF SOUTH AFRICA

South Africa Society of Clinical
  Hypnosis
Ms. Pam Tilley, Secretary
P.O. Box 52893
Saxonwold, Johannesburg, 2132,
Republic of South Africa

SWEDEN

Swedish Society for Clinical and
  Experimental Hypnosis
Mr. Kjell Waara, Correspondent
Box 269
Nykoping S-611 26,
Sweden

UNITED STATES OF AMERICA

The American Society of Clinical
  Hypnosis
William F. Hoffman, Jr.
Executive Vice President
2250 East Devon Avenue
Suite 336
Des Plaines, IL 60018

Telephone: (312) 297-3317

ASCH membership and associate membership are open to professionals holding the degrees of M.D., D.D.S., D.M.D., D.O., or a Ph.D. or equivalent doctoral degree with psychology as the major study from accredited institutions, who are licensed to practice in their state of residence and are members of or eligible for membership in a professional society consistent with their degree. Appropriate professional training and experience in clinical or experimental hypnosis are required for full membership. Associate and student affiliate memberships are also available for qualified professionals and professional students who are in the process of acquiring the clinical experience, education, and training for full membership status.

The Society for Clinical and
  Experimental Hypnosis
Mrs. Marion Kenn
Administrative Director
129-A Kings Park Drive
Liverpool, NY 13090

Telephone: (315) 652-7299

SCEH membership is open to professionals holding the degrees of D.D.S., D.M.D., M.D., D.O., Ph.D. or Ed.D. (Psychology), Psy.D., M.S.W. (Clinical), or D.S.W., who are members of the American Dental, Medical, or Psychological Associations. Social workers must be listed or eligible for listing in either the *NASW Register of Clinical Social Workers* or the *National Register of Health Care Providers in Clinical Social Work*. Associate members must have completed one or more approved courses in hypnosis. Full members, in addition, must have provided evidence of competence in practice and/or research (on the basis of approved publication or national level presentation) in the field of hypnosis. Student affiliate memberships are also available for qualified students in the above professional disciplines.

WEST GERMANY

Deutsche Gesellschaft für Ärtzliche
  Hypnose und Autogenes Training
Dr. med. E. Schafgen, Secretary
Brinderkrankenhaus
Saffig D-5471
West Germany

Deutsche Gesellschaft für Klinische
  und Experimentelle Hypnose
Mrs. J. Buchanan, Correspondent
Gerokstrasse 65
Stuttgart 1 D-7000
West Germany

German Society of Hypnosis
Dr. Walter Bongartz, Correspondent
University of Konstanz
Konstanz 7750
West Germany

Qualified professionals in nations that do not have Constituent Societies may apply directly to the ISH for membership:

International Society of Hypnosis
Central Office
111 North 49th Street, Box 17
Philadelphia, PA 19139

Telephone: (215) 748-2161

Wherever you live, you should be able to meet and learn from colleagues associated with one of these ISH Constituent Societies. Even if you do not have a local society convenient to where you are, you can still attend a workshop sponsored by one of them. These are usually held as part of their annual meetings, and include both beginning and advanced workshops for members of the major professional disciplines who use hypnosis. Specialized workshops are often available in areas such as pain control, forensic hypnosis, and hypnoanalysis.

If for any reason you are unable to attend a meeting or workshop sponsored by an ISH constituent society, the best standard for evaluting workshops or professionals offering supervision is their affiliation with a university, hospital, or clinic that you trust and that has a good reputation in your community. A number of these institutions regularly offer excellent workshops or special lectures on hypnosis either using members of their own staffs or bringing in recognized outside experts.

APPENDIX B

Annotated Basic Bibliography

This introduction to the clinical uses of self-hypnosis has intentionally kept scientific references to a minimum. However, as you begin to work with the technique, you will want to know more about hypnosis in general and about other views of self-hypnosis. For this reason, I have included brief reviews of what I consider the most useful books in the area, focusing on how and why a particular book is relevant to a user of the B.H.E. exercise.

Basic Books

1. Bowers, K. S. *Hypnosis for the seriously curious* (second edition). New York: W. W. Norton & Company, 1983. (176 pp., references and indices)

For the clinician who is looking for an introduction to the literature dealing with the nature of hypnosis and who has a limited research background, Kenneth Bowers' succinct book would be my first recommendation. Despite its succinctness, the book is scholarly and scientific — the phrase "for the seriously curious" in the title is an apt one. A number of the issues that I have mentioned but have not discussed, such as the debate over whether and how hypnotic behavior can be faked, or hypnosis as a state vs. hypnotic responsivity as a trait, are dealt with in detail here.

The discussions are clear, move along in a logical way, and contain well-chosen quotations and examples that give the reader a good flavor of the original sources. There is a nice balance between simplification and technical detail, without too much of either. Clinicians will find the summary and discussion of the research on hypnotic analgesia particularly interesting; it provides a nice complement to the clinical material on this subject presented in this book.

2. Crasilneck, H. B., & Hall, J. A. *Clinical hypnosis: Principles and applications* (second edition). Orlando: Grune & Stratton, 1985. (486 pp., references and index)

This is, in my opinion, the best of the available books that attempt to present a comprehensive guide to clinical applications of hypnosis. The 1985 second edition includes some of the more recent research and clinical contributions that are missing from other standard works of this type. The authors have a medical orientation, and this book will be especially useful to clinicians who work in hospitals or with hospitalized patients.

There are specific chapters on pain control, anesthesia, cancer patients, pediatric problems, dermatological problems, dental hypnosis, and other specialized applications. These sections, as well as the ones on hypnosis in general and on specific hypnotic techniques, are clearly written and contain enough specific scripts to give you an idea of just how to proceed. Although there is a chapter on self-hypnosis and several applications of self-hypnosis to specific clinical problems, most of the material in this book involves hetero- rather than self-hypnosis. After you have mastered some of the basic applications of the B.H.E. exercise, it is probably a good idea to try some hetero-hypnotic techniques, as well as some other approaches to self-hypnosis.

Crasilneck and Hall write with the authority of long and varied clinical experience, and of participation in and leadership of the wider community of clinicians and researchers involved with hypnosis. One of the most valuable features of this book is that it reminds clinicians of what *not* to do as well as giving positive "how-to" advice. These precautions are contained both in a chapter on the topic and in specific cautions inserted into the sections where they apply. Although Crasilneck and Hall are open to and describe a variety of hypnotic approaches, they insist on professionalism, which is the best protection for *both* clinicians and patients.

3. Frankel, F. H. *Hypnosis: Trance as a coping mechanism*. New York: Plenum Medical Book Company, 1976. (185 pp., bibliography and index)

You can get an idea of the high regard in which I hold Fred Frankel's book from the number of times I have referred to it in my own discussions in these pages. For mental health clinicians, it is the wisest, most realistic presentation of the clinical applications of self-hypnosis that I know of. To make it even more useful, the first 54 pages are devoted to a balanced and readable presentation of the history of hypnosis, major theoretical positions about the nature of hypnosis, and specific issues including susceptibility scales, correlates of hypnotizability, concepts of hypnotic depth, altered states of consciousness, and Ernest Hilgard's neodissociation theory.

All this historical, research, and theoretical material is integrated into a clinical approach to patients that has been, and will continue to be, a model to be emulated. A theme that runs through the book concerns the hypnosis-like phenomena that appear in a number of syndromes, including those of some hysterical and phobic patients, and the possibility of using hypnosis to convert these experiences in a treatment context to sources of reassurance and self-control.

What makes this book so especially useful to practicing clinicians is the remarkable series of detailed case histories. The fact that there is a chapter devoted to therapeutic failures merely emphasizes a tone throughout of appropriate scientific and clinical humility that makes me, for one, much more confident in the positive findings and suggested explanations. The cases described range from hysterical fugue to fear of dentistry, but all include a clear presentation of the clinical problem, the application of hypnosis to that problem in that patient, and the subsequent clinical course. My own favorite is the presentation of the extended treatment of a 37-year-old accountant with psoriasis (pp. 156–162) that embodies almost all of the clinical principles that I have stressed in these pages. In particular, the case makes it clear that self-hypnosis, sensibly and sensitively applied, can make a significant positive difference in the lives of people with chronic illness who are not cured, and perhaps never will be.

4. Gardner, G. G., & Olness, K. *Hypnosis and hypnotherapy with children*. New York: Grune & Stratton, 1981. (397 pp., appendices including Children's Hypnotic Susceptibility Scale and Stanford Hypnotic Clinical Scale for Children, and index)

For clinicians who work with children, this collaborative effort of a clinical child psychologist and a pediatrician is the standard source on clinical hypnosis. As with

Crasilneck and Hall's *Clinical Hypnosis*, the range of subjects covered and the basic approach are distinctly medical, making it especially valuable for clinicians who work in hospital settings or with seriously ill children.

The book includes brief and readable sections on the major issues in hypnosis research and practice as they apply to children. Chapter 5 is an excellent presentation of hypnotic induction techniques for children that includes plenty of specific quotations to provide guidance for age-appropriate wording. There are detailed sections on appropriate hypnotic interventions in a wide range of specific conditions ranging from needle phobia to hemophilia. These include discussions of applications, such as attempts to increase I.Q. in children with primary mental retardation, where hypnosis is *not* effective. Sections like these may allow a clinician to help a parent reach emotional closure in accepting a handicap, rather than stimulating unrealistic expectations.

A special and valuable feature of this volume is the inclusion of two of the standard hypnosis scales for children as appendices. The relatively brief Stanford Hypnotic Clinical Scale for Children may be especially useful for clinicians who have learned and used the B.H.E. induction and evaluation form with adults.

5. Hilgard, E. R. *The experience of hypnosis*. New York: Harcourt Brace Jovanovich, 1968. (A shorter version of *Hypnotic susceptibility*. New York: Harcourt, Brace & World, 1965.) (353 pp., bibliography and index)

Ernest Hilgard's classic is one of the basic books in any serious library about hypnosis and a good introduction to the combination of scientific elegance and clearly communicated common sense that have made him a leader in the field. There are chapters on the nature of hypnosis, the role of an induction, aftereffects, attitude and personality factors, and a number of things that "the hypnotized person can do and experience."

Beginning clinicians will find this latter section (Part II of the book) an excellent introduction to the many aspects of hypnosis that the B.H.E. induction and the clinical applications that I have presented leave unexplored. These include challenge items, negative hallucinations, hypnotic dreams, age regression, post-hypnotic amnesia, and other post-hypnotic suggestions. This list includes several inherently dramatic and chronically controversial phenomena, making a sensible, scientifically based approach like Dr. Hilgard's even more important than usual. The exploration of what is normal, in the research sense of this term, for each of these phenomena formed the basis of the various Stanford hypnosis scales (described elsewhere in this appendix), which are mentioned in *The Experience of Hypnosis* and discussed in greater detail in *Hypnotic Susceptibility*.

The final section of the book offers parallel discussions of developmental, interactive, and state aspects of hypnosis. The concept of dissociations and their role in hypnosis has been developed and extended in clinically relevant ways in Dr. Hilgard's later book, *Divided Consciousness: Multiple Controls in Human Thought and Action* (New York: John Wiley & Sons, 1977).

6. Hilgard, E. R., & Hilgard, J. R. *Hypnosis in the relief of pain*. (Revised Edition) Los Altos: William Kaufmann, Inc., 1983. (294 pp., appendices including SHCS, references, and index)

If you are using the B.H.E. exercise clinically for pain relief, I would recommend this book as a solid theoretical and practical foundation on this topic. The Hilgards have produced an excellent combination of research and clinical perspectives along with enough case examples to provide clinicians with useful guidance.

The book is divided into three parts. Part I deals with theoretical issues of hypnosis, pain, and their interaction. Part II is concerned with hypnosis and clinical pain, and devotes sections to cancer, obstetrics, surgery, and dentistry. This last section will be especially useful to practicing dentists, and like the others includes references to a number of significant research projects and case studies.

The final section of this book describes the discovery of the "hidden observer" of covert pain and its implications for the dissociative aspects of hypnosis, which are developed even further in *Divided Consciousness*. The 1983 Revised Edition concludes with a succinct update (Chapter 11) on developments in the research and clinical aspects of this field since the 1975 original publication date. There is a clarification of the role of hypnosis in the treatment of psychogenic vs. organic pain, and a valuable set of criteria for clinicians to use in preparing case reports on the use of hypnosis in pain (p. 236). A special feature of this book is the inclusion as Appendix A of the Stanford Hypnotic Clinical Scale (SHCS), a brief, clinically oriented scale that includes a scripted induction and complete scoring instructions. The SHCS is a useful contrast and supplement to the B.H.E. induction and evaluation form, and is described in greater detail below in the section on standardized scales.

7. Hilgard, J. R. *Personality and hypnosis: A study of imaginative involvement* (second edition). Chicago: The University of Chicago Press, 1979. (309 pp., bibliography and indices)

Josephine Hilgard's book is a model for the creative interaction of clinical and research skills. It is based on an extensive series of carefully rated interviews that brought her to the concept of "imaginative involvement" in activities such as reading, drama, sports, or nature, and to an understanding of the developmental roots of these involvements through the influence of an involved parent. The concrete, human details that fill this book are useful for any clinician working with the B.H.E. or any self-hypnosis exercise that patients are expected to use on their own. They provide guidelines for exploring and encouraging linkages between hypnosis and related "positive, pleasurable experiences" that patients engage in and enjoy in their own time and space. The concept of imaginative involvement presented by Dr. Hilgard is similar to the personality factor of "absorption" elucidated by Tellegen and Atkinson, and which has also been related to hypnotizability.

8. Hilgard, J. R., & LeBaron, S. *Hypnotherapy of pain in children with cancer*. Los Altos: William Kaufmann, 1984. (250 pp., appendices and indices)

For clinicians who work with children suffering from any serious and/or painful condition and who plan to include hypnosis in their treatment approach, this book is essential. As with the other works that have emerged from the Stanford program, it skillfully moves back and forth between the clinical and research domains. The last three chapters present an excellent integration of current perspectives on what hypnosis is, how hypnotic abilities develop, and opportunities for research in the area. The discussion of enactive, relaxation, and imagination components in hypnotic induction and their relationship to waking suggestion and hypnosis without formal induction (pp. 146–153) is a particularly lucid exposition of an area usually clouded by proprietary claims and personal preferences.

Any clinical work with children requires sensitivity to developmental changes and their effect on the clinical task at hand. Josephine Hilgard and Samuel LeBaron provide a wealth of practical help to clinicians in just these areas, including specific techniques that are useful with very young and older children, with those who possess high levels of hypnotic talent and with those who lack it entirely. Examples are the preference of very young children to keep their eyes open, the creative use of whispering to hold a child's attention, the roles of religion and humor, and the imaginative transformation of the odor of alcohol to that of flowers.

9. Sheehan, P. W., & Perry, C. W. *Methodologies of hypnosis: A critical appraisal of contemporary paradigms of hypnosis.* Hillsdale, NJ: Lawrence Erlbaum Associates, 1976. (329 pp., references and indices)

If you have had some background in research or are comfortable reading research literature, this book is probably the best substantial introduction to the different and often conflicting approaches that have been taken to the nature of hypnosis and how it works. The major views that have been listed in this book are discussed in detail, as are a number that have not been mentioned.

The book's coverage includes Ernest Hilgard's modified altered state of awareness model, the operational model of Theodore Barber, the role enactment model of Theodore Sarbin, the credulous vs. skeptical approach of J. Philip Sutcliffe, the real-simulating methodology of Martin Orne, and the interactive research designs of Perry London and Marcus Fuhrer. The most important feature of this presentation is that these views are compared and contrasted in a dispassionate way that emphasizes what each brings to a view of hypnosis and what each leaves unexplored.

10. Shor, R. E., & Orne, M. T. (Eds.) *The nature of hypnosis: Selected basic readings.* New York: Holt, Rinehart and Winston, 1965. (504 pp., references and index)

This is the place to find well-chosen excerpts from the classics on hypnosis. It begins with the "Secret Report on Mesmerism, or Animal Magnetism" that grew out of the commission chaired by Benjamin Franklin and containing Lavoisier and Guillotin among its members. In addition to examples of a number of the research approaches reviewed in *Methodologies of Hypnosis*, two of my favorites are a brief discussion by Sandor Ferenczi of "paternal and maternal hypnosis" and a section covering Milton Erickson's approach that makes it clear why he has had such a major influence on the field.

11. Spiegel, H. S., & Spiegel, D. *Trance and treatment: Clinical uses of hypnosis.* New York: Basic Books, 1978. (382 pp., references and indices)

This book contains the most comprehensive presentation of the methods and theories of a father-son team who have been major exponents of the clinical use of brief self-hypnosis procedures; an early version of the material in this book was one of my own starting points in clinical work with self-hypnosis. The Spiegel method is known as the Hypnotic Induction Profile (HIP). It includes a scripted induction procedure that uses an upward roll of the eyes, eye closure, and hand levitation in fairly rapid sequence. The subject is given a signal for a second hand levitation in a "postceremonial trance" after he has been instructed to open his eyes, and the technique includes structured inquiries about dissociation, control and amnesia. The HIP procedure includes a scripted transition from this hetero-hypnotic induction to instruction in a simple self-hypnosis exercise that shares many features with the B.H.E. exercise that I have presented in this book.

In addition to the basic material on the HIP, *Trance and Treatment* includes sections on the Spiegels' approach to a typology of personality (Apollonians, Odysseans, and Dionysians) and detailed discussions of the hypnotic treatment of a number of important clinical conditions. I have already referred in Chapter 8 to the Spiegel approach to habit disorders. Their approach to smoking control is set out in detail (with a sample session script) in Chapter 13 of *Trance and Treatment*. The following chapter on eating disorders extends their approach to this group of problems without any of the extravagant claims that are so common among clinicians who offer treatment approaches to obesity.

12. Weitzenhoffer, A. M. *General techniques of hypnotism.* New York: Grune & Stratton, 1957. (460 pp., references and indices)

I have emphasized a number of times in these pages that although the procedures associated with the B.H.E. are presented in great detail, this reflects my view on the best way to get beginners at clinical hypnosis started, rather than a conviction that I have discovered the best way to do hypnosis. Despite its age, Andre Weitzenhoffer's standard work remains, in my opinion, the best single source of hypnotic induction techniques and standard suggestions. Here you will find all the items you used to think hypnosis was about: postural sway, locked hands, inability to stand up, burning coins, and even (p. 356) the subject suspended rigid between two chairs. Dr. Weitzenhoffer, an eminent researcher and clinician, is a much better source of information on these phenomena than the popular press or nonprofessional books.

There are plenty of explicit scripts and detailed descriptions to broaden your horizons. In addition to the standard demonstrations described above, there are sections on the use of metronomes and pendulums, group hypnosis, Schultz's autogenic training, and the Chevreul pendulum that are difficult to find in other sources. Most of the induction procedures use sleep terminology ("Your eyes are now closed and you are going deep asleep . . . "), but this can be modified to simple relaxation if, like myself, you prefer not to identify hypnosis with sleep. I should mention that a number of sophisticated clinical hypnotists continue to use sleep terminology because they feel that it still provides the best model for some clinical purposes.

Book Chapters and Papers Referred to in Text

1. Dinges, D. F. The nature and timing of sleep. *Transactions & Studies of the College of Physicians of Philadelphia*, 1984, *6(3)*, 177–206.
2. Orne, M. T. and Dinges, D. F. Hypnosis. In P. D. Wall and R. Melzack (Eds.), *Textbook of Pain.* New York: Churchill Livingstone, 1984, pp. 806–816.
3. Orne, M. T., Soskis, D. A., Dinges, D. F., and Orne, E. C. Hypnotically induced testimony. In G. L. Wells and E. F. Loftus (Eds.), *Eyewitness testimony: Psychological perspectives.* New York: Cambridge University Press, 1984, pp. 171–213.
4. Orne, M. T., Soskis, D. A., Dinges, D. F., Orne, E. C., and Tonry, M. H. *Hypnotically refreshed testimony: Enhanced memory or tampering with evidence?* Washington, D.C.: U.S. Department of Justice, National Institute of Justice, Office of Development, Testing and Dissemination (Issues and Practices in Criminal Justice report), 1985.
5. Wadden, T. A. and Anderton, C. H. The clinical uses of hypnosis. *Psychological Bulletin*, 1982, *91*, 215–243.

Journals

Articles about hypnosis appear occasionally in the major professional journals in medicine, dentistry, psychology, social work, and other disciplines that use or study hypnosis. Each of the major legitimate American hypnosis societies puts out an excellent journal, and these would be my recommended source for the most up-to-date published material on specialized aspects of the field. These journals are:

American Journal of Clinical Hypnosis
    published quarterly by
The American Society of Clinical Hypnosis
2250 East Devon Avenue, Suite 336
Des Plaines, IL 60018

A useful special issue of the AJCH will be mentioned later in this appendix: October 1978/January 1979 (vol. 21, nos. 2 & 3): Measures of hypnotizability.

Three other special AJCH issues frequently requested by clinicians are:
1. July 1977 (vol. 20, no. 1): Milton H. Erickson
2. October 1982/January 1983 (vol. 25, nos. 2 & 3): Hypnosis and cancer.
3. October 1983 (vol. 26, no. 2): Multiple personality.
   These issues may be obtained from the ASCH central office.

The International Journal of Clinical
and Experimental Hypnosis
    published quarterly for
The Society for Clinical and Experimental Hypnosis
Journal address:
The International Journal of Clinical
    and Experimental Hypnosis
111 North 49th Street
Philadelphia, PA 19139

Three special issues of the IJCEH have been mentioned in this book:
1. April 1979 (vol. 27, no. 2): Clinical assessment of hypnotic responsivity.
2. July 1981 (vol. 29, no. 3): Self-hypnosis.
3. October 1982 (vol. 30, no. 4): Measurement of hypnosis in the clinical context.
   Four other IJCEH special issues may be of interest to readers:
1. October 1977 (vol. 25, no. 4): Altered states of consciousness.
2. October 1979 (vol. 27, no. 4): The forensic use of hypnosis.
3. October 1982 (vol. 30, no. 4): 30-year cumulative author index.
4. April 1984 (vol. 32, no. 2): Multiple personality.
   Copies of these special issues may be obtained through the journal office.

Standardized Scales of Hypnotic Responsivity

The Brief Hypnotic Experience induction and evaluation form share a number of features in common with most standardized hypnosis scales: a scripted induction, a series of test suggestions, and several questions about the hypnotic experience whose answers can be combined into a numerical score. If you have learned about hypnosis and its clinical applications through the B.H.E., these common features will make it relatively easy for you to use one or more of the standard scales for clinical or research purposes.

As pointed out in Chapter 5, the B.H.E. evaluation form and the quantitative rating of hypnotic talent that it provides do not have the range or precision of the well established standard scales. In this section, I have provided a brief sketch of the major scales. For readers interested in using and/or learning more about them, I would recommend the special issues of the *American Journal of Clinical Hypnosis* and of *The International Journal of Clinical and Experimental Hypnosis* devoted to this topic which have been listed in the previous section of this appendix (AJCH October 1978/ January 1979; IJCEH April 1979 and October 1982).

The foundation of the hypnosis scales in current use are the various *Stanford Hypnotic Susceptibility Scales* developed by Ernest Hilgard, Andre Weitzenhoffer, and their colleagues:

SHSS (forms A, B, and C): The A and B forms are alternates, and consist of a scripted hetero-hypnotic induction and a series of test suggestions. Each of 12 test items is scored by the hypnotist as pass or fail, yielding a score of 0–12. The 12 items are: postural sway, eye closure, hand lowering, arm immobilization, finger lock, arm rigidity, moving hands together, verbal inhibition (can't say name), fly hallucination, eye catalepsy (can't open eyes), post-hypnotic suggestion (changes chairs), and temporary amnesia for the hypnotic experiences. The C form contains some items similar to the A and B, but also moves beyond motor-type suggestions to include positive and negative hallucinations and a hypnotic dream. The content of the dream may be clinically relevant, especially if the test is administered in the context of a therapist-patient relationship. An especially useful feature of the C form is its arrangement in an ascending order of item difficulty. If a subject fails the first few items, the procedure can be stopped with a relatively low risk of missing large areas of hypnotic talent, and without exposing the subject to multiple failures.

The *Stanford Profile Scales of Hypnotic Susceptibility, Forms I and II (SPS:I and II)* go even further than the C form in exploring special aspects of hypnotic talent and phenomena such as selective deafness and automatic writing; a modification of form C called *The Tailored SHSS:C* permits the use of one of these specialized items in place of one of the 12 standard items on the C form in order to tap the benefits of both approaches.

For the clinician interested in a scale of greater range than the B.H.E. evaluation form, the *Stanford Hypnotic Clinical Scales (SHCS: Adult and Child)* may provide an ideal transition to the longer standardized scales. The adult scale includes a scripted, eyes-closed induction that focuses on progressive muscular relaxation and a deepening count from one to 20. This induction is perfectly appropriate for most clinical applications. The test items are: moving hands, a hypnotic dream, an age regression to a happy day in elementary school, a post-hypnotic suggestion (subject coughs or clears throat when hypnotist taps pencil twice), and temporary post-hypnotic amnesia for the hypnotic experience. These items go far beyond those included in the B.H.E. (a hand levitation and an imagined pleasant scene) both in terms of the cognitive distortions involved and the number of dimensions of hypnosis that are explored.

The entire procedure can be administered in 20 minutes or so, making it practical for even a busy clinician. The children's versions contain similar items adapted appropriately. An additional positive feature of these scales is their publication in books that are valuable for clinicians in their own right: the adult form in *Hypnosis in the Relief of Pain* by Ernest and Josephine Hilgard, and the children's form in *Hypnosis and Hypnotherapy with Children* by Gail Gardner and Karen Olness. The latter book also contains Perry London's longer *Children's Hypnotic Susceptibility Scale* as an appendix. Both books are listed in the first section of this appendix. The SHCS: Adult and Child are also included in the October 1978/January 1979 AJCH special issue on measures of hypnotizability.

A well-validated group scale with a tape-recorded induction is available in the *Harvard Group Scale of Hypnotic Susceptibility: Forms A and B (HGSHS:A and B)* developed by Ronald Shor and Emily Orne. The 12 test items on the scale are: head falling, eye closure, hand lowering, arm immobilization, finger lock, arm rigidity, moving hands together, communication inhibition (unable to shake head), fly hallucination, eye catalepsy (can't open eyes), post-hypnotic suggestion to touch ankle, and temporary post-hypnotic amnesia for the hypnotic experiences. As with the B.H.E. evaluation form, the subject scores the test himself. For the HGSHS, each item is scored pass or fail for a total score of 0 to 12. The HGSHS is widely used in research studies as an initial screening device.

Two scales that grew out of the work of Theodore Barber and his colleagues are the *Barber Suggestibility Scale (BSS)* and the *Creative Imagination Scale (CIS)*. Both scales have similar test items to the Stanford scales, but place less of an emphasis on the role of a formal hypnotic induction. The CIS, as its name implies, emphasizes thinking and imagining along with the suggestions to make them happen. It is scored by the subject using a graded rating of the reality of the item during the test compared to its reality if it had actually occurred. The BSS and CIS can both be found in the October 1978/January 1979 AJCH special issue.

Finally, there are two other published scales that are as brief, or briefer, than the Brief Hypnotic Experience induction and evaluation form. The first is the *Hypnotic Induction Profile (HIP)* developed by Herbert Spiegel and presented fully in *Trance and Treatment: Clinical Uses of Hypnosis* (described and referenced earlier in this appendix). The HIP can be scored in several different ways, and includes a transition to a self-hypnosis exercise that the patient does on his own.

The second very brief scale is the *Stanford Hypnotic Arm Levitation Induction and Test (SHALIT)* developed by Ernest Hilgard, Helen Crawford, and Amy Wert. This six-minute procedure involves a scripted, eyes-closed arm levitation induction, with the scoring derived from the measurement of how far the arm rises. The SHALIT is described and contrasted with the HIP and the SHCS:Adult in the April 1979 issue of IJCEH (see previous section of this appendix).

In using a standardized hypnosis scale with a patient, I have generally found it preferable to administer the scale during one of our early sessions. This allows the information from the scale to be used in treatment planning, and also minimizes the importance to the ongoing treatment relationship of how the patient scores on the test. Later on in treatment, when transference factors may be more significant, the content and performance on the test may require some working through. In my own experience, use of a standardized measure of hypnotic responsivity does not interfere with either the process or the results of treatment. I present the scale in a matter-of-fact way, much as an internist would present a glucose tolerance test as a standardized procedure that can supplement the clinical history and physical examination.

* * *

APPENDIX C

Brief Hypnotic Experience
Scripts and Forms

The scripts and forms on the following pages may be reproduced for clinical use, without infringing on the author's copyright.

The Hand-Separation Test

"Look at your hands and note their position . . . Now, close your eyes and listen to what I say. I will be providing the thoughts and images in this exercise, and all you need to do is to concentrate actively on what I say and let whatever happens happen . . . Now, focus your attention on the feelings in your arms and hands and imagine that your right arm is growing heavy and at the same time your left arm is growing light . . . Your right arm is growing heavy . . . heavier and heavier . . . heavier and heavier . . . *very* heavy. At the same time your left arm is growing light . . . lighter and lighter . . . lighter and lighter . . . *very* light."

WAIT FIVE SECONDS AT THIS POINT AND WATCH FOR A RESPONSE. IF THERE IS NO DEFINITE RESPONSE, CONTINUE AS FOLLOWS:

"Concentrate on your hands and arms, just listen and concentrate. You may want to imagine a huge buoyant balloon attached by a soft string or ribbon to your left wrist, gently pulling it up into the air . . . up and up . . . lighter and lighter . . . higher and higher . . . Now shift your attention to your right hand and arm and imagine that several heavy, boring books are attached by a book-strap to your right wrist, pulling it down . . . down . . . further and further down . . . heavier and heavier."

* * *

AT THIS POINT NOTE THE VERTICAL SEPARATION OF THE PATIENT'S HANDS (CENTER TO CENTER) IN INCHES. THE BASIC RATING IS A SEPARATION OF SIX INCHES OR MORE (POSITIVE) VS. A SEPARATION OF LESS THAN SIX INCHES (NEGATIVE). AFTER YOU HAVE RATED THE HAND-SEPARATION, CONCLUDE THE PROCEDURE:

"Now, without moving your hands or arms, open your eyes and note the relative positions of your two hands . . . Now open and close your hands a few times to restore your usual sensation and control."

Visual Target for Chevreul Pendulum

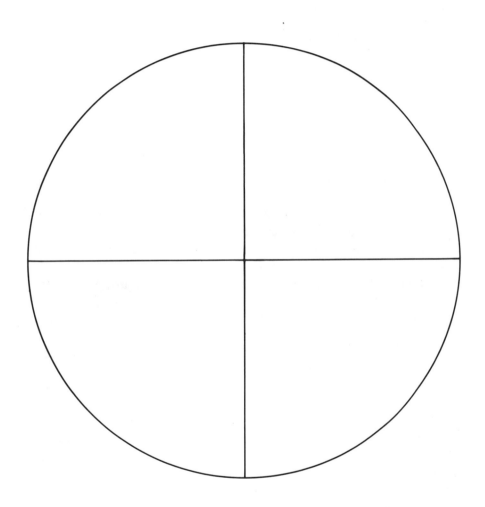

Brief Hypnotic Experience Induction

Just sit comfortably and close your eyes. . . . Listen to what I say and try to think along with and imagine the things I mention. . . . Don't try to force anything; just let things happen as they occur. . . . In this session, I will act as a coach and guide you, so that you will be able later to learn to enter hypnosis yourself. . . . Now focus your attention on your left hand. . . . Become aware of all the sensations in your hand and of any movements that occur. . . . These sensations and movements are always present, but we are not usually aware of them. You may notice a mild tingling sensation, or feel some small twitches in the muscles of your hand . . . or the feeling of weight as your hand rests on the chair (your leg, bed), or perhaps the sensation of your pulse beating in one of your fingers. You are curious about what will happen and open to the experience.

Now, as you continue to focus on your left hand, you will notice a sensation of lightness developing. First in the fingers and then spreading to the entire hand. As the lightness spreads, your hand will gradually float off the arm of the chair (your leg, the bed) and up into the air as your wrist or elbow bends to allow the hand to float upwards. Pay close attention and see which finger will move first. . . . A pleasant sensation of lightness . . . lighter and lighter, floating upward effortlessly . . . lighter and lighter. . . . As the sensation of lightness spreads, the fingers begin to lift, bit by bit . . . bit by bit . . . up into the air . . . floating . . . floating . . . higher . . . higher.

If you like, you can imagine that a huge buoyant balloon is attached by a soft string or ribbon to your left wrist. Imagine the balloon tugging gently at your hand. Gently lifting it up . . . higher . . . higher . . . gently lifting. Or, you may want to imagine some other image that is more comfortable for you, such as a magnetic force, or a gentle breeze with your hand light as a feather. Just let it float upwards gradually . . . higher and higher . . . lighter and lighter . . . higher and higher.

Now, take three deep, relaxing breaths and let the floating feeling in your left hand spread throughout your body as the left hand settles back down. As it does, your usual sensation and control in your left hand return.

Now, I'm going to begin counting slowly from one to ten. As I count, you will feel your body relaxing more and more, as you feel yourself floating into a deeper and deeper state of hypnosis, until at the count of ten you will be deeply relaxed and in a pleasant, comfortable hypnotic state.

ONE – Let your hands and forearms relax. . . .

TWO – Let the relaxation spread to your upper arms. . . .

THREE – Let all the muscles in your shoulders and neck relax . . . more and more relaxed . . . deeper and deeper. . . .

FOUR – Your scalp and your forehead. . . .

FIVE – Now, let the relaxation spread to the muscles of your face . . . to your eyes, your nose and mouth, to your jaw. . . .

SIX – Let your chest and your upper back relax, deeply and comfortably. . . .

SEVEN – Your lower back and abdomen . . . deeper and deeper. . . .

EIGHT – Let the relaxation spread down through your upper legs to your knees. . . .

NINE – To your lower legs, all the way down to your feet. . . .

TEN – If there are any areas of tension remaining anywhere in your body, just let the relaxation extend to these areas now as well . . . to your whole body, now deeply, evenly, completely relaxed. . . .

You are now in a relaxed, pleasant hypnotic state. You can hear what I say clearly, and respond to ideas and images that I will present that are acceptable to you. You are in complete control and will always be able to respond appropriately in any emergency. Deeply relaxed, and in a calm, pleasant hypnotic state. You will be able to remember the feeling that you have now and return to it when you want to.

Now, you are going to be able to use hypnosis to experience a very pleasant scene. Just let yourself travel in your imagination to a warm, pleasant beach. Perhaps it is a beach that you have actually visited in the past, or it may be an imaginary beach that you construct for yourself. . . . It's very pleasant, safe and warm.

You are sitting or lying comfortably. Above you, the sky is clear and blue with a few fluffy white clouds floating overhead. . . . Out in front of you is the water. You watch the waves coming in and perhaps some sailboats out in the distance. You can hear the sound of the waves . . . a very regular, soothing sound. The air smells and tastes fresh and clean. . . . The sun is warm and comfortable. You can feel it warming your body and warming the beach beneath you. . . . It's a beautiful day – you're feeling at peace and relaxed. . . . Just enjoy this scene now for a while on your own. . . .

(*Wait one minute while the patient enjoys the beach scene, then continue:*)

You will be able to return to this pleasant scene in hypnosis whenever you want to. Remember how you feel right now. . . . You may want to think of one or two words that express how you feel . . . words like "clear and calm" or "warm and relaxed" . . . (or [the patient's key phrase, if you are using one]) . . . whatever words are best for you. . . .

Next, I am going to teach you a simple self-hypnosis exercise that will allow you on your own to do and experience all the things we have just done now. Just listen as I describe the experience and let it enter your mind. Don't worry about responding or about remembering the details; I will give you the exercise later in written form to take with you.

The exercise I am going to teach you now follows directly and naturally from what you have just experienced and done. To do the exercise, find a time of day when you can have ten minutes without interruptions. Get into a comfortable position in a location as free as possible from noise and distractions; make sure that your left hand can move freely. If you are using a timer, set it for ten minutes.

When you are ready, close your eyes and let yourself remember the feeling of hypnosis. Direct your attention to your left hand. Allow it to become light and experience the feeling of it floating upwards. If you are in a public place, you can allow just your left forefinger to float up, or merely experience the feeling without any actual movement.

When you have the feeling of floating in your left hand, that will be a signal for you to take three breaths. When you do the exercise on your own, say to yourself: "I'm taking three deep, relaxing breaths and letting the floating feeling spread throughout my body." As the floating feeling spreads, your left hand will settle back down, with its usual sensation and control.

You then continue to yourself: "Now, I'm deepening the experience by counting slowly from one to ten." As your count, you let your body relax more and more, until at the count of ten you are in a deeply relaxed, pleasant, comfortable hypnotic state.

At *one*, you let your hands and forearms relax. . . . *Two*: let the relaxation spread to your upper arms. . . . *Three*: let all the muscles in your shoulders and neck relax. . . . *Four*: your scalp and your forehead. . . . *Five*: let the relaxation spread to the muscles of your face

. . . to your eyes, your nose and mouth, to your jaw. . . . *Six*: let your chest and your upper back relax. . . . *Seven*: your lower back and abdomen. . . . *Eight*: let the relaxation spread down through your upper legs to your knees. . . . *Nine*: to your lower legs, all the way down to your feet. . . . And — *ten*: if there are any areas of tension remaining anywhere in your body, just let the relaxation extend to those areas as well, so that your whole body is deeply, evenly, completely relaxed.

You can then use the hypnotic state to help yourself achieve whatever goals you have chosen. You can say to yourself: "Now I'm experiencing a pleasant, peaceful, relaxing time, just as when I was at the beach. I can even see the clear blue sky with the fluffy white clouds; I can hear the soothing sounds of the waves and feel the warm sun. I feel clear and calm (*or key phrase, if using one*); . . . I am at peace." Let yourself enjoy this experience while you remain comfortably relaxed until you hear the sound of the timer or decide that the time is up.

When you are ready, you can end the exercise and come out of hypnosis by counting backward to yourself slowly from five to one, just as I will be counting for you in a little while. At the count of two your eyes will open, and at the count of one you will be fully awake, alert, feeling pleasantly refreshed, and with your usual sensation and control. You should flex and relax your muscles a few times before standing up.

The more you practice this exercise, the easier it will become to do and the more effective it will be to help you achieve your goals.

([*If using key phrase:*] Even when you are not doing the exercise, you will be able to use your key phrase to bring back some of the feeling of being _____ and _____ , . . . _____ and _____ .)

Now, I am going to count backward from five to one, just as you will do when you do the exercise by yourself. At the count of two your eyes will open, and at the count of one your hypnotic experience will be over and you will be fully awake, alert and refreshed. Ready now . . .

FIVE — You are beginning to become more alert. . . .

FOUR — Coming out now. . . .

THREE — Feeling good. . . .

TWO — Eyes open. . . .

ONE — Alert and refreshed!

* * *

(Make sure the patient flexes and relaxes his muscles a few times before standing up, and that you take time to inquire about his experience and answer any questions he may have. This is the time to have the patient fill out the Brief Hypnotic Experience evaluation form if you will be using it. The self-hypnosis exercise instructions should be given to the patient before he leaves.)

Brief Hypnotic Experience Evaluation Form

Please choose the response option that best describes your experience, and circle the appropriate number to the left of the option (1-4).

Hand Lightness and Rising:

A. To an outside observer, my hand would have appeared
   1. not to have moved at all.
   2. to have moved a little but not really risen.
   3. to have risen less than 6 inches.
   4. to have risen 6 inches or more.

B. My hand
   1. did not feel light at all.
   2. felt a little light.
   3. felt moderately light.
   4. felt very light.

C. When my hand felt light and/or floated up,
   1. I felt like I was helping it along.
   2. though I felt like I was helping it along, there was some movement on its own.
   3. my hand seemed to move by itself, but I felt like I was helping it along somewhat.
   4. my hand seemed to move up by itself, without effort on my part.

Experience of the Beach Scene:

D. For me, the sensory experiences of the scene (sights, sounds, body feelings, smells, temperatures, tastes) were
   1. absent.
   2. faint.
   3. moderately vivid.
   4. very vivid.

E. During the beach scene
   1. I had no feeling of actual participation.
   2. I was mostly an observer with a slight sense of participating.
   3. I had some sense of actually participating in the experience.
   4. I felt like I was really there.

General Evaluation:

F. I found the experience of hypnosis
   1. unpleasant.
   2. neutral.
   3. moderately pleasant.
   4. quite pleasant.

Self-Hypnosis Exercise Instructions

1) Find a time of day when you can have ten minutes without interruptions.

2) Get into a comfortable position in a location as free as possible from noise and distractions. If you are using a timer, set it for ten minutes.

3) Close your eyes and let yourself remember the feeling of hypnosis.

4) Direct your attention to your left hand. Allow it to become light and experience the feeling of it floating upwards.

5) Say to yourself, "I'm taking three deep, relaxing breaths and letting the floating feeling spread throughout my body."

6) Continue, "Now, I'm deepening the experience by counting slowly from one to ten. As I say *one*, I begin by relaxing my hands and forearms. . . . *Two*, I let the relaxation spread to my upper arms. . . . *Three*, I let my shoulders and neck relax . . . more and more relaxed, deeper and deeper. . . . *Four*, my scalp and my forehead. . . . *Five*, now I let the relaxation spread to the muscles of my face, to my eyes, my mouth, and my jaw. . . . *Six*, I let my chest and my upper back relax, deeply and comfortably. . . . *Seven*, my lower back and abdomen. . . . *Eight*, I let the relaxation spread down through my upper legs to my knees. . . . *Nine*, to my lower legs, all the way down to my feet. . . . *Ten*, to my whole body, now deeply, evenly, completely relaxed."

7) Say to yourself, "Now I'm experiencing a pleasant, peaceful, relaxing time, just as when I was at the beach. I can even see the clear blue sky with the fluffy white clouds; I can hear the soothing sounds of the waves and feel the warm sun. I feel clear and calm; I am at peace." (Key Phrase: _____)

8) Let yourself enjoy the experience, remaining comfortably relaxed, until you hear the sound of the timer or decide that the time is up.

9) Say to yourself, "Now, I'm going to end the exercise by counting backward slowly from five to one. As I say *five*, I begin to become more alert . . . *four*, coming out now . . . *three*, I feel good . . . *two*, eyes open . . . *one*, alert and refreshed!"

10) Flex and relax your muscles a few times before standing up.

Sample Scripts for Numbing Images

1) *Pure numbness*: "Focus your attention now on your right hand. . . . As you do, you will begin to notice that it is growing numb . . . growing numb. You may notice some tingling sensations at first, or feel some twitches, but soon feeling will gradually leave the hand so that it grows more and more numb . . . more and more numb. . . . The more you concentrate on the hand, the more numb it gets . . . numb and without feeling . . . numb and without feeling."

2) *Cold*: "Focus your attention now on your right hand. . . . As you do, you will begin to notice that it is gradually growing cooler and cooler . . . cooler and cooler. As the hand gets cooler, a not unpleasant sensation of numbness begins to envelop it . . . cooler and more numb . . . cooler and more numb. You might even want to imagine that pure white snow is falling on your hand, covering it up and making it cool and numb . . . cool and numb. Or you might prefer to imagine that you are immersing your hand in an icy mountain stream. . . . As the water flows over the hand it gets cooler and cooler . . . cooler and cooler . . . more and more numb . . . cool and numb."

3) *Injection of Novocain*: "Imagine now that you are in your doctor's office and that he is giving you an injection of Novocain in your right hand. You feel a slight prick from the needle, then a little pressure as the medication flows into your hand. . . . Now, as the Novocain begins to work, you feel a sensation of numbness gradually spreading through your hand from the point of the injection . . . more and more numb . . . gradually spreading . . . more and more numb. . . . Now your entire hand is growing numb . . . more and more numb . . . more and more numb."

4) *Change to inert substance*: "Focus your attention now on your right hand, and let yourself imagine that it is beginning to change gradually into a piece of wood . . . a piece of wood just like the arm of a department store mannequin. . . . You can feel the change taking place, and as it does, your hand gradually becomes numb — just like a piece of painted wood. . . . It may look the same on the outside, but on the inside it is becoming more and more numb and without feeling . . . more and more numb . . . just like an inert piece of wood . . . without feeling and numb . . . numb . . . more and more numb."

Remember always to cancel a suggested numbness in any application of hetero-hypnosis with a statement like "Now, let the image of your hand as X fade gradually, as your usual sensation and control in your right hand return," and to add the following (or a similar) qualifying statement:

"As you practice the exercise more and more, it will become easier and easier for you to make your X as numb as it needs to be to relieve your pain. When the pain is gone and you no longer need the numbness, the numb feeling will gradually fade and your usual sensation and control will return. No matter how much you use the self-hypnosis exercise to make your X numb, you will still be able to be aware of any changes in the type or pattern of the pain so that you can report them to your doctor. Part of you will always be aware of the signals that your body is sending you, so that you can protect your health and still be able to do the things that you want."

Index

acupuncture, 150
adjustment disorder with anxious mood, 105
affective disorders, 105
age, hypnotic responsivity and, 14
agoraphobia, 33–34, 105
alcohol abuse, 32, 158, 162
American Journal of Clinical Hypnosis, 101
amnesias, 17, 20, 46
amputees, as patients, 90–91
Anderton, Charles, 153
anesthesia, hypnosis as, 135, 149
antianxiety medications, 121, 122–24
anticipatory anxiety, 28, 30
antidepressant medications, 122, 157
anxiety, 63, 126, 155
    behavioral approaches to, 124
    case examples of, 24–27, 28, 30, 33–34,
        115–17, 118–21
    cognitive therapy for, 124
    with constant or steady symptoms, 107,
        112–17
    with episodic, predictable symptoms,
        107–8, 117–19
    with episodic, unpredictable symptoms,
        107, 108, 110, 119–21
    during hand-separation test, 71
    as ideal application for B.H.E. exercise,
        103–4
    in pain experience, 132–33
    patient's descriptive name for, 54–55
    pharmacological treatment of, 121, 122–24
    psychodynamic approach to, 124–25
    recording system for symptoms of, 56–57
    relationship-based, 33–34
    self-hypnosis in treatment of, 24–27, 28,
        30, 32, 33–34, 103–25, 175
    sexual problems and, 163, 164–65
    as term, 104–5
anxiety disorders, 104–5, 106, 107–8
asthma, 153–54
athletic performance, 28–29, 30, 162–63
atypical anxiety disorder, 105

audiotapes:
    of hypnosis sessions, 88
    for learning self-hypnosis, 179
avoidant personality disorder, 40, 105
awakening, B.H.E. exercise practiced after,
    171–72

baseline occurrence, of target symptoms,
    54, 55–56
bathroom, practicing B.H.E. exercise in, 172
bed, practicing B.H.E. exercise in, 171–72,
    175
behavioral approaches, 9, 124
behavior modification:
    self-hypnosis, effectiveness in, 29–30
    see also habit disorders
Benson, Herbert, 31
bipolar disorder, 32, 156
borderline personality disorder, 105
Bowers, Kenneth, 63
Braid, James, 126
brain waves, during hypnosis, 15, 17
Brief Hypnotic Experience (B.H.E.) evalua-
    tion form, 9, 96–98, 99–101, 134–35,
    211
    numerical scoring of, 100–101
Brief Hypnotic Experience (B.H.E.) exer-
    cise, 14, 16–17, 65, 167
    anxiety, tension, or stress alleviated by,
        25–27, 30, 103–25, 168, 172, 173, 175
    beach scene in, 96, 98–99, 155, 163, 164,
        165
    behavioral approaches integrated with, 124
    for constant or steady symptoms, 112–17
    dosing of, 108, 112–14
    for episodic, predictable symptoms, 117–
        19
    for episodic, unpredictable symptoms,
        119–21
    falling asleep during, 175
    family and interpersonal issues precipitat-
        ed by, 184–86

215